'Challenging recent interpretations of the *Gospel of Thomas*, Nick Perrin offers a new, provocative hypothesis. According to his approach this ancient gospel does not provide new information about the earthly Jesus. Originally written in Syriac, it is rather a document of earliest Syriac Christianity. *Thomas, the Other Gospel* is a very readable book with much valuable information and many fresh insights.'

Jens Schröter, Professor of New Testament
University of Leipzig

'*Thomas, the Other Gospel* is a well-written, thought-provoking examination of current scholarship on the *Gospel of Thomas*. Perrin's own hypothesis of *Thomas'* origins cuts against the grain of most recent scholarship, but he advances it clearly, carefully and modestly. *Thomas, the Other Gospel* is must reading for students of the New Testament and early church history, indeed for all those who care about who Jesus is for us today.'

Robert Van Voorst, Professor of New Testament
Western Theological Seminary

THOMAS,
THE OTHER GOSPEL

NICHOLAS PERRIN

Westminster John Knox Press
LOUISVILLE • LONDON

In Memory of Nancy Ann Brown
(1942–2007)

First published in Great Britain in 2007
by the Society for Promoting Christian Knowledge

First published in the United States in 2007 by Westminster John Knox Press
Copyright © Nicholas Perrin 2007

First U.S. edition
Published by Westminster John Knox Press
Louisville, Kentucky

This book is printed on acid-free paper that meets the
American National Standards Institute Z39.48 standard. ♾

PRINTED IN THE UNITED STATES OF AMERICA

07 08 09 10 11 12 13 14 15 16—10 9 8 7 6 5 4 3 2 1

Library of Congress Cataloging-in-Publication Data is on file
at the Library of Congress, Washington, D.C.

ISBN: 978-0-664-23211-5

Contents

About the author

Nicholas Perrin is Assistant Professor of New Testament at Wheaton College Graduate School, Illinois. He was formerly research assistant to Tom Wright, internationally renowned New Testament scholar and Bishop of Durham. Nick has taught at Biblical Seminary (Hatfield, PA) and served as senior pastor at the International Presbyterian Church, London. He completed his PhD at Marquette University in 2001.

In addition to writing numerous articles, Nick is the author of *Thomas and Tatian: The Relationship between the* Gospel of Thomas *and the* Diatessaron (SBL, 2002) and is the joint editor, with Mark Goodacre, of *Questioning Q* (SPCK and IVP, 2004).

Nick lives in Wheaton, Illinois, with his wife, Camie, and their two sons, Nathaniel and Luke.

Preface

If postmodernity has taught us anything, it has taught us that there is no such thing as *just* a story. Nor are there *just* texts. Whatever stories we possess, whatever texts have come to our attention, they do not come down to us innocently. Texts are interpreted things. And just as the Bible comes down to us through the media of tradition and traditional interpretation, the same thing goes for an intriguing ancient text called *The Gospel of Thomas*. Today most people who know anything at all about this Coptic gospel know what they do because they have heard what others have already said about it. From authoritative-looking web sites, to off-the-cuff comments made by a university professor, from Muslim–Christian debates at Hyde Park, to office water-cooler conversations about the *Da Vinci Code* and Gnostic gospels – *Thomas* has earned a name for itself. Not just a name, but a popular interpretation as well, a street-level reception. And what typically drives the opinions of those who have insufficient time or interest to investigate the matter for themselves is, at the end of the day, scholarly opinion.

I have written this book for two reasons. First, I write because there needs to be a scholarly yet accessible treatment of what researchers have been saying lately about the *Gospel of Thomas*. A long time has passed since the Nag Hammadi discovery some six decades ago. It's time to pause and see where we have got to in the discussion, but not without critique. It is not enough to ask, 'What are they saying these days about the *Gospel of Thomas*?' We must also ask whether 'what they're saying' makes the most sense.

The second reason I write this book is that in North American discussions there is an unsettling homogeneity within Thomas scholarship; were it not for the fact that there are at least a few dissenters, one might even be tempted to call it a monopoly. Despite the conflicting evidence presented by the *Gospel of Thomas*, we have somehow arrived at a basic paradigm which does not always take that conflict seriously. Rather than continuing to work *the* basic question ('When was this gospel written?') from fresh angles, many have sought to make *Thomas*'s alleged first-century roots their fundamental principles. Somewhere along the way, the insightful contribution of non-American researchers from the 1960s and 1970s has, like Cinderella's carriage on the stroke of midnight, vanished from the discussion. In reading so many of today's works, the efforts of fine scholars like Han Drivjer

Tjitze Baarda and J.-E Ménard are unfortunately all but ignored. I write this book because their basic suggestion, that the *Gospel of Thomas* issued from a mid-to-late second-century Syriac milieu, needs to be revisited. While my published dissertation, *Thomas and Tatian: The Relationship between the Gospel of Thomas and the Diatessaron* (2002), has provoked some discussion along these lines, it seems as if Thomas scholarship is returning to 'business as usual' without seriously engaging the scholarship of those who depart from the contemporary standard line, which was first laid out by James M. Robinson and Helmut Koester in their highly influential *Trajectories through Early Christianity* (1971).

Having spent a good part of the past seven years thinking about the *Gospel of Thomas*, I am today more convinced of my thesis than ever. If I can make these ideas accessible to the lay reader of this book, my efforts in writing it will be well repaid. My thanks first go to all those who have challenged me and disagreed with me along the way. Were it not for the erudition and robust argumentation of those who have shared my interest in *Thomas* but disagreed with my viewpoint, I would be nowhere at all in my thinking. Thanks too go to those colleagues and friends who have encouraged and made helpful suggestions along the way, including not least Dr David Vinson. But it is my wife, Camie, who far and away earns the lion's share of my thanksgiving. Were it not for her, I would be nowhere at all. I dedicate this book to the memory of her mother.

Nicholas Perrin
Wheaton, Illinois
St Valentine's Day, 2007

Abbreviations

General abbreviations

AAWG	Abhandlungen der Akademie der Wissenschaften in Göttingen
AcA	*Acta Antiqua*
AcBib	Academia Biblica
ANRW	*Aufsteig und Niedergang der römischen Welt: Geschichte und Kultur Roms im Spiegel der neueren Forchung*
Atpub	*Atti pubblicati degli accademici segretari delle due classi*
BBJ	Beiheft der Bonner Jahrbücher
BCNH	Bibliothèque copte de Nag Hammadi
BETL	Bibliotheca ephemeridum theologicarum lovaniensium
BJS	Brown Judaic Studies
BSFN	*Bulletin de la Société française de Numismatique*
BZAW	Beihefte zur Zeitschrift für die alttestamentliche Wissenschaft
BZNW	Beihefte zur Zeitschrift für die neutestamentliche Wissenschaft
CJ	*Classical Journal*
CJA	Christianity and Judaism in Antiquity
CSCO	Corpus Scriptorum Christianorum Orientalium
CurBS	*Currents in Research: Biblical Studies*
Dialogue	*Dialogue*
ECC	Early Christianity in Context
EPRO	Études préliminaires aux religions orientales dans l'empire
EThL	*Ephemerides theologicae lovanienses*
EvTh	*Evangelische Theologie*
ExpTim	*Expository Times*
FF	Foundations and Facets
FFF	*Foundations and Facets Forum*
FGNK	Forschungen zur Geschichte des neutestamentlichen Kanons und der altkirchlichen Literatur
GTS	Grazer theologische Studien
GTT	*Gereformeerd theologisch tijdscrift*
HDR	Harvard Dissertations in Religion
HistDAC	Histoire des doctrines de l'Antiquité classique
HTR	*Harvard Theological Review*

HUT	Hermeneutische Untersuchungen zur Theologie
HvTSt	*Hervormde teologiese studies*
Int	*Interpretation*
JBL	*Journal of Biblical Literature*
JECS	*Journal of Early Christian Studies*
JETS	*Journal of the Evangelical Theological Society*
JRS	*Journal of Roman Studies*
JSHJ	*Journal for the Study of the Historical Jesus*
JSJSup	Journal for the Study of Judaism in the Persian, Hellenistic, and Roman Periods Supplement
JSNTSup	Journal for the Study of the New Testament: Supplement Series
JSOTSup	Journal for the Study of the Old Testament: Supplement Series
JTECL	Jewish Traditions in Early Christian Literature
JTS	*Journal of Theological Studies*
LNTS	Library of New Testament Studies
MS	Manichaean Studies
Mus	*Muséon: Revue d'études orientales*
NedTT	*Netherlands theologisch tijschrift*
NHS	Nag Hammadi Studies
NovT	*Novum Testamentum*
NovTSup	Novum Testamentum Supplements
NTAbh	Neutestamentliche Abhandlungen
NTS	*New Testament Studies*
OLP	*Orientalia lovaniensia perodica*
OTM	Oxford Theological Monographs
REG	*Revue des études grecques*
RevistB	*Revista biblica*
RevScRel	*Revue des sciences religieuses*
SA	*Studia anselmiana*
Salm	*Salmanticensis*
SBLDS	Society of Biblical Literature Dissertation Series
SBLSP	Society of Biblical Literature Seminar Papers
SECA	Studies on Early Christian Apocrypha
SecCent	*Second Century*
Semeia	*Semeia*
SHR	Studies in History of Religions (supplement to *Numen*)
SSS	Semitic Study Series
ST	*Studia Theologica*
StPatr	Studia patristica
Str	*Stromata*

StudPhil	Studia philonica
Theoph	Theophaneia
ThTo	*Theology Today*
TRu	*Theologische Rundschau*
TS	*Theological Studies*
VC	*Vigiliae Christianae*
VCSup	Supplements to Vigiliae Christianae
WBC	Word Biblical Commentary
WMANT	Wissenschaftliche Monographien zum Alten und Neuen Testament
WUNT	Wissenschaftliche Untersuchungen zum Neuen Testament
ZKG	*Zeitschrift fur Kirchengeschichte*

Non-biblical ancient authors

Athenagoras
Leg.   *Legation for the Christians*

Augustine
Contra Faustum   *Against Faust the Manichaean*

Clement of Carthage
Stromateis   *Miscellanies*

Cyprian of Carthage
De idol. vanit.   *Concerning the Vanity of Idols*

Cyril of Jerusalem
Cat.   *Catecheses*

Ephraem
Contra haer.   *Against Heresies*

Eusebius
Hist. ecc.   *Ecclesiastical History*

Hippolytus
Haer.   *Refutation of All Heresies*

Ignatius
Mag.   *To the Magnesians*
Phil.   *To the Philadelphians*

Irenaeus
Adv. Haer.   *Against Heresies*

Jerome
Comm. Gal.   *Commentary on the Epistle to the Galatians*
Jo. Hier.   *Book against John of Jerusalem*

Justin
1 Apol.   *First Apology*
Oratio ad Graecos   *Oration to the Greeks*

Origen
Hom. Luc.   *Homilies in Luke*

Philo
Abr.   *On the Life of Abraham*
Mos.   *On the Life of Moses*

Tatian
Oratio   *Oration to the Greeks*

Tertullian
An.   *The Soul*

Non-biblical ancient texts

Acts Thom.	*Acts of Thomas*
C. H.	*Corpus Hermeticum*
Discourse on the Eighth and Ninth	*Discourse on the Eighth and Ninth*
Doctrina Addai	*Doctrine of Addai*
Gos. Phil.	*Gospel of Philip*
Gos. Thom.	*Gospel of Thomas*
Lat. Asc.	Latin *Asclepius*
P. Oxy.	Oxyrhyncus fragments
Peter to Philip	*Letter of Peter to Philip*
Pist. Sophia	*Pistis Sophia*

Introduction:
The quest of the historical
Gospel of Thomas

Our story begins on a winter's day in 1945 just outside the Egyptian town of Nag Hammadi, not terribly far from the site in which the *Gospel of Judas* was to be found some thirty years later, and not at all far from the former stomping ground of Pachomius, the fourth-century ascetic who was among the first of Christian monks. Muhammed Ali (not the famed boxer) and his brother were foraging for fertilizer in the jagged rocks of the hills when suddenly they came upon a pale red jar. The jar was about chest-high, crusted with dry dirt and no doubt very ancient. Curiosity would have compelled them to break the jar open at once, but they hesitated, and wondered. What could be in the jar? Perhaps there was an evil spirit, that is, a *jinn* (genie) trapped inside?[1] Or perhaps there was gold?

Somehow it was the prospect of the latter that emboldened the brothers to take their chances with an escaped *jinn*. Not exactly the trained archaeologist, Muhammed Ali raised his mattock in the air, swung it down and tore into the jar. There were no obvious signs of a *jinn*, much to the brothers' relief; nor was there any evidence of gold, much to their disappointment. Instead, the jar was found to contain sheaves of papyrus bound by leather covers. They were merely books, some dozen of them. Still, the brothers thought the leather-bound books must be of some value. So they wrapped them carefully in cloth, mounted their camels, and went home.

About this time, life for the Ali family (Muhammed, his six brothers and his mother) was to become somewhat complicated. Six months earlier, Muhammed's father had been killed in retribution for his killing an intruder on a property that he was guarding the night before. This was just the beginning of a serious local feud. It was not long after Muhammed had found these ancient books that he was informed of the identity of the person who had killed his father. In turn, the murdered man's son and his brothers cornered the suspect, held him

---

[1] It is commonly thought that a *jinn*, despite its powers, cannot remove the lid to a vessel.

1

down, and, probably using the same mattock with which Muhammed had smashed the jar, began hacking off the man's limbs one at a time. When there were no further limbs to remove, all that was left was to do was plunge the mattock into the man's chest, remove his warm, beating heart and eat it.

Meanwhile back at home, Muhammed's mother was busy stoking the fire with pages from one of the books (Codex XII). It may have been that for her these old books portended bad luck. But perhaps too it was the distraction of recent family-related events that prevented her from using the whole lot for oven fuel. Following this close call, Muhammed then decided to remove the books to the house of the local Coptic priest. After all, the books were written in Coptic, Muhammed was told, and if there was anyone who knew what to do with these Coptic texts, it would be a Coptic priest. Muhammed also reasoned that his chances of holding on to the books would be slim if he kept them on his person, especially with the local police stopping by every now and again.

That was the last time Muhammed would handle what is now called the Nag Hammadi library. Had he any idea what he had found, surely he would have held out for a much better deal, for he had in fact struck gold. Not gold exactly, but the books – more properly called codices (the plural of codex) – would surely prove to be worth their weight in gold. But if the value of the newly discovered artefacts was not immediately obvious to Muhammed, neither was it obvious to those who first trafficked the ancient codices. Over time the bound documents were variously traded among the villagers, sold to overseas antiquities dealers and marketed to Cairo booksellers.

When in the early 1950s the Egyptian Department of Antiquities became wise to the existence of the collection, it did a remarkable job of gathering them, making sure that the twelve books and one tractate would find their way safely back to Egypt and into Cairo's Coptic Museum. The books had by this point attracted attention outside the country. By 1956 an international team of scholars had begun to set its sights on translating the texts and by 1959 one of them, the *Gospel of Thomas*, was published. Translations of the other Nag Hammadi codices would follow soon enough. But the publication of the *Gospel of Thomas* was to take priority. It was felt that this text, among all those contained in the collection recovered at Nag Hammadi, was the most significant of all.

Today, *Thomas*'s perceived significance is only growing stronger. Any other gospel from the Nag Hammadi trove, for example the *Gospel of Philip* or the much more recently discovered *Gospel of Judas*, simply pales in comparative importance. This no doubt largely has to do with the fact that in the *Gospel of Thomas* we have 114 sayings or 'logia' (sing. logion) mostly attributed to Jesus, and that roughly half of these sayings bear some resemblance to the synoptic gospels (Matthew, Mark and Luke). There even seems to be terminology and themes that are shared between *Thomas* and the fourth canonical gospel (John). Of all the so-called apocryphal gospels, this Thomasine gospel from Nag Hammadi seems the most gospel-like, in that it gives every impression of conveying the very words of Jesus himself. Because of its potential for shedding light on the authentic words of Jesus' teaching, the *Gospel of Thomas* has, on both a scholarly and a popular level, attracted far more attention than any Nag Hammadi text or non-canonical gospel.

To be sure, there have been other gospels, outside of *Thomas* and the canonical four (Matthew, Mark, Luke and John), composed down through the ages. And, obviously, we continue to find them. But *Thomas* has acquired the reputation of being a kind of gospel alongside the canonical gospels, a 'fifth gospel', the 'other gospel'.[2] It is because of *Thomas*'s importance that I have written this book. The stakes are too high to allow only a few prominent voices to corner this area in the marketplace of ideas. It's time, I thought, to offer an alternative viewpoint on the so-called 'other gospel', one that I am convinced makes best sense of the available data.

But when I or someone else calls *Thomas* the 'other gospel', it is not entirely clear what that means. After all, the word 'other' can be used simply to distinguish one thing as opposed to another ('For this exam use this pencil not the *other* one'), or it can refer to something that is other precisely because it is of a different category ('For this exam use something *other* than a pencil'). Sometimes otherness denotes variations on the same theme; sometimes otherness means a different theme altogether. Beagles are something *other* than basset hounds, but both are in a much more fundamental way *other* than cats. The term 'other' denotes distinction, but may or may not signify a difference of categories.

Of course, disagreements sometimes occur as to whether two given objects belong to the same category, and these disagreements typically arise not so much from the failure to observe differences, but from a divergent interpretation of those observed differences. For example, my eight-year-old son who wants a cat does not think that the differences between dogs and cats are all that great. And certainly he has a point. Both are vertebrates, both are mammals, both can be trained

---

[2] As suggested, respectively, by the titles of a well-known book published through the Jesus Seminar (Funk and Hoover 1996) and Cameron 1982.

to live inside a house. But as far as I'm concerned, the similarities just about stop there. 'Son,' I tell him, 'we already have three hamsters, three hermit crabs, a chinchilla, and a dog. We have enough animals. And by the way, don't you know we're a "dog family", not a "cat family"?' I don't mind cats terribly. Some of my best friends have cats. But for some reason or another, rather than getting a cat, I would rather complement our beagle with a basset or retriever. Cats, in my mind, are just *other*. My eight-year-old sees it differently. When it comes to drawing the line between what house pets are appropriate ('That's us!') and inappropriate ('That's other!'), it more often than not boils down to personal tastes.

For this very reason, sometimes 'other' can be used as part of a rhetorical strategy to challenge people's tendency to perceive differences without good grounds for doing so. This is the very point of Jacob Riis's 1890 title, *How the Other Half Lives*. In his exposé of life in the slums of New York City, the 'other half' was not – as we are now accustomed to use the phrase – the wealthy, but instead the very poor. In this case, the 'other half' is *other* simply because the more fortunate have consciously or unconsciously marginalized them. Riis hoped to shock his readers into reclaiming a forgotten segment of humanity. In our post-colonial world, where imperialistic powers are being reminded of the gravitational force they have been exerting, the 'other' is that which needs to be freed from having to tread an orbit around the centre as defined by the dominating culture. Here the 'other' is reclaimed, embraced and celebrated on its own terms.

But otherness is not always a matter of personal perception. If, to take another example, my ten-year-old son were to come home and announce that it was Vladimir Lenin who signed the 'Emancipation Proclamation', thereby freeing the American slaves, I would have to conclude that either he or his teacher was confused. Even if he were to prefer that Lenin were American, this would not make it any the more true. Likewise, while to include Lenin in the roll of important American figures would be, I suppose, more inclusive than not including him, to do so simply for inclusivity's sake would be absurd. Obviously there are similarities between Lenin and Lincoln, some of which are notable (both sought a freedom of sorts), some of which are superficial (both sported beards). But such similarities, whether important or trivial, have no bearing on the fact that Lincoln played a crucial role in nineteenth-century American history and Lenin did not. That Lenin is something *other* than a nineteenth-century American hero is intrinsically the case; it is a matter of historical fact, and no argument from personal judgment or moral imperative can change that fact.

So, when we encounter on the bookstore shelves such titles as *The Other Gospels* or *Four Other Gospels*, we may be forgiven for asking what such titles really imply.[3] Do they suggest that the *Gospel according to the Egyptians*, the *Gospel according to the Ebionites*, and the rest are 'other' in the sense that they are truly and objectively different in kind? Or do they mean that these gospels are texts which, for better or worse, have been forgotten, but which too, like distant and largely unknown cousins with whom we suddenly pick up an email correspondence, are worth retrieving to our collective consciousness? Or do they mean that these gospels are more like unjustly treated stepsisters who need to be brought back into the mix of their more famous siblings (Matthew, Mark, Luke and John)?

The difference between the second option ('Let's get to know the other gospels again, for they too, historically speaking, are part of our heritage') and the third option ('Let's celebrate the other gospels, for they too, theologically speaking, have much to teach us') is not all that great. To maintain that these other gospels are part of our tradition but have been wrongfully suppressed is to suggest, at least in principle, that these gospels be included in our theological reflection about Jesus and the early church. Here historical judgments have certain theological entailments, but not vice versa. While *Thomas* may be argued to be either fundamentally other or only seemingly other on material grounds, the starting point must be within the realm of history. Where does the *Gospel of Thomas* sit on the trajectory of early Christianity?

The title of the present book is intentionally ambiguous. This is in keeping with my two-fold purpose. In the first place, now that some sixty years have passed since its discovery, and less than fifty years since its first publication, I wish to show how scholars have come to think about the *Gospel of Thomas* and how this gospel has been used as a datum in all kinds of fascinating discussions. Insofar as scholars have been conferring on *Thomas* an important role in establishing the theological diversity of early Christianity, the discussions are also very significant. The Coptic collection has according to the recent trend, especially in North America, become the disenfranchised step-sister. And, according to the same trend, it is time for her to emerge from her small, dingy room of obscurity and come out for all to admire.

But this has not been the only way of looking at *Thomas*. At first, despite the initial exhilaration surrounding the discovery of the sayings collection and the rest of the Nag Hammadi library of which it is a

---

[3] The latter title is Crossan 1985.

part, scholars were not entirely sure what to make of this strange text. It is as if, while working on not one but several jigsaw puzzles, not least among these the puzzle of Christian origins, scholars had caught something peeking back up at them from out of the carpet. 'What is it?' we ask, as we reach for it with trembling fingers. We are not sure, but are excited nonetheless. 'Could it be? Yes, I think it is! It's a stray piece to one of the puzzles. Jolly good thing we found it!' Such excitement is understandable, especially since there has been a lot of labour spent on piecing these odd shapes together.

But now, having been retrieved from under the coffee table and pressed against the box-tops of the various puzzles, the *Gospel of Thomas* still awaits final consensus from the broader world of scholarship as to where it should really go. Some scholars say, 'Yes, this indeed is a missing puzzle piece. It's just the kind of thing we might be looking for in our Second-Century Gnosticism puzzle.' Others remain unconvinced. Instead they decide that the piece belongs to the First Century/ Era of Christian Origins puzzle. Among these there are some who claim that this gospel is more than a missing piece; it is in fact a corner piece. Of course, if this is true, it is extremely important. Once you have the corners, and only once you have corners, can you reasonably proceed with the rest of the puzzle.

While I am not fully convinced by either position, it has become clear that the 'Thomas is a corner piece' viewpoint is gaining in ascendancy, again, especially among North American scholars. Sometimes such tidal shifts have a way of dragging countless laypeople and scholars along. Those who do not specialize in Thomasine scholarship (and I suspect that there are more than a few in this category!) may well – like Dan Brown's *The Da Vinci Code* heroine in her meeting with Leigh Teabing – have little choice but to acquiesce to what the experts are saying when it comes to the truth of Christian origins. That is why it is important to lay out clearly what is being said, evaluate the claims, and then take a fresh look at the text. This, in a nutshell, is my intention.

I begin in Part 1 by describing how three important Thomas scholars have recounted the story behind *Thomas*. All three see *Thomas* as crucial to a proper reconstruction of Christian origins, but interestingly all three have lined up the edges of the puzzle in different ways. There are strengths to each of their arguments, but also weaknesses. The first two scholars under review will recognize that *Thomas* has been seen as theologically 'other', but will implicitly or explicitly insist that this otherness is a matter of unfounded prejudice. For them, it is time to bring *Thomas* back into the mix and put it on the table, front and centre, where it belongs. The approach of the third scholar is more purely historical, but the implications of her views, if correct, are profound.

But are today's leading voices on *Thomas* getting the history of *Thomas* right? This is the question I take up in Part 2. Of course one may embrace the Coptic gospel simply because one prefers its teachings to those contained in, say, Matthew. And while I suspect that arguments could be made as to why Matthew's theological outlook is preferable to that of *Thomas* (or vice versa), this again is not where the discussion ought to start. To speak to the comparative merits of both texts apart from any consideration of the historical settings will prove just as fruitless as a strictly substantive comparison of Lenin's *New Economic Developments in Peasant Life* with the 'Emancipation Proclamation'.

It is even less convincing to argue that *Thomas* should be theologically appropriated precisely because it has been suppressed and then ignored all these years. (While it is true that history is generally written by the winners, this fact does not make the losers any more right.) Whatever sympathies one might have for an individual puzzle piece that has been lost under the coffee table and indeed even kicked there, I am first and foremost interested in settling the question as to which puzzle *Thomas* actually belongs to. I think most people are. What is the *Gospel of Thomas*? When was it written? Where was it written? And to whom? These are the sorts of questions with which we must begin before deciding on the otherness of *Thomas*.

Getting our bearings

Let us start with what we can see and touch for ourselves: the brute facts of the actual manuscripts. Within the Nag Hammadi library there are a number of duplicate works.[4] There are six versions of a well-known Gnostic text called the *Apocryphon of John*. There are also three tractates which, while only occurring once in the Nag Hammadi library, find parallel in other extant literature; these include among other texts a portion of Plato's *Republic*, the *Sentences of Sextus*, a *Prayer of Thanksgiving*, and fragments from *Asclepius*. The last two items, interestingly enough, derive from the world of Hermeticism, an Egyptian religion concerned with preserving and exploring the secrets of the legendary Hermes Trismegistus ('Hermes the thrice-great'). The Coptic

---

[4] Within the so-called Nag Hammadi library, composed of 12 codices and one separate tractate, are 52 tractates, all written in Coptic. *The Gospel of Thomas* was only one of a number of texts discovered in this cache: the second tractate of the second codex, i.e. II,2.

codex in which *Thomas* is contained probably dates to the middle of the fourth century CE. Of course the Coptic text is probably only a translation of other texts which in turn were presumably copies. The date of the original composition of each of these texts must have been still earlier, perhaps considerably earlier.

The text of the *Gospel of Thomas*, as it came to light at Nag Hammadi, was not something *completely* new. Some fifty years earlier, two British explorers by the names of Grenfell and Hunt were sorting through papyri finds at the village of Oxyrhynchus in Egypt. Amidst these they found three Greek fragments relevant to our Coptic *Thomas*: they are catalogued *P. Oxy. 1, 654*, and *655*. The oldest of these three, *P. Oxy. 1*, which Grenfell and Hunt very reasonably supposed to have been written some time just after 200 CE, contains Greek sayings very close in content to what is recorded in *Gos. Thom.* 26–33 and 77a.[5] Another Greek fragment, *P. Oxy 654*, which parallels *Gos. Thom.* 1–7, has been dated toward the middle of the third century.[6] Finally, there is *P. Oxy. 655*, which is roughly identical with *Gos. Thom.* 24, 36–39. This text apparently may be dated at some time in the first half of the third century.[7] Like their Coptic counterpart, these Greek fragments too were found alongside Hermetical writings. What is particularly striking on any comparison between the Greek fragments and the later discovered Coptic text is that, even accounting for the obvious fact that the two recensions are in different languages, there are dissimilarities in wording. At points the Greek text is more expansive; at other places, it is more abbreviated than its Coptic counterpart. There are also a few dissimilarities in sequence.[8]

The Oxyrhynchus fragments are particularly useful in that they provide a *terminus ad quem* for the dating of the *Gospel of Thomas*: the first copy could not have been written any later than the first few decades of the third century (200–20 CE). This is confirmed by the witness of Hippolytus of Rome, who in his *Refutation of All Heresies*, written in either the second or the third decade of the third century, states:

> They [the Naassenes] say that not only the mysteries of the Assyrians and the Phrygians, but also those of the Egyptians support their account of the blessed nature of the things which were, are, and are yet to be, a nature which is both hidden and revealed at the same time, and which he [the Naassene believer] calls the sought-for kingdom of

---

[5] Grenfell and Hunt 1897: 16. So too Attridge 1989: 96–7.

[6] Attridge 1989: 97–8.

[7] Attridge 1989: 98–9.

[8] Attridge 1989: 99–101. For further discussion, see also Fitzmyer 1959; Munck 1960; Fallon and Cameron 1989: 4201–4; Neller 1989: 4–7; Perrin 2004.

heaven which is within man. They transmit a tradition concerning this in the Gospel entitled '*According to Thomas*', which states expressly: 'The one who seeks me will find me in children from seven years of age and onwards. For there, hiding in the fourteenth aeon, I am revealed.'
(*Haer.* 5.2.20)

Not too long after Hippolytus wrote these words, Origen (*c.* 233 CE) chimes in, mentioning that 'there is passed down also the *Gospel according to Thomas*, the *Gospel according to Matthias*, and many others'.[9] Then just under a century later, near the opening of the fourth century, Eusebius includes Thomas and Matthias, along with the *Gospel of Peter*, on his list of heretical writings.[10] Apparently, whenever the *Gospel of Thomas* was first written, it enjoyed considerable popularity as early as the beginning of the third century and was around the same time declared to be heretical by important church leaders.

So if the *Gospel of Thomas* was composed no later than the early 200s, what might be its earliest possible dating? Here, when we turn to the text itself and see the repetition of the phrase 'Jesus said . . . ,' we find our answer: the text could not go back any earlier than the ministry of Jesus of Nazareth. This leaves us with a rather broad window: *c.* 30 – *c.* 210 CE. Is there any way we can further narrow things down?

Grenfell and Hunt, the discoverers of the Greek fragments of *Thomas*, thought that there was. It is worthwhile considering their judgment in their own words, for it was to have a lasting effect on later scholarship:

> The primitive cast and setting of the sayings, the absence of any consistent tendency in favour of any particular sect, the wide divergences in the familiar sayings from the text of the Gospels, the striking character of those which are new, combine to separate the fragments from the 'apocryphal' literature of the middle and latter half of the second century, and to refer it back to the period when the Canonical Gospels had not yet reached their pre-eminent position.
> (Grenfell and Hunt 1897: 16)

Grenfell and Hunt decided that the original text could not have been written any later than 140 CE on the basis of four considerations: (1) the 'primitive cast and setting of the sayings', (2) no consistent indication of any known sect, (3) the differences between the Thomasine sayings and the canonical counterparts, and (4) the 'striking character' of the sayings that are new. The second point, the absence of any sure and consistent sign of any known sect, is fair enough, but presumes a

---

[9] *Hom. Luc.* 1
[10] *Hist. Eccl.* 3.25.6.

good degree of knowledge of the second- and third-century sects, knowledge that neither Grenfell and Hunt, nor even researchers today, can confidently espouse. Reason number 3 (the differences between the synoptic-like material in *Thomas* and the synoptics themselves) is an interesting point and one that would take centre stage in future debates. The newly discovered cache of sayings that deviates from the canonical records, Grenfell and Hunt surmise, can be best assigned to a period before the notions of canonical authority attached themselves to the gospels. But this presumes, mistakenly in my view, that any author living after the mid-second century would out of holy reverence refuse to tamper with the received wording of Matthew, Mark, Luke and John. Finally, points 1 and 4, the 'primitive cast' of the settings and their 'striking character', are simply impressions, a flimsy basis for inferring firm dates.

This is not to fault Grenfell and Hunt. When you find a 1700-year-old fragment, you do your best to answer the 'who?', 'why?', 'where?', and 'when?' questions. They are doing no different. But it still remains that their case (if we call it that) is extremely fragile. For all intents and purposes, the question of the dating of the autograph remains very much open.

Fortunately, as far as the Coptic version is concerned, we are able to fix some pegs in the ground here and there. The very odd *Gos. Thom.* 7 ('Blessed is the lion which the man will eat so that the lion becomes a man and cursed is the man whom the lion will eat so that the lion becomes a man'),[11] for example, has been convincingly demonstrated to have derived from a second-century confluence of Platonic, Hermetic, Pauline and ascetical thought forms.[12] Another saying, *Gos. Thom.* 102 ('Woe to the pharisees, for they are like a dog asleep in the manger of oxen, for he does not eat, nor does he let the oxen eat'), clearly draws on an Aesop fable hailing from a second-century Syrian setting.[13] In *Gos. Thom.* 44 ('Whoever speaks against the father will be forgiven, and whoever speaks against the son will be forgiven. However, whoever speaks against the holy spirit will not be forgiven neither on earth nor in heaven') we find Jesus speaking not just in Trinitarian terms, but in Trinitarian terms that find analogy in the late second-century gospel harmony, the *Diatessaron*.[14] Clearly, it would be misguided to argue that these sayings prove that *Thomas* derives from a second-century context. Just because parts of it come from a

---

[11] All translations of the *Gospel of Thomas* in this book are my own.
[12] Jackson 1985.
[13] Priest 1985; cf. Moravcsik 1964.
[14] Baarda 1997b.

particular setting does not mean the whole text did so as well. It is certainly possible, as a good number of scholars maintain, that the present collection was the end result of a long evolution. These same scholars remain convinced that the roughly half of Thomasine sayings that find parallel in the synoptic tradition derived not from any written gospel texts, but from a separate oral tradition, perhaps even reaching back to Jesus himself. On the other hand, the presence of sayings that patently show the impress of second-century texts and traditions raise the question as to whether the whole text originated in the second century.

The problem might be illustrated by imagining that one day you are cleaning out a desk that has been handed down through the family line but which has not been cleaned out for years. In the main drawer of the desk is not one or two or even three, but four boxes of paperclips, all partially opened. Judging by the various degrees of fading on each paperclip box, you infer that each box was purchased at a different time. Then you notice amidst the many paperclips that cover the bottom of the drawer a paperclip chain. And because you are dreading the prospect of cleaning the desk and looking desperately for any means of procrastination, you begin to examine the paperclip chain. By your count there are 114 paperclips. You think to yourself, 'Who would take the time to sit around and make a chain of 114 paperclips?' You think back over the previous generations that owned and used the desk. You look again at the paperclip chain: some paperclips all along the chain look old and a bit rusted, others look shinier and relatively new. This observation suggests one of two scenarios. On the one hand, it is possible that someone fairly recently put the chain together using paperclips old and new. The presence of older paperclips would lend the misleading appearance that this paperclip chain was formed some time ago. On the other hand, it is equally possible that the chain was an intergenerational project. Great-grandfather in his idle moments started it, then later Grandfather, disassembling and reassembling, added on a few dozen paperclips of his own, then Father added even more to the chain from the newest box.

Likewise, it may be argued, if *Thomas* came together over time, with one saying being attached to another, and one chain being connected to another, it is impossible to judge *Thomas's* date on the basis of the dating of the last sayings to be attached. *Thomas* may be a text that was long in the making, or *Thomas* may be a text that was composed in a relatively brief span. If the former is the case, then there are good grounds for thinking that a number of its sayings, being very old, actually go back to Jesus of Nazareth. If the latter is the case, a second-century dating is more likely in view. The issue of dating must remain, for the moment anyway, an open question.

As for provenance, *Thomas* has regularly been assigned to Edessa, the ancient city that would become modern-day Urfa (Turkey), due east of Syrian Antioch.[15] As for its language, most scholars have also been of the opinion that the original text was indeed Greek, which gave rise on one side to the Greek tradition (preserved in the Oxyrhynchus fragments) and on the other side to the Coptic tradition (preserved in the Nag Hammadi text). In a later chapter, I will explore how provenance and original language of composition are more closely correlated than we have customarily thought.

The text is made up of some 114 sayings, most of which begin, 'Jesus said'. At several places there is instead, 'he said' (*Gos. Thom.* 8, 65, 74). And when Jesus is not taking the lead in conversation, it is his disciples who are coming to him, either to ask Jesus a question (e.g. *Gos. Thom.* 6, 18, 20) or, less frequently, to make a statement or suggestion that Jesus rebuffs (*Gos. Thom.* 52, 114). Thus, strictly speaking, it is not entirely accurate to call the *Gospel of Thomas* a 'sayings collection'. There are sayings, indeed, but alongside these are a number of miniature scenes or dialogues.

There are further difficulties when it comes to Thomas's theology. In the earliest research on the gospel commentators generally were of the mind that the text was 'Gnostic'. There are problems with this term. While for most of modern scholarship, writers and scholars alike were quite unselfconscious in bandying about the term 'Gnostic', matters are somewhat different today. Because 'Gnostic' has been used to describe so many different movements that bear only the slightest comparisons to each other, it has been suggested that we dispense with the term altogether.[16] While I agree that 'Gnostic' and 'Gnosticism' makes for a pretty unwieldy rug under which to sweep all those sects that are not ostensibly proto-orthodox,[17] the term has its place, at least if defined accurately enough. All the same, I disagree with those who say that the *Gospel of Thomas* is Gnostic.[18] To be sure, the sayings gospel shares many elements with purported Gnostic texts (elements of

---

[15] This was first argued by Puech (1978 [1957]: 286–7) with the vast majority of scholars following suit. Dehandschutter (1975: 25–31) and a few of the earliest commentators (e.g. Cerfaux 1957: 319; Wilson 1960: 39) suggest Egypt.

[16] Williams 1996.

[17] Because orthodoxy was never formally established until the Council of Nicea (325 CE), I use the term 'proto-orthodox' to refer to the socio-theological trajectory leading up to Nicea.

[18] So too DeConick 1996: 11–27; Marjanen 1998b.

anti-Judaism, hatred of the body, secret knowledge, etc.), but there is no hint that Thomas's Creator God is the same sadistic deity or pompous idiot that we meet in the Gnostic materials. Lacking these features, Thomas must be judged to be non-Gnostic. If it were Gnostic, that would certainly help those arguing for a second-century date to make their point. But the case is otherwise.

Perhaps the most pressing question, and the most hotly debated one, is how the Coptic gospel relates to the canonical gospels. At first, during the 1960s, it looked as if most scholars would conclude that *Thomas* was a Gnostic text that drew on and distorted the text of the synoptic texts. And perhaps things would have gone this way were it not for James M. Robinson's signal essay: 'LOGOI SOPHON: On the Gattung of Q'.[19] In this piece, Robinson compares *Thomas* to the alleged sayings source Q (from the German *Quelle* meaning 'source'), upon which both Matthew and Luke supposedly independently drew.[20] Q and *Thomas*, Robinson argues, must have been examples of the same sayings genre, *logoi sophon* ('sayings of the wise'). Robinson's co-author, Helmut Koester, takes this further: because *Thomas* contains sayings attributed to Jesus and the collection as a whole lacks the narrative elements that were later introduced by the likes of Matthew, Mark and Luke, the Coptic collection gives us the very earliest and most authentic Jesus tradition.[21] It is a tradition without cross or resurrection or any apocalyptic Son of Man language. To date, Koester and Robinson have had a profound influence on Thomas studies, so much so that one may even speak of a 'Koester school'. Most scholars arguing that *Thomas* was independent of the synoptic tradition have done so by reiterating the basic argument laid out by Koester and Robinson. We will explore one particular development of the Koester-Robinson thesis when we come to Stephen Patterson in Chapter 1.

While most scholars have been interested in the possible connection between *Thomas* and our synoptic gospels, others have been drawn to the more subtle connections between the Coptic text and John. One book that broke new ground in this discussion is Gregory Riley's *Resurrection Reconsidered: Thomas and John in Controversy* (1995). Riley sees the fourth gospel as having been written in response to the Thomas community, especially its views that the risen body was impalpable. While Thomas holds to the typical and therefore original Greco-Roman view of post-mortem existence, John represents a wave of

---

[19] Robinson 1971 [1964].
[20] But see Goodacre and Perrin: 2004.
[21] Koester 1971 [1965].

thinking that inexplicably comes to insist on bodily resurrection. The notion that John was written as a polemical against Thomas is later taken up by April DeConick and after her Elaine Pagels.[22] We explore Pagels's reworking of Riley's argument in Chapter 2.

In Chapter 3 we review and assess the argument put forth in DeConick's recent monograph, *Recovering the Original Gospel of Thomas: A History of the Gospel and its Growth* (2005). Here DeConick emphasizes the importance of orality in ancient culture and the necessity of thinking of *Thomas* as an oral collection. DeConick's work makes for quite a contrast to another important work, written more than forty years earlier: Wolfgang Schrage's *Das Verhältnis des Thomas-Evangeliums zur synoptischen Tradition und zu den koptischen Evangelien-Übersetzungen* (1964).[23] Working with the Coptic New Testament versions, Schrage saw places at which *Thomas* is influenced by the Coptic NT text. While there are some major limitations to this argument (namely, if the Coptic translation occurred very late in the process of transmission, these observations prove very little), Schrage gave rise to a tradition that sees *Thomas* from the standpoint of redaction criticism. This approach asks, 'How and to what extent has the editor of *Thomas* shaped his sayings in accordance with the synoptic tradition?'; it generally characterizes Thomas scholarship on the continent. While there are recent notable exceptions, most European scholars would probably not object to Silke Petersen's statement that 'the majority of German exegetes . . . presuppose the dependence of the *Gospel of Thomas* on the synoptic Gospels and date it correspondingly late'.[24]

The remainder of the book, Part 2, serves the purpose of affirming the observations made by the scholars reviewed in Part 1, but providing a rather different interpretation. It is an interpretation that begins with a linguistic analysis of the text coupled with a study of the ritualistic practices in *Thomas* (Chapter 4). Then in the next chapter (Chapter 5) I pay close attention to *Gos. Thom.* 13 and explain how this saying with its portrayal of the apostles provides an important key in understanding how Thomas Christians understood themselves vis-à-vis a less-than-sympathetic proto-orthodox community. Finally, in the last chapter (Chapter 6), we begin to home in on the burning historical question: what does *Thomas* have to do with the historical

---

[22] DeConick 2001; Pagels 2003.

[23] The English for this title is: 'The Relationship of the Gospel of Thomas to the Synoptic Tradition and to the Coptic Gospel Translations'.

[24] Petersen 1999: 184. Liebenberg 2001 and Nordsieck 2004 are two German scholars who have sympathies with the Koester school.

Jesus? Not surprisingly, there are some theological implications here too. If the nature of *Thomas*'s 'otherness' hangs squarely on the text's relationship to the most famous of Galileans, here we can close by describing the ways in which the *Gospel of Thomas* is like and unlike the four gospels that have been handed down for nearly two thousand years.

Conclusion

We recall that Muhammed Ali, the discoverer of the Coptic *Gospel of Thomas*, was not quite sure what to think of the jar that he had stumbled upon. Did it contain riches or a *jinn*? We are quite sure that on that December day some sixty years ago, Muhammed had found a valuable trove of materials. How valuable and in what manner valuable are they for future theological and historical reflection? These questions remain before us. But at least there was no *jinn*, that mythological spirit who plays deceptive tricks on human beings.[25] Or was there?

A lot has been written on the *Gospel of Thomas* over the years. Many of the ideas put forward have been hotly contested. I suspect my own thesis will be no exception. My goal is to make my case plainly and convincingly. But at the end of the day, it is either my conversation partners, with whom I respectfully disagree, or it is I who have met the *jinn* of the *Gospel of Thomas*. When he was about to swing his mattock, Muhammed was not sure whether his reward would be tricks or treats. Even if he received neither, those who have followed the scholarly and popular discussion on the *Gospel of Thomas* have undoubtedly received measures of both. May the reader of this book be only the richer for it! Now as we approach this rather impenetrable gospel with mattock in hand, we must first consider how others have taken their swing.

---

[25] The western concept of a genie (derived from the plural *jinnī*) is typically depicted in friendly and positive terms; this is quite opposite in character to the *jinn*.

Part 1

WHAT THEY ARE SAYING ABOUT THE *GOSPEL OF THOMAS*

1

The Thomas community on the move: Stephen J. Patterson

Having glanced at some of the landscape of Thomas scholarship in the previous chapter, we now relax the pace in order take a closer look. From a distance the range of scholarly opinion on the Coptic gospel almost defies sorting out. Like an overgrown wood it may appear vast, dense and confusingly variegated. Here in this the first part of the book, amidst the tangled branches of ideas and hypotheses clamouring for the light of recognition, I want to focus on three writers: Stephen J. Patterson, Elaine Pagels and April D. DeConick. While there are certainly a few other oaks in the forest (Risto Uro and Marvin Meyer come to mind), I single these out for special consideration for a number of reasons. First, each of these scholars is well recognized in the sub-discipline of Thomas studies and has made a noticeable impact either on academic or the popular-level discussion. Second, all three have published book-length treatments that seek to explain the gospel both as a theological and a socio-historical reality; their contributions are a winsome blend of textual sensitivity and historical imagination, the carefully wrought products of broad-stroke thinkers. In Thomas studies such big-picture historians are hard to find. But if Koester and Robinson have set the discussion for current Thomasine studies in North America, Patterson and DeConick may be seen as two of the most important interlocutors at the table. Meanwhile Pagels, the author of a *New York Times* bestseller on the gospel, is to be credited not only for her innovative hypotheses, but also for doing more than any other scholar in getting talk about *Thomas* beyond the arcane world of academia into the workaday world of local book clubs and water-cooler discussions. In reviewing these three historians, I will attempt to give an account that is both fair and accurate. At the same time, I believe that their positions suffer significant weaknesses, so that while there are a good number of points on which I am happy to agree, there are, as will become clear soon enough, a number of counts on which I fundamentally disagree.

The first scholar under consideration is a prolific one. Stephen J. Patterson, a professor of New Testament at Eden Theological Seminary in St Louis, has published numerous articles and a half-dozen books on not only the *Gospel of Thomas*, but also the historical Jesus. In his most recent book, *Beyond the Passion: Rethinking the Death and Life of Jesus* (2004), Patterson joins a recent wave of thinkers calling into question traditional theories of atonement and participates in another, much older, discussion that sees Jesus' primary theological significance lying in his tenacity of conviction. But it is his first book, developed out of his dissertation work on *Thomas* and Jesus under the auspices of James Robinson, that seems to provide the basic framework for his thought. As such it will be my sole focus.

Review

The Gospel of Thomas and Jesus (1993), its introduction tells us, is an attempt to move beyond the impasse on the questions of dating and sources. As Patterson rightly points out, until *Thomas* can be located with more chronological precision, important issues like genre and the social situation behind the text will likely remain shrouded in doubt. However, once *Thomas* is dislodged from between the loggerheads of competing scholarly judgments on dating, it becomes much easier to explore other matters of interest.

Putting the matter squarely, our author asks: 'Does the Gospel of Thomas represent an exotic spin-off from the main-stream of synoptic Christianity, or is it, like John, the document of yet another early Christian school of thought, what one might call "Thomas Christianity"?'[1] Patterson declares his preference for the latter option: *Thomas's* independence. Then, in an interesting move, he throws down a gauntlet before those who subscribe to the alternative, namely, *Thomas's* dependence:

> My assumption is that in order to be convincing, a theory of literary dependence must show not just that two texts share a good deal of material in common, but specifically that 1) between the texts in question there is a consistent pattern of dependence, i.e., that one author can be seen regularly to build upon the text of the other, rather than on yet another, shared source (oral or written); and that 2) the sequence of individual pericopae in each text is substantially the same.
>
> (Patterson 1993: 16)

By shifting the burden of proof on to the shoulders of those who affirm *Thomas's* indebtedness to the synoptic gospels, Patterson has forestalled any smug attempt to point to the ostensive similarities

---

[1] Patterson 1993: 16.

between the Thomasine and synoptic traditions and cry, 'See! *Thomas* is later!' Those who hold that Thomas knew and used the canonical texts must show *why* the form of the Coptic gospel should be judged as secondary and later. They can only begin to do so by proving that the Thomasine sayings regularly build on the written synoptic texts.

Knowing that the best defence is a good offence, Patterson continues his assault on the argument for dependence by appealing to the order of the Thomasine sayings, more precisely, its lack of order. Whereas Matthew and Luke march along, albeit with faltering step, according to the sequence of Mark, there appears to be no method to Thomas's madness.[2] If the author of the collection had in fact used the synoptic gospels, it is almost as if he had snipped the pages of the gospels into a small heap of something like Chinese fortune-cookie messages, thrown the lot into a barrel, given the barrel a good roll down the street, and then started picking out sayings one by one. This or something like this, according to our author, is what the view of dependency seems to demand. The desultory order of the Thomasine sayings, in other words, serves as *prima facie* evidence that these sayings came from a source other than the well-known synoptic gospels, namely, an oral tradition unsullied by direct or indirect influences from Matthew, Mark or Luke.

In describing the comparisons between *Thomas* and the parallel NT materials, Patterson employs family metaphors. Synoptic *twins* represent those Thomasine sayings that are extremely close to the parallel form found in the canonical texts.[3] Synoptic *siblings* are those logia that show a somewhat hazier resemblance. While sharing a 'common outline' or 'key terminology', in the final analysis 'these pairs simply do not show the kind of verbal correspondence that point to the literary dependence of one text upon another'.[4] Finally, synoptic *cousins* are those Thomasine sayings that 'have no synoptic parallels, but which, in terms of their traditional form and content, offer no grounds for distinguishing them chronologically or topically' from

---

[2] By 'Thomas' I simply mean the author responsible for our collection. I am not aware of any scholar who holds that this is one and the same as Jesus' disciple. As we shall see, that 'Thomas' is the Aramaic word for 'twin' proves to be significant.

[3] Patterson 1993: 18–71. These are as follows: *Gos. Thom.* 4.2; 5.2 (par. 6.5–6); 9; 10; 14.4–5; 16; 20; 21.5, 9; 26; 31; 33.1–2; 34; 35; 39.1–2, 3; 41; 44; 45; 46; 47.2–5; 54; 55 (par. 101); 57; 61.1; 62.2; 63; 65; 66; 68–69; 71; 72; 73; 76; 79; 86; 89; 90; 91; 93; 96; 99; 100; and 107.

[4] Patterson 1993: 71–81. These include *Gos. Thom.* 3.1–3 (par. 113); 8; 11.1; 22.1–3; 25; 32; 36; 40; 42; 64; 78.1–3; 95; 103; 104; and 109.

the synoptic materials.[5] The categorical shift from formal similarities (twins and siblings) to chronological and material similarities (cousins) is somewhat confusing, but nonetheless illustrates how Patterson's conception of the problem differs from that of so many previous scholars. Up to this point, Thomasine scholars have generally been content to divide the Coptic sayings into two categories: those that look as if they came from the synoptic gospels and those that do not. But Patterson's metaphorical taxonomy suggests that the Thomasine and synoptic tradition are of common descent; next to this historical fact, formal similarities or dissimilarities are more or less incidental.

For the next seventy-five pages, our author submits these twins, siblings and cousins to rigorous source-critical analysis. Along the way he is relentless in teasing out weaknesses in his opponents' arguments. For example, against one scholar's judgment that *Gos. Thom.* 5.2 reflects the Lucan redaction of Luke 8:17a (thus strongly suggesting dependence on Luke), Patterson states that the same construction can be better understood as belonging not to the author of the third gospel but to Q.[6] Inasmuch as Patterson can show Thomas's indebtedness to Q rather than Luke, he succeeds in pushing the source of the Thomasine tradition well behind the Matthean/Lucan tradition. But Thomas is also said to have drawn on pre-Marcan material. For example, in discussing *Gos. Thom.* 14.5 ('After all, what goes into your mouth will not defile you; rather, it is what comes out of your mouth that will defile you'), Patterson points out that form critics have generally theorized the Marcan parallel (Mark 7:15) to have been free-floating tradition, passed down independently of the account of Jesus' pronouncement regarding dietary laws. From this he concludes that the Thomasine editor must have laid hold of the saying preserved in Mark 7:15 while it was still in oral free fall and before it was inscribed and embedded in its Marcan context.[7] In like manner, drawing on form-critical methodologies and source-critical reconstructions of Q, our author works through the Thomasine sayings one at a time. In the end, he makes a plausible case for the oral origins of a good number of the logia he treats.

There are other evidences that Thomas drew from a primitive oral tradition. At times, the Coptic collection shows no awareness of redactional additions which we surmise the evangelists to have added to the original form of the text. For example, following Crossan,

---

[5] Patterson 1993: 18, 82–91. These include *Gos. Thom.* 4.1; 5.1; 6.1–4; 12; 13; 14.1–3; 17; 21.6–7; 24; 27; 29; 38; 47.1; 48; 51; 53; 58; 62.1; 74; 81; 82; 92.2; 97; 98; 102; and 112.

[6] Patterson 1993: 21–2. The original argument was made in McArthur 1959–60: 287.

[7] Patterson 1993: 24–5.

Patterson takes the absence of Mark 4:5−6 in the Thomasine Parable of the Sower (*Gos. Thom.* 9) to mean that Thomas was not privy to Mark's 'convoluted explanation of the fate of the seed' (Mark 4:5−6).[8] Likewise it is Thomas's version of the Parable of the Wicked Tenants (*Gos. Thom.* 65), as opposed to the three versions passed down in the canonical gospels, that preserves the simplest and therefore − form criticism tells us − the most primitive version.[9] In comparing *Gos. Thom.* 55 and 101, which are close enough to be considered doublets, Patterson finds strong evidence of independence: 'how is it to be explained that the Thomas author/editor created two different versions of the same saying, including them both as single, independent sayings? This alone seems to rule out dependence on the synoptics.'[10] Apparently, the existence of doublets constitutes an 'overwhelming problem' for the case for dependence.[11] As we shall see, this point is also taken up by others.

Of course, it is not all smooth sailing for the argument of independence. There are, in the first instance, places where *Thomas* incontrovertibly preserves synoptic influences. In *Gos. Thom.* 39.1, for example, one reads that 'the Pharisees and the scribes have taken the keys of knowledge and have hidden them'; meanwhile, in *Gos. Thom.* 45.3 Jesus says that 'a bad person brings forth evil things from the corrupt store house which is in his heart . . .'. The phrase 'scribes and Pharisees' in 39.1 is commonly said to be distinctive of Matthew's style, just as the wording 'which is in his heart' in 45.3 is widely agreed to be Lucan. Patterson himself admits as much. But how are Matthean and Lucan traces in *Thomas* to be explained if, as he argues, the author behind the Coptic collection never knew these gospels? On the one hand, Patterson realizes that to write this off as coincidence would be akin to hiding an elephant under a rug; on the other hand, if he concedes that Thomas knew and used Matthew and Luke here and elsewhere, this opens the door to countless other places where the Thomasine editor may also have used the written synoptic tradition − indeed, why would any other explanation be necessary? To avert the dilemma, our author stays the course with a third possibility, namely, that the trademark language of Matthew and Luke crept in at a fairly late stage in the process of textual transmission.[12] In other words, in those places where the Thomasine

[8] Patterson 1993: 22. See Crossan 1973: 147−8.
[9] Patterson 1993: 49.
[10] Patterson 1993: 45.
[11] Patterson 1993: 45.
[12] Patterson 1993: 36.

language can only be explained by knowledge of Matthew's or Luke's gospel, this knowledge is to be connected with a second-, third-, or fourth-century scribe who consciously or unconsciously conformed the text to the language of the synoptic tradition. According to Patterson, later corrupting influences also seem to have entered in on the level of theology, for example in *Gos. Thom.* 44, which appears to have been reworked under the influence of the Trinitarian terminology found in Tatian's *Diatessaron*.[13] The synoptic gospels' ordering of pericopae has also influenced the order of certain Thomasine sayings. One may think here, for example, of *Gos. Thom.* 65–66, which, conveying the Saying of the Rejected Stone on the heels of the Parable of the Wicked Tenants, follows the order of the triple tradition (Matt. 21.33–46//Mark 12.1–12//Luke 20.9–19).[14] Because it is 'scarcely imaginable that the synoptic tradition did not come to affect the text of Thomas in some way, especially during the period in which the canonical gospels were experiencing great popularity', Patterson prefers to speak of the Thomasine tradition as 'autonomous' rather than 'independent'.[15]

In the next step of his argument, Patterson draws attention to the phenomenon of catchwords. Catchwords, that is, the on-again-off-again repetition of word-sounds or word-meanings that link one saying to the next, are evidence for *Thomas's* oral pedigree; it is the 'principle upon which the sayings in the Gospel of Thomas were originally collected'.[16] Had we found no gaps in the pattern of catchwords, we would more naturally attribute them to a 'conscious design on the part of the editor'.[17] But because of the gaps and the irregularity with which catchwords are employed, it makes most sense to think of the collection as having oral origins.

Here Patterson draws on Robinson's category of *logoi sophon* ('words of the wise'), a term that, as mentioned in the Introduction, was coined by Robinson to describe the genre of various sayings collections, from those embedded in the *Didache* and Mark 4, to the *Testament of the Twelve Patriarchs* and the Gnostic dialogues. Within this trajectory of *logoi sophon* comfortably sit not only Q, but also the *Gospel of Thomas*. Along with Robinson and Koester, Patterson is convinced that there is something special about this genre and therefore there is something special about *Thomas*:

---

[13] Patterson 1993: 38.
[14] Patterson 1993: 51.
[15] Patterson 1993: 93. I will, however, remain with the conventional term 'independent'.
[16] Patterson 1993: 102.
[17] Patterson 1993: 102.

Insofar as the synoptic gospels absorb and defuse the sayings tradition by embedding it in a biographical narrative, they represent a critical detour from the literary and theological development traceable in a more direct line from Jewish and early Christian sayings collections, such as Q, to the Gospel of Thomas. In other words, any continuity between Thomas and the early stages of the Jesus tradition is not to be traced through the synoptic gospels, but rather directly to the collections of sayings used as sources by the synoptic evangelists.

(Patterson 1993: 105)

Patterson does not stipulate a genetic relationship between Q and *Thomas*, but rather sees them running in parallel universes. The most important historical difference between the two collections is that while Q fell victim to an unfriendly takeover at the hands of Matthew and Luke, *Thomas* evaded any such merger. This same *Thomas*, like the earliest layer of Q, represents the most accurate representation of Jesus. Far from being an apocalyptic preacher as he is made out, say, in Mark 13, the Jesus in *Thomas* actually looks more like an eschatological sage, one for whom the eschaton (i.e. God's decisive in-breaking into our reality) is not the end of the time–space continuum, but an ever-present, experiential, reality.[18] It is this presentation of Jesus, never having been bought out by the theological competition, that stays true to its origins.

For Patterson, the issues of provenance and dating are problematized by the supposition that *Thomas* is an evolving collection, changing its shape and contents from one generation to the next. Some sayings most assuredly go back to Jesus; others are very much later, for example, *Gos. Thom.* 7, which was created by a second-century Egyptian encratite.[19] In the end, on the basis of *Gos. Thom.* 12 and 13, which cast James and Thomas in very favourable lights, Patterson concludes that the collection came together at a time when the authority of the apostles was still being worked out. This leads him to favour a date in the 70s (first century CE), roughly the same time the synoptic gospels were being written.[20] While this date would be seen as too late for some (e.g. Crossan and DeConick) and far too early for others (Dehandschutter and Fieger), on the question of provenance our author is not the least bit controversial. Like the vast majority of

---

[18] Patterson 1993: 106–10.

[19] Patterson 1993: 115 n10. 'Encratism' was an ascetical movement, especially popular in eastern Christianity after the end of the second century, whose adherents would deny themselves earthly pleasures like alcohol, meat and sexual activity.

[20] Patterson 1993: 113–20.

scholars, he sees the collection as bearing the indelible stamp of Syrian provenance, the area around Edessa.[21]

From here Patterson goes on to offer a social description: what can we know about the community that gave birth to this *Gospel of Thomas* and what were they like? In the first place, our author surmises that the Thomas community was one that stressed the itinerant life (*Gos. Thom.* 14.4, 42, 86, etc.), as well as the cutting of family ties (*Gos. Thom.* 31, 55, 101). Signing up with the Thomas sect also meant taking up a life of poverty and begging (*Gos. Thom.* 36, 54, 95, etc.). No Donald-Trump-wanna-bes here: the Thomas community was one in which the obtaining and possession of mammon were eschewed.[22] This ancient community was also one in which the presence of the living Jesus was prioritized over traditional Jewish rituals and disciplines (*Gos. Thom.* 14, 52), rulers big and small were put in their place (*Gos. Thom.* 71, 78, 100), and organizational structure was kept to a minimum (*Gos. Thom.* 30, 49). Finally, it was a community open to women – well, sort of. The bad news, as the last logion in the collection tells us, is that women had to 'become like men' first (*Gos. Thom.* 114). While this saying has been variously interpreted, Patterson sees it as fitting his theory to a tee: 'It would have been difficult for a woman to live the itinerant life unmolested by the various characters inhabiting highway and byway. Disguise as a man would have offered at least some protection from these dangers.'[23] Obviously, life among the Thomas Christians would have been difficult even by ancient standards of comfort. It was a community in which 'men were men' – and come to think of it, so were the women.

Following a description of the sect's social life, Patterson goes on to argue that this Thomas community, governed by norms of itinerancy and asceticism, was the historic continuation of the Jesus movement as described by the well-known New Testament scholar Gerd Theissen; it was a movement of wandering radicalism.[24] Eventually the Thomasine movement became a shaping force in early Syriac Christianity, which, as is well known from texts like *Acts of Thomas* and Pseudo-Clement's *To the Virgins*, also had a decidedly ascetical aspect.[25] As history would have it, however, the Thomas community was not able to maintain its lifestyle for very long. For as Christianity became increasingly settled, local leaderships began to resent the

---

[21] Patterson 1993: 118–20.
[22] Patterson 1993: 126–46.
[23] Patterson 1993: 155. See fuller discussion in Marjanen 1998a.
[24] Patterson 1993: 158–70. See Theissen 1977 [1978].
[25] Patterson 1993: 166–8.

incursions of the wandering charismatic itinerants and conflict broke out. The traces of such conflict, Patterson claims, can be found in *Didache* 11–13, James, 2 John and 3 John.[26] In fact, the high-impact collision between the wandering charismatic leaders and local institutionalized leadership structures seems to have left burn marks on the *Gospel of Thomas* itself. First, as the Thomas community began facing an increasingly domesticated church, one that was in effect 'selling out' on the original ideals of the Jesus movement, it had little choice but to radicalize its own demands of forsaking family and possessions. This call to leave all for the cause, Patterson maintains, was best leveraged by the notion that material wealth, family bounds, and other such earthly ties were to be regarded as unnecessary evils, ones left behind. Second, as it became clear to the Thomas Christians that fewer and fewer Christians were appreciative and supportive of the their wandering lifestyle, they sought to respond – as beleaguered sects sometimes do in such circumstances – by intensifying the privileged nature of their truth claims. This worldly renunciation combined with radical claims to esoteric truth lent itself almost inevitably to Gnosticism.[27] The *Gospel of Thomas*, in other words, tells a story of a community in social and theological flux, one that was transitioning from primitive Christianity as it was taught by Jesus into Gnosticism.

Nonetheless, one thing that remained as true for Jesus as for his spiritual heirs in the Thomas community was the presence of the kingdom:

> If eschatology is a mythological challenge to the world as it exists, the mythological expression of hope for something better, asceticism offers a real, present challenge to the world. It calls into question the ways of the world, its standards, its goals, its notion of what is meaningful in life. Thomas Christianity's social radicalism, as a form of asceticism, has precisely this effect . . . Everything that the world of early Christianity has to offer is called into question. This is eschatology demythologized and actualized. Wandering radicalism does not proclaim the (future) coming of the kingdom, it brings it directly to the front door. With the knock of the itinerant radical, the old world has already passed away, and the kingdom of God has arrived.[28]

Such is the vision of Thomas Christianity; such, according to Patterson, is the vision of Jesus too. The author cannot resist pressing the point and its implications for research. Jesus scholarship to date, he tells us,

---

[26] Patterson 1993: 171–95.
[27] Patterson 1993: 196–206.
[28] Patterson 1993: 211.

has been hampered by its remaining within the confines of the synoptic gospels and it is time to step out. By comparing *Thomas* with the synoptics, it is possible to arrive at some common ground of material that is 'at a very early stratum in the sayings tradition, which stands the best chance of preserving some continuity with the preaching of Jesus.'[29] Amidst that cache of authentic Jesus materials may be discerned first and foremost an ethos of social radicalism.[30] It would be in his later books that Patterson would be able to develop more fully what this Jesus looks like and what difference his life and message makes to our lives.[31]

Response

On the face of it, there is a certain beauty to Stephen Patterson's explanation for our Coptic collection. Whereas so many Thomas scholars content themselves with treating the gospel in piecemeal fashion, bringing their critical skills to bear on one logion at a time, but daring to go no farther, Patterson achieves a big picture, a vision of the whole gospel, without sacrificing attention to detail. Although his account is obviously indebted to Koester and Robinson in a number of ways, he has taken the work of these two scholars considerably further by granting their general outline fresh plausibility. His distinctive synthesis of theological and sociological realities makes *The Gospel of Thomas and Jesus* one of the most brilliantly argued works on the collection to date.

But the question at the end of the day is whether Patterson has got it right. Well, yes and no. Positively speaking, I am convinced that Patterson has correctly identified asceticism as *the* self-defining activity of the Thomasine community. The glorification of poverty, the talk regarding reconstituted families, the low view of the body – all these add up to asceticism of some kind or another. Secondly, our author is equally correct to maintain that the author of *Thomas* had an outlook that might be characterized as actualized eschatology. Quite apart from the question as to how Jesus conceived the coming of the kingdom (future, present or something in between), for Thomas and his hearers the kingdom was indeed a present reality that carried with it no hint of a future apocalyptic crisis or upheaval or even resurrection. While the expectation of such an event in the mind of

---

[29] Patterson 1993: 241.
[30] Patterson 1993: 241.
[31] Patterson 1998, 2004.

Thomas's author cannot be ruled out altogether (this would be an argument from silence), the focus is clearly on the present realization of the kingdom. Third, Patterson's comparison between Thomasine Christianity and early Syrian Christianity is a useful one. There are indeed, as our author notes, telling points of comparison between the asceticism that can be inferred from, say, the Syrian text the *Acts of Thomas* and the kind of asceticism discernible in the *Gospel of Thomas*.[32] He may have even gone further to show how the realized eschatology in Thomas also bears striking resemblance to what we know of the second- and third-century Syriac Christians.[33] If some kind of historical linkage is to be inferred from these comparisons, the crucial question (and one that deserves more attention than Patterson is able to give here) is whether the pathway of influence is to be construed diachronically or synchronically. In other words, are the similarities between the *Gospel of Thomas* and early Syrian Christianity to be explained by their sharing a common historical trajectory, or are they to be explained by their sharing a common milieu?

This pushes us back once again to the issues of sources and dating. And here, regarding precisely these issues, it is questionable whether Patterson has in fact made his case. Patterson begins, as I have pointed out, by reframing the question. 'For those of you who say that *Thomas* is dependent on the synoptic tradition,' he seems to say, 'show me (1) a "consistent pattern of dependence", and (2) some account as to why the sequence of material in *Thomas* is so wildly divergent from that of the synoptic tradition.' Fair enough. But what does '*consistent* pattern of dependence' mean? He allows that there are more than a handful of places where Thomas preserves the distinctive touches of Matthew and Luke. This is, as Patterson would presumably concede, a pattern of sorts. But it is apparently not a 'consistent pattern'. But then what should a *consistent* pattern look like? For any given pericope in Matthew or Luke, certifiable Mattheanisms or Lucanisms are relatively uncommon. How many sure such marks of written synoptic tradition would one need in order for Patterson to reverse himself?[34] For lack of an objective and verifiable standard by which the conditions of 'consistent pattern' could be met, the argument is hardly satisfying. One might justifiably be wary of such an argument, much as one might be wary of being challenged to a high-jump competition where the opponent gets to hold the bar at an undisclosed (and for all one knows quickly adjustable) height.

---

[32] Patterson 1993: 167.

[33] See, e.g. Sivertsev 2000.

[34] So too Tuckett 1991: 359 in regard to Koester's similar argument.

The argument relating to the unusual sequencing of *Thomas* vis-à-vis the triple tradition is more compelling. If it is true that Thomas drew on the synoptic materials, it would indeed be natural enough to expect some reflection of this fact in his ordering of that material. It is of course theoretically possible that the editor who assembled the 114 sayings into their current order did so by moving madly back and forth through the text. But it is, as I pointed out above, quite hard to imagine him or her doing so simply for the sake of doing so. The irregular order of the Thomasine logia provides *prima facie* grounds for assuming that whoever put this collection together did not do so by slowly unrolling a scroll of the gospels (actually it would take a few scrolls) and working from there.

Ultimately, Patterson's source-critical case rises and falls on these two points: the absence of consistent dependence (however that is defined) and the absence of shared sequence. And of these two, the latter is much the stronger. In claiming this, I am asserting that while Patterson's extensive source-critical analysis shows how the data may be compatible with Thomasine independence (not an insignificant point), it does not prove as much. This is so because if one begins with the assumption that *Thomas* is substantially made up of sayings that have evolved independently of the synoptic tradition, form-critical analysis can substantiate this assumption but it cannot by itself rule out alternative explanations. Just as Schrage's application of redaction-critical principles to the *Gospel of Thomas* ineluctably led to the conclusion that the final editor was simply reworking synoptic materials, form-critical analysis of the same text will inevitably tend to generate the opposite conclusion, *viz.* that *Thomas* was orally and independently derived. Both methodologies, unless they are triangulated against other lines of inquiry, can only confirm what they have already assumed. To expect any different would be like telling the gardener with the pruning shears, 'You missed digging a few weeds here!' and the other gardener with the weeder, 'You really need to cut the rose bushes back some more.'[35] Thus in the attempt to move beyond the impasse between independence and dependence, Patterson cannot issue a decisive verdict on the evidence of form criticism. What he can do, and what he has done admirably, is to give fresh currency and coherency to the view of Thomasine independence. This is no mean feat, but plausibility should not be confused with proof. We are driven back to the question of 'consistent dependence'

---

[35] Or, as the late Robert Funk (1971: 151) put it: 'Methodology is not an indifferent net – it catches what it intends to catch.'

and why the Thomasine order is so strikingly different from that of the synoptic witness.

A review of Patterson's book would not be complete without taking a closer look at some of the shoulders on which he stands. We have already met one pair of shoulders in James Robinson. Robinson, along with Koester, believes that since the sayings genre (*logoi sophon*) to which *Thomas* belongs is by definition free from narrative elements, elements which accrued to other texts like Q, it stands to reason that these Thomasine logia are the closest thing to what Jesus actually said. Simply on account of its genre, the Thomas collection is to be prized as preserving the message of the historical Jesus without the embellishments of theologically tendentious narrative. Obviously, for Patterson or anyone else seeking to build an argument for the *Gospel of Thomas*'s independence relative to the canonical gospels, Robinson and Koester's identification of *Thomas* as *logoi sophon* makes for attractive support. Because *Thomas* may be classed among the untainted *logoi sophon*, its primitiveness and therefore its independence virtually speak for themselves.

There are, however, several glaring fissures in the support. First of all, Robinson has been criticized, rightly, for playing fast and loose with the categories of form and genre.[36] Because Bultmann and the classic form critics envisaged their task as being distinct in principle from the literary investigation of genre, they employed the term 'form' strictly for describing the rhetorical shape and structure of discrete oral performances. This means, very simply and sensibly, that form has to do with the hypothesized isolated oral unit behind the final text, while genre has to do with the literary product that is the final text. On the face of it, it makes no more sense to collapse the distinction between 'wisdom saying' and 'wisdom saying collection' than it does to think that an interview transcript is one and the same as the version that ends up on glossy pages in the magazine racks. Practically ignoring the *Gospel of Thomas*'s status as an edited document (along with any substantive consideration of the theological, literary and social agenda that drove the selection, arrangement and editing of that document), Robinson and Koester choose instead to see the Coptic text as a naïvely compiled and rather long-winded wisdom saying. One might say this is a kind of form criticism that has forgotten its limits.

The justification for taking up literary concerns on form–critical premises is arrived at neither by the path of critical thinking nor by

---

[36] See, e.g. Schröter 1997: 34–5.

a self-consciously articulated rationale, but by an intuition that traces itself to a romantic notion reaching at least as far back as the late eighteenth-century thinker Herder.[37] For Herder, as for Giambattista Vico a generation earlier, the oral utterance, whether lost on the sound waves or preserved in ink, possessed a kind of inherent innocence, primitiveness and originality that defied all subsequent attempts to impose refinement. Surely, were Vico and Herder alive today and interested in learning about the real David Beckham, their instincts would tell them to forgo the biography in favour of an article like 'Beckham in His Own Words'. Why? Because the path to one's true self, so their intuition would say, is through his or her words. Examining the transmission of Jesus' words on analogy with folklore, Bultmann was heir to this romantic tradition. Therefore, it is hardly surprising if for Koester and Robinson, the premier modern-day perpetuators of the same legacy, the words of the *Gospel of Thomas*, precisely because they are just words without *obvious* mediation or manipulation, seem like the real Jesus. Here we have critical naïveté creating the presumption of textual naïveté, but the presumption is unwarranted.

The privileging of recorded words (sayings collections) over recorded actions (narrative) as bearers of historical fact finds its roots in certain other philosophical commitments which are equally liable to criticism. The most obvious critique, and one that has been developed in a more sophisticated way by Wittgenstein and later by speech-act theorists, pertains to the observation that a sharp dichotomy between words and actions is finally unsustainable.[38] At the end of the day, words act (i.e. are intrinsically performative) and actions talk (i.e. are intrinsically communicative). To deny as much is to remain strangely blinkered by the post-Enlightenment notion that mind and body occupy two separate universes. The form-critical approach to the synoptics and *Thomas*, taken up by the Patterson–Koester–Robinson line, is ultimately driven by a dualism that has been drawing fire in philosophical and hermeneutical circles for some time now.

But there is more to Bultmann's influence (via Robinson and Koester) on Patterson than his romantic idealism. There are also built into the argument certain preconceptions regarding the person of Jesus. According to Bultmann, when Jesus preached the kingdom, he was not preaching a historic event; he was preaching an ever-present existential reality, and the words of Jesus were less signifiers of

---

[37] Berger 1984: 63–7.
[38] See Kerr 1986; Arens 1997.

historical realities than vehicles of the person of Jesus himself. It was through his words that Jesus made himself present to his hearers and this is the only reason that the early church later on bothered to rehearse them. Of course, this take on Jesus and his message leaves large swathes of the gospels unexplained, particularly those portions – for example, the Olivet Discourse in Mark 13 – where Jesus seems to be intimating some kind of divinely initiated rupturing of history. But for Bultmann such content would have to take a back seat as far as authenticity was concerned. As reticent as Bultmann was to speak of what we can know about the historical Jesus, his thin-lined, charcoal sketch of the man from Galilee finally gave the impression that the real Jesus can be seen not through any mythological claim to be the Son of Man but through his wisdom sayings.

As students of Bultmann, Koester and Robinson have been – *mutatis mutandi* – faithful to their master's vision of Jesus. And what better vindication of Bultmann's Jesus than the *Gospel of Thomas*? Having neither apocalyptic material nor talk about Jesus being the Son of Man, *Thomas* is the one gospel in which the post-Bultmannian tradition would find Jesus, once duly set on his feet and scraped of his Gnostic overlay, at his truest and best. Thus, it is no coincidence that this Bultmannian Jesus plays as important a role in Patterson's argument as he does for Koester and Crossan. These scholars are simply cashing out a perceived reciprocity between Jesus the Sage and the Jesus of *Thomas*. Thanks to the Nag Hammadi gospel, the non-apocalyptic, existential Jesus has finally received the hard backing of historical artefact. Conversely, when it comes to getting into the very exclusive club called 'Texts That Can Actually Tell Us Something About Jesus', all Thomas has to do is point to this same non-apocalyptic Jesus, say, 'I'm with him', and his foot is more than in the door. Struck by the semblance between a de-apocalyptized Jesus and the Thomasine Jesus, Patterson and several others before him have realized that, between the Bultmannian vision and the text of *Thomas*, this could be the beginning of a beautiful, symbiotic relationship.

At the same time, inasmuch as Patterson relies on Gerd Theissen, who envisions Jesus as a wandering itinerant, the leader of a social movement characterized by *Wanderradikalismus*, his Jesus also undergoes important modifications. To be clear: if Theissen has accurately characterized the historical Jesus movement, and if what can be gathered from *Thomas* coheres with the details of Theissen's thesis, then this provides a sound explanation as to when, how, and why the Thomas movement got its start. However, if both these conditions are unfulfilled, Patterson is left without an explanation as to why the first-century Thomas Christians believed what they did and acted the way they did. More to the point, he falls short of his goal of securing a socio-historical reason for locating Thomas Christianity in the first century. It is as if Patterson, in seeking to return the glass slipper of *Thomas* to its rightful owner, has decided that the shoe best fits Theissen's Jesus.

But sometimes Cinderella is not so easy to find. While Theissen's argument has undoubtedly won some converts, there has also been quite a lot of scholarship written since the publication of *The Sociology of Early Palestinian Christianity* (1978) and his later *The Shadow of the Galilean* (1987) that takes a decidedly different view of Jesus and his mission.[39] To put it mildly, there is a lively difference of opinion among scholars as to who Jesus was and his rationale for gathering followers. Were there fewer young maidens in the land, at least were there fewer who could make a passable Cinderella, Patterson's dependence on Theissen would be less precarious.

But even if for a moment it were granted that Theissen was correct, that the Jesus movement was deeply ascetic, it seems that Cinderella's foot is being sized up at too great a distance. For on closer inspection, it seems that *Thomas*'s brand of asceticism is rather different from anything we find in the first decades of Christianity. First, *Thomas*'s insistence on celibacy (*Gos. Thom.* 16, 30, 49, 75) squares poorly with the well-known fact that early Christianity's leaders were almost all married (1 Cor. 9.5).[40] Second, while Patterson maintains that the call to Thomas Christianity entailed denouncing worldly possessions, the canonical traditions consistently depict Jesus' closest disciples as having means. One might think, for example, of Lazarus, Mary and Martha (Luke 10.38–42), James and John (Mark 1.20), Peter (John 21), or a number of women who supported Jesus out of their own pockets (Luke 8.1–3). When Jesus says, 'The poor you will always have with you' (Mark 14.7), this implies that the poor were people other than the disciples. Third, if the Jesus movement developed out of John the Baptist's desert movement, and both sects affirmed certain Jewish rituals (including prayer, fasting and almsgiving), how is it that the community behind *Thomas* stood staunchly opposed to such rituals (e.g., *Gos. Thom.* 14, 53, 89)?[41] *Thomas*'s stark rejection

---

[39] Evans (2006) is correct in maintaining that the most dominant trend in Jesus research emphasizes, in a way quite different from Theissen, Jesus' Jewishness.

[40] See Patterson 1993: 152–3.

[41] See the comments of A. Marjanen (1998c: 180): 'With regard to these [Jewish] religious practices, the author thus belongs to those early Christians who reject their Jewish legacy altogether.'

of marriage, possessions and distinctively Jewish practices coheres poorly with what we know about Jesus.

Finally, even if the Jesus movement was itinerant in the way Theissen conceives (a big 'if'),[42] there is in fact no compelling evidence that Thomas Christianity took up the practice in the same way. Patterson infers that they did so on the basis of *Gos. Thom.* 42 ('Be passers-by') and 14.4 ('When you go into any region and walk about in the countryside, when people take you in, eat what they serve you and care for the sick among them'). *Gos. Thom.* 42 is notoriously difficult and, being subject to a wide variety of translations and interpretations, seems too uncertain to weigh heavily in consideration.[43] *Gos. Thom.* 14.4 may have served any number of functions in the Thomas community, just as the parallels in Luke 10.8–9 and Matthew 10.5–8 have presumably served a function in two thousand years of Christianity without necessarily being understood to entail a lifestyle of itinerant teaching.[44] And even if we admit *Gos. Thom.* 86 ('. . . but the Son of Man has no place to lay his head and rest') into consideration, this together with the other logia provide all too slender a basis for inferring that Thomas Christians wended their way through the towns in the manner of Jesus' disciples with essentially the same goals.

The explanatory power of Patterson's argument is constrained not only by the fact that Theissen's Jesus has failed to win the day, but, more substantially, by the contradictions between the practices of the Jesus movement and those of Thomas Christianity. To his credit, Patterson is *not* saying that Thomas Christianity and the historical Jesus movement are to be linked on account of the fact that they are both ascetical groups. Asceticism was widely practised in the ancient world and so to have staked this claim would be something like postulating a historical link between two churches by virtue of their both having a steeple. But any explanatory power Patterson derives from the parallels between Theissen's Jesus and Thomas Christianity is offset by the patent incongruities. If you find that the glass slipper goes on only after considerable tussling, shoving and shoe-horning, perhaps it's time to take the shoe back and keep looking. Either you have not found your elusive Cinderella or the quest is misguided altogether, that is, the glass shoe never belonged to the famed pauper in the first place.

---

[42] See a critique of this point in Witherington 1995: 139–40.

[43] See, e.g. the survey on *Gos. Thom.* 42 in Sellew 2006.

[44] But see Quispel 1985: 248 on itinerancy in the early Syriac church.

Conclusion

To summarize, Patterson has successfully established the following points. First, if the *Gospel of Thomas* is dependent on the synoptic gospels, the present order of Thomasine sayings cries out for explanation. Until such an explanation is provided, we may well, at least on these grounds, be best served by supposing that the gospel hailed from an independent, oral, stream of tradition. Second, Thomas Christianity was characterized by a thoroughgoing asceticism of some kind, even if the details of that asceticism do not line up with the practices of the Jesus movement. Third, the Thomasine community espoused what may be accurately termed a realized eschatology. The kingdom was not primarily a future event (if it was a future event at all): it was a present reality. Fourth, there are certain semblances between Thomas Christianity and early Syriac Christianity, as can be seen in such texts as the *Acts of Thomas*. The best historical explanation for *Thomas* will somehow link it, as Patterson has done, with Christianity as it was practised in the environs of late second- or early third-century Edessa. These are all, I believe, important points.

Unfortunately, our author has fallen short of making a compelling case for tracing the *Gospel of Thomas* back to the Jesus community. Yet the glass slipper must belong to *somebody*. As we consider Elaine Pagels and April DeConick, we will ask whether and in what ways these two scholars have come any closer to a good fit.

2

The Thomas community on the run: Elaine Pagels

It is no secret that the vast majority of contemporary biblical and theological scholarship is written for a very small audience. In part the inability of biblical-theological scholarship to popularize itself has to do with the ever-increasing degrees of specialization in human knowledge. But, to my mind, the guild's broad failure to resonate with and market itself to the everyday faith concerns of the layperson is more the result of a methodological divide in scholarship. For a number of years now, history and theology have been locked away in two separate towers, so that the one has not been able to speak to the other. After reading a systematic-theological piece, I often find myself whimsically wishing that the author had taken more time to describe the historical setting in which the scriptures took shape. Likewise, on my shelves there are innumerable books dealing with the history behind the Bible and the early church, but, I find myself sighing, if only there were a greater willingness to deal with the broader question, 'So what?' The separation of 'what it meant then' and 'what it means today' is unfortunate, because history and theology need each other, at least if they ever hope to descend from the ivory heights to the firm earth of cultural relevance.

Of course, in speaking of the split between faith and history in modern scholarship, I am generalizing, and as with any generalization there are important exceptions. Elaine Pagels, the Harrington Spear Paine Professor of Religion at Princeton University and the author of the *New York Times* bestseller *Beyond Belief: The Secret Gospel of Thomas*, is one such exception. Fearless in combining historical research with personal reflection, Pagels's overall approach is a breath of fresh air. Hers is a tale told both by scholar and seeker, historian and woman of faith; her boldness and honesty are to be commended. Surely, whatever reservations I or any other reader may have concerning this book, a writer who unapologetically synthesizes historiography and faith – all things being equal – is surely to be preferred to one who pretends to speak to such subjects apart from any personal involvement. Although, as will become clear soon enough, I disagree with

Pagels at a number of turns, no reader could fail to appreciate how Pagels, in her crisp and lucid style, takes pains to show why the *Gospel of Thomas* matters. Now on to the book itself.

Review

In the opening chapter, Pagels reminisces on the personal and spiritual crisis set in motion through the suffering and eventual death of her young son. Her account is as touching as it is poignant for its raw candour. She recounts how in those days people in her church would come to her and say, 'Your faith must be of very great help to you.' Our author wonders, 'What do they mean? What is faith?'[1] In essence, the remainder of the book is dedicated to answering that very question in a way that attempts to be both deeply personal and historically responsible.

Faith, so it seems for the author, can be conceived of in one of two ways. There is the kind of faith that can be found within oneself and there is the kind of belief that entails allegiance to certain external propositions. For Pagels, these two kinds of faith represent, respectively, the best and worst aspects of Christianity. 'What is it about Christian tradition that we love?' she asks, and then, somewhat acidly, 'What is it that we *cannot* love?'[2] That which she loves, the reader gathers, is the expressions of hope and community she finds both in her own church experience and in the recorded acts of the pre-Nicean church. That which Pagels cannot love – here the author is more explicit – is the 'tendency to identify Christianity with a single, authorized set of beliefs' and 'the conviction that Christian belief alone offers access to God'.[3]

At bottom, Pagels's goal is to show that in the first three hundred years of the church's existence, certain notions attached themselves to Christian tradition, notions which, insofar as they unduly circumscribed legitimate spiritual expression, were alien to earliest Christian belief. These doctrinal accretions, imposed by an ecclesiastical hierarchy bent on consolidating an increasingly diverse Christian movement, spelled the reversal of an earlier willingness to embrace a great diversity of faith communities, including the mystically inclined movement represented by the *Gospel of Thomas*. In her account of church history from the *Gospel of Thomas* to Nicea, it becomes clear that Pagels is interested in reclaiming those strains of Christianity which

---

[1] Pagels 2003: 5.
[2] Pagels 2003: 6.
[3] Pagels 2003: 29.

have been de-legitimized and suppressed by the ecclesiastical powers. That the harbingers of Nicene Christianity had successfully eclipsed alternative belief systems is not so much a tribute to the inherent persuasiveness or truthfulness of their position as a reminder that some ideas attain the status of truth simply through the fortunes of history. Pagels suggests that, when one examines the turn of events leading up to Nicea, it becomes apparent that at least the first creeds, so foundational to the church's beliefs, are but the accidental truths of history.

But this is no mere revisionist history for revisionist history's sake. Our author cannot conceal her longing to return to a pre-Nicene Christianity, a primitive and pristine faith without the elaborate theological formulations and constraining canons – without, in short, the suggestion that some have God right, others have God wrong. It seems that Pagels, essentially rehabilitating the project of the well-known Enlightenment figure Rousseau, is seeking to extract the primitive core of Christian faith from the Christological and soteriological overlays that supposedly had accumulated with time. In order to arrive at this authentic Christianity, we must first peel off the extraneous husk of later ecclesial history, fraught as it is with intrigue and political coercion.

To this end Pagels brings to bear her own research on *Thomas* and in particular the theory, already proposed by Riley and DeConick, that the fourth gospel was written as a response to the Thomasine collection or at least the theology that the collection espoused.[4] A first step involves showing that John's soteriology and Christology constituted a radical break from what had hitherto been believed about Jesus, including what had been believed by the authors of the synoptic gospels. Towards underscoring the disparity between the fourth and the first three gospels, Pagels employs a number of examples to argue that 'John's gospel directly contradicts the combined testimony of the other New Testament gospels.'[5] More significantly, John differs from the synoptics in that while the latter saw Jesus as 'merely God's human servant', the fourth evangelist saw him as 'God himself revealed in human form'.[6] According to Pagels, the radical message of John (that salvation is to be found in Christ alone) would have been completely unanticipated by the writers of the first three gospels, for 'Mark's contemporaries would most likely have seen Jesus as a *man*.'[7] Pagels intends to show that the author of the fourth gospel is an isolated

---

[4] Riley 1995; DeConick 1996: 72–3.
[5] Pagels 2003: 35.
[6] Pagels 2003: 37.
[7] Pagels 2003: 38.

figure; when he does allude to the other apostles, it is only to snipe discretely at them.[8]

As important as the differences are between John and the earlier (synoptic) gospels, equally important are the similarities between the fourth gospel and *Thomas*. Both John and Thomas seem to know the storyline preserved in Mark. John, like Thomas, preserves secret sayings (John 13–18). Moreover, when compared to the synoptic tradition, John and Thomas are less interested in eschatology (doctrine of last things) than they are in protology (doctrine of first things): for John and Thomas both, Jesus is the primordial light.[9] Likewise, also against the synoptic witness, John and Thomas share a realized eschatology: the kingdom is not a future event, but a present reality.[10]

Despite their shared misgivings with the synoptic portrait of Jesus, John and Thomas are far from being two peas in a pod. Indeed, 'John's gospel was written in the heat of controversy, to defend certain views of Jesus and to oppose others.'[11] What John the evangelist stood *for* was his readers' belief, that they might have life through the name of Jesus. But what

> John opposed, as we shall see, includes what the Gospel of Thomas teaches – that God's light shines not only in Jesus but potentially at least, in everyone. Thomas's gospel encourages the hearer not so much to *believe in Jesus*, as John requires, as to *seek to know God* through one's own, divinely given capacity, since all are created in the image of God. For Christians in later generations, the Gospel of John helped provide a foundation for a unified church, which Thomas, with its emphasis on each person's search for God, did not.
>
> (Pagels 2003: 34)

Whereas John depicts Jesus as the unique bearer of light and salvation, Thomas tells another story: 'that the divine light Jesus embodied is shared by humanity, since we are all made "in the image of God"'.[12] According to Pagels, who here is undoubtedly drawing very deeply on DeConick's *Voices of the Mystics*, Thomas is advocating a vision of faith that involves turning to the truth of God within, while John, uncomfortable with this kind of natural theology, insists on finding salvation only in Jesus. The deepest truth of all, Thomas would have us know, is that true salvation is to be found within oneself.

---

[8] Pagels 2003: 60–4.
[9] Pagels 2003: 39–40.
[10] Pagels 2003: 49–51.
[11] Pagels 2003: 34.
[12] Pagels 2003: 40–1.

But why is it that John is said to be a refuter of Thomas and not vice versa? The answer in short is that Riley's argument, which I have already briefly discussed, has convinced her of Thomas's priority.[13] It is the fourth gospel, not the synoptics, that goes out of the way to cast Thomas in a negative light (John 11.16; 14.3–4; 20.24–31). Nor to be missed is the absence of Thomas the *dramatis persona* during Jesus' appearance behind closed doors (John 20.19–24):

> The implication of the story is clear: Thomas . . . is not an apostle, has not received the holy spirit, and lacks the power to forgive sins, which the others received directly from the risen Christ. Furthermore, when they tell Thomas about their encounter with Jesus, he answers in the words that mark him forever – in John's characterization – as Doubting Thomas: 'Unless I see the mark of the nails in his hands, and put my finger in the mark of the nails, and my hand in his side, I will not believe.' (Pagels 2003: 71)

A week later, as the biblical account goes, when Jesus appears to all the disciples, he says to Thomas, 'Do not be faithless, but believe.'

> For John, this scene is the coup de grâce: finally Thomas understands, and Jesus warns the rest of the chastened disciples . . . Thus John warns all his readers that they *must* believe what they cannot verify for themselves – namely, the gospel message to which he declares himself a witness – or face God's wrath. John may have felt some satisfaction writing this scene; for here he shows Thomas giving up his search for experiential truth – his unbelief – to confess what he sees as the truth of his gospel: the message should not be lost on Thomas Christians. (Pagels 2003: 72)

Comparing John with Thomas, Pagels, like Riley and DeConick, finds evidence that the former has a bone or two to pick with the latter. John must be considered later.

Pagels then picks up the story again with Irenaeus. When the Bishop of Lyons became disturbed by a charismatic sect called Montanism and began to exert an overwhelming influence on the late second-century church, he did so with the intent of making John the '*first and foremost of the gospels*'.[14] And succeed he did. Eventually, the whole church came to interpret the synoptic gospels and indeed the whole New Testament canon through the Johannine lens. The great irony is that, although John's views on Jesus were hardly characteristic of the Christian movement at the end of the first century, by the end of the second it would be John's views that would

---

[13] Pagels 2003: 58. See Introduction, pp. 13–14.
[14] Pagels 2003: 112.

prevail, and continue to prevail to this day.[15] On Pagels's reckoning, then, if orthodox Christians have the Gospel of John to thank for setting the agenda for the formation of orthodoxy, a provocative assertion in its own right, we have the *Gospel of Thomas* to thank for sparking the controversy that led to the writing of John.

For her part, Pagels is not particularly thankful for how early Christian history turned out, neither for the repression of Thomas Christianity nor for the fact that John's views would become normative in Christian circles. But the point of her historiographical exposé is clear: because of this turn of events, the more mystically inclined Thomas-style Christians, those more comfortable with 'experiential truth', have been tragically excluded. At the heart of this history is a forceful plea, a call for a return to a halcyon period of broad theological diversity, where Thomas Christians could happily worship with Matthean or Lucan Christians, a period where Christians did without such things as creeds and formulations. Pagels seems to be saying, 'To this Christianity we must go; to these kinds of Christians we must turn in imitation.'

Response

If there is one thing that Pagels is absolutely right about, it is that Thomasine Christianity is fundamentally an interiorized religion, one that clearly identifies self-knowledge with salvation. In broad terms, this is what the *Gospel of Thomas* is 'about'. In the Thomas community salvation seems possible not only quite apart from external revelation, but quite apart from community as well. She is equally right to insist that this was *not* what the likes of Irenaeus were about. In his five-volume *Against Heresies*, Irenaeus could hardly have come out any more strongly against the various sects that he saw as heretical, not least because of their views on revelation (how one learns about God) and soteriology (how one becomes rightly related to God). Obviously, Irenaeus's successors would have to decide whether the boundary lines drawn by Irenaeus and earlier writers like him were appropriate. As history would have it, the orthodox church stuck with Irenaeus, and has stuck to this day.

Two more points need to be brought out. First, Pagels is also on to something when she highlights Thomas's interest in protology, that is, beginnings. Like John, and in fact seemingly sharing much of John's

---

[15] Pagels 2003: 45.

vocabulary, the author of *Thomas* is attracted to creational images. Second, Pagels does well to recognize the need to explain why this is the *Gospel of Thomas*, and not, say, the *Gospel of Thaddeus* or the *Gospel of Fred*. Why did the Thomasine Christians decide to be *Thomas* Christians? While I challenge her interpretation of the data, this should not eclipse the fact that she has focused in on the right data.

A proper consideration of Pagels's argument must begin by giving some thought to how her argument works. She lays the groundwork for her case by isolating the fourth evangelist, theologically and historically. First John is played off against the synoptics, only to be coupled in some unusual ways with *Thomas*. Then he is distanced from *Thomas* on account of his failure to accept Thomas Christianity for (what Pagels sees as) some rather narrow-minded reasons. Like Tolkien's Gollum, John is painted as a rather strange, lonely and peevish figure, made to grouse along the margins of first-century Christianity. Once *Thomas* has been comfortably ensconced between the synoptics and John on the first-century timeline, John can then be portrayed not only as a theological odd-man-out, but as a late odd-man-out to boot. As fate would have it, we are told, it is precisely this peripheral Johnny-come-lately (no pun intended) that towards the end of the second century would catch the eye of Irenaeus, just as the bishop was scrambling to seize control over a church that had fallen into epistemological chaos. It was only in response to the Montanist crisis that Irenaeus insisted on the sole authority of the four now-canonical gospels, the most important of which was the Gospel of John. Those gospels disagreeing with John would have to go.

Of course there is more moral to the story than 'Some gospels have all the luck.' Pagels is making a much more fundamental and provocative point. It is in fact a two-fold claim: first, that Christianity-as-we-have-known-it owes its origins much more to a historical accident involving an isolated and misguided figure we call John than it does to anything else that may have gone on in the first century; and, second, that the mysticism witnessed in the *Gospel of Thomas* is earlier than and not the least bit inferior to what we find in John and later orthodoxy. In fact, if we get the hint, *Thomas* is more Christian than and theologically superior to anything John has to offer. Needless to say, if Pagels is right, a lot of people have a lot of rethinking to do, not to mention a good bit of back-pedalling.

A proper assessment of Pagels's thesis should begin with her construal of the relationship between John and the synoptics. To be sure, it is evident on even the most cursory reading that the fourth gospel stands apart from the synoptic texts in a number of ways.

John's arrangement of the material, his geographical focus, his relative omission of Jesus' parables and kingdom pronouncements – all these factors, among others, mark off the fourth gospel as distinctive. It is also unquestionable that the terminology and thrust of Johannine Christology is different from that of the other canonical gospels. But what Albert Schweitzer a hundred years ago saw as an 'antithesis' between John and the synoptics, a conceptual framework that gained prominence in the first half of the twentieth century, has in more recent years often been perceived as complementarity.[16] More importantly, despite Pagels's finding irreconcilable differences between the respective Christologies of John and the synoptic texts, the early church, while quite aware of differences between the gospels, did not seem to be quite so bothered.[17] Of course, one might, as Pagels does, chalk this up to a certain obtuseness on the part of the first few centuries of Christendom. But which is more likely, it may be asked, that the early church was blind to the existence of two mutually contradictory Jesuses (one only human, one only divine) in the same four-fold gospel collection, or that certain modern scholars have been determined to cast the synoptic Jesus and the Johannine Jesus together on a peculiar procrustean bed, framed by western, post-Enlightenment, assumptions as to what a God-man would really do and say? On general grounds, we ought to be duly suspicious of a twenty-first-century scholar who on a point like this says to the first readers of the gospels, 'Let me take the speck out of your eye!'

That the synoptic writers had no conviction of Jesus' divinity and that it was the author of John who introduced this notion at the expense of Jesus' humanity is a hard point to make stick. Even though the synoptic writers were driven by a different agenda than that of John, and by different questions than the ones that would later occupy the bishops at Nicea, this does not mean that the synoptic writers would have found John's characterization of Jesus or the Nicene definition at odds with their own. The earliest gospels, Mark and

---

[16] See, e.g. the comments of Thomas L. Brodie (1993: 33): 'John's Jesus is ultimately Mark's Jesus.' Similarly, Kammler 1996 and Bauckham 1998. Also, see now Anderson 2006.

[17] On the differences see Eusebius, *Hist. Eccl.* 6.14.7. Pagels's argument (2003: 37–8) in part turns on the claim that Son of God was originally a messianic title which the church, no doubt through the lens of John, erroneously took to be a claim of deity. Against this, the early church fathers' tendency to link Son of God with Son of David suggests that they knew the phrase as a messianic epithet but, like the gospel writers themselves, were not averse to capitalizing on the *sensus plenior* that may have been drawn from the term. Irenaeus (*Adv. Haer.* 3.11.6), at any rate, seems to be completely aware of the distinction between the two senses of 'Son of God': messiah and co-equal with God.

Matthew, both make statements testifying to a high Christology.[18] Paul himself, one of the earliest and most influential voices in the early Christian movement, speaks in the mid-first century with no less equivocation than John regarding Jesus' role as divine *kurios*, the Greek word translated 'Lord' (Rom. 9.3; 1 Cor. 8.3; Phil. 2.6, 11). (The omission of any treatment of Paul in *Beyond Belief* is striking indeed.) The author of Hebrews too could not have expressed a higher Christology (Heb. 1.1–4). As it turns out, the Christology of John is not the anomaly Pagels would have us believe.

What about John's soteriology? John's concern, our author tells us, is to inform his readers of the salvific necessity of belief in Jesus. No argument here. But then Pagels goes on to suggest that this notion is also peculiar to John, and that it would be this component of early Christian belief together with the notion of Jesus' divinity that would later serve as the hermeneutical lens through which later Christendom would understand all the other gospels. But against this it should be said that whatever special interest the fourth gospel might have in faith, and whatever bold and stark strokes it employs to separate those who are in the light from those who are in the darkness, such themes are discernible in just about every book of the New Testament canon. On any construal of New Testament theology, salvation by faith in Jesus is simply a rampant theme.

Moreover, any evidence for Pagels's related claim, that John acquired something like 'hermeneutical lens' status and that at the hands of Irenaeus, is simply lacking. First, if there was anything like a gospel of choice in the early centuries, it was Matthew – by far the most quoted gospel – and not John.[19] Second, that Irenaeus was plotting the redundancy of other gospels through a promotion of John runs afoul of the fact that, in one of the very first mentions of the fourth gospel by name, the bishop explicitly inveighs against those (the Valentinians in this case) who gave John privileged status among the gospels.[20] For the Bishop of Lyons, it was to be all four gospels or nothing at all. Irenaeus's insistence on four and only four gospels smacks of the sense that he is simply reinforcing a notion already well accepted by his readers; it is unlikely that he is setting forth a novel argument, at least on such slim grounds.[21] Judging by the evidence

---

[18] Consider (one need go no further) how Mark begins his gospel by implicitly equating Jesus with the 'Lord' of Isaiah 40.3 (Mark 1.3); Matthew (3.3) and Luke (3.4) do no less. See Gathercole 2006: 46–79.

[19] Hengel 2000: 76–8.

[20] *Adv. Haer.* 3.11.7.

[21] *Adv. Haer.* 3.11.8.

it seems that the church already had an established tradition of using four gospels a good thirty or so years before the time or Irenaeus.[22] Even if we are not sure when Christians first started using John authoritatively alongside Matthew, Mark and Luke, it must have been a good bit before the day of Irenaeus.

Finally, we come to the question of the chronological ordering of John and *Thomas*. For a number of years, *Thomas* scholars doubted that there was any relationship at all between these two texts. But more recently there has been a willingness to suppose a connection of some kind. If a link does exist, there are basically three options: either John knew *Thomas*, Thomas knew John, or both independently drew on the same sources. While it is not my intention to offer a thorough answer here, I might say that I find the argument that John was writing to refute *Thomas* less than compelling, especially as it is laid out by Riley, DeConick and Pagels.

Riley's thesis depends in the first place on the assumption that first-century belief concerning the resurrection body underwent an important change over time: from impalpable resurrection (so *Thomas*) to corporeal resurrection (so Luke and John). This is an old thesis but one that has not escaped a battering from more than a few careful exegetes. If, as the best evidence seems to suggest, the consensus position of the mid first century was that Christ was raised bodily, with spiritualizing interpretations coming later, Riley's thesis cannot get off the ground.[23]

Second, if the key evidence for John being an anti-Thomas polemic is the evangelist's intentionally negative portrayal of Thomas, the evangelist has done a rather bumbling job at it. In John 11.16, in urging the disciples to follow Jesus to Jerusalem, the apostle Thomas waxes heroic.[24] Later, in a scene in which he comes off measurably better than Philip, Thomas is informed by Jesus that 'from now on' he is among those who know God (John 14.7). Finally, if the figure of Thomas is John's foil for representing how *not* to act and believe, it makes no sense for the evangelist to have made him the mouthpiece for one the clearest statements within the New Testament canon pertaining to the divinity of Christ: 'My lord and my God!' (John 20.28). If John is really painting a bull's-eye on the chest of the *dramatis persona* of Thomas, and by extension the community he represents, it can only be in a fit of confusion that the evangelist accords

[22] Stanton 2003.

[23] Benoit 1973: 221–2; Watson 1997: 127–8; Wright 2003.

[24] See, e.g. Schnackenburg 1982: 328; Beasley-Murray 1987: 189.

to Thomas the honour of articulating John's culminating Christological point.[25]

Third, quite aside from the questionableness of John *contra* Thomas, there is no firm basis for inferring the existence of any Christians who identified themselves with Thomas as early as 100 CE, roughly the time John's gospel was written. New Testament scholars are quick to point out that the titles of the New Testament gospels (According to Matthew, According to Mark, etc.) were appended to copies some decades after the composition of the original autographs. The historical distance between the point at which these gospels were first written and the time when they acquired titles has led many to doubt that the gospels were in fact penned by their traditional authors, especially in the case of the apostolic titles, Matthew and John. On this majority view, the apostolic names were attached to the otherwise anonymous gospels so as to grant them added authority. It seems, however, that Riley, DeConick and Pagels are wishing to grant *Thomas* a pedigree and legitimacy that is seldom granted to the canonical gospels. While none of these scholars holds that the *Gospel of Thomas* was actually written by the apostle Thomas, it is implied or entailed in all their arguments that whoever penned the Thomasine sayings did so as an authoritative disciple of the historical Thomas, for the benefit of a community that saw itself as heirs to the same figure.

But the problem here is that if the only evidence we have for such a Thomasine school is within the text of *Thomas* itself, then those portions of the text that do speak to the possibility of such a Thomas school – the appended title ('The Gospel according to Thomas'), the Prologue ('These are the secret sayings of Didymus Judas Thomas. . . .'), and *Gos. Thom.* 13 – are either hopelessly late or inconclusive as evidence. Most scholars surmise that the title now found on the tail end of the Coptic collection, very simply, *to peuangelion pkata toma*, the *Gospel according to Thomas*, was appended fairly late in the textualizing process. How late, we cannot be sure. Fortunately, Hippolytus, writing around 220 CE, mentions this *Gospel of Thomas*, which confirms the existence of a text of the same name and, presumably, at least one community that used it (see Introduction, pp. 8–9). While this provides a *terminus ad quem*, it does not bring us very close to the time of the writing of John.

Most likely, the wording of the title was based on the Prologue: 'These are the secret sayings of Didymus Judas Thomas . . .' But scholars agree that if the Prologue belongs anywhere on *Thomas*'s evolution

---

[25] See also the criticisms of Dunderberg 1997, 1998a.

as a sayings collection (assuming for a moment there was an evolution), it belongs at the final stage, for its wording presupposes that the collection was already in hand.[26] Moreover, if one insists on *Thomas's* independence and oral origins, then one must also insist that the Prologue was added as one of the final touches. This becomes clear on consideration of the Prologue and *Gos. Thom.* 1:

> These are the secret sayings which Jesus the living one spoke and Didymus Judas Thomas wrote down. (Prologue)

> And he said, 'Whoever finds the interpretation of these sayings will not taste death.' (*Gos. Thom.* 1)

It can hardly be doubted that the Prologue and *Gos. Thom.* 1 together form a unit. The catchword repetition of 'sayings', the contrast between 'living one' (Prologue) and 'death' (*Gos. Thom.* 1), the way in which 'these sayings' (*Gos. Thom.* 1) looks back to the 'sayings' of the Prologue, the sense in which the first logion functions almost as an extension of the Prologue – all these factors conspire to show that the Prologue and *Gos. Thom.* 1 are of a *literary* piece. I emphasize literary simply because the Prologue tells us that Thomas '*wrote* the sayings' down: it is virtually inconceivable to think of Prologue/*Gos. Thom.* 1, which explicitly claims to preserve written tradition, as having oral origins. Thus, on the theory that in *Thomas* we have an original oral core that later accrued scribal overlays of one sort or another, the Prologue/*Gos. Thom.* 1 complex must have been added at the final stage of this protracted metamorphosis.

The literary quality and lateness of Prologue/*Gos. Thom.* 1 are corroborated by their hermeneutical function within the collection. With Prologue/*Gos. Thom.* 1 in place, we now have something more than a naïvely wrought sayings collection: we have a text, and we have an editorial voice establishing a relationship with the reader and promising the same reader great reward on the successful interpretation of the sayings that follow. Again, this all suggests that the words contained in Prologue/*Gos. Thom.* 1, while not necessarily the last words to be added to the gospel, were probably very close to it.

Now whatever our judgments concerning the dating of the core of the *Gospel of Thomas*, the evidence compels us to conclude that the collection could not have been compiled in its final form much earlier than 150 CE. This is simply because we know that at least two of the sayings, *Gos. Thom.* 7 and *Gos. Thom.* 102, are traceable to mid second-century contexts.[27] Now if the collection took final shape no

---

[26] So too Sevrin 1995: 263–5.
[27] See discussion in Introduction. So too Patterson 1993: 115.

earlier than the middle of the second century, and if the Prologue was appended precisely to give the collection its hermeneutical shape, then the Prologue itself must also be dated no earlier than the middle of the second century, some five to seven decades after the writing of the fourth gospel. Whatever the evidence there is in the *Gospel of Thomas* that John was responding to a community that identified with the apostle of the same name, the Prologue simply cannot reasonably be included as part of that evidence.

This means that the only remaining admissible evidence for a first-century Thomas community is to be found in *Gos. Thom.* 13. The text reads as follows:

> Jesus said to his disciples, 'Compare me to someone else and tell me whom I am like.' Simon Peter said to him, 'You are like a righteous angel.' Matthew said to him, 'You are like a wise philosopher.' Thomas said to him, 'Teacher, my mouth is entirely incapable of saying whom you are like.' Jesus said, 'I am not your teacher. Since you have imbibed, you have become drunk on the bubbling spring which I have dug.' And he took him, withdrew and told him three words. When Thomas came back to his friends, they asked him, 'What did Jesus say to you?' Thomas said to them, 'Were I to tell you even one of the things which he told me, you would pick up stones and throw them at me. Then a fire would come out of the stones and consume you.' (*Gos. Thom.* 13)

There is no doubt that, among the three disciples, Thomas is made to steal the show at the expense of Matthew and Simon Peter. But this can hardly be taken as evidence for a 'Thomas community'. In the first place, the valorizing of the *dramatis persona* Thomas seems to have much more to do with the final editor's intended symbolism than with the claim to historic continuity with the apostle himself. In *Gos. Thom.* 108, when Jesus promises, 'The one who drinks from my mouth will become like me. I myself will become he,' it becomes clear that the goal for the Thomas Christian is to be like Jesus, that is, to become his twin. And this is precisely what 'Thomas' means: 'twin'. Thus, it is no surprise that Thomas and only Thomas can claim to have drunk from the 'bubbling spring' which Jesus has dug (*Gos. Thom.* 13), for Thomas symbolizes the one who has become like Jesus. We suspect then that Thomas is heroicized in this saying not so much to honour the memory of the apostle for what he had done, but rather to capitalize on the significance of his name. To infer the existence of a first-century Thomas community on the basis of *Gos. Thom.* 13, as the Riley-DeConick-Pagels thesis must do, is to attempt to weave a tapestry of history from a single thread of mythography.

An added problem for finding a Thomas community behind *Gos. Thom.* 13 is *Gos. Thom.* 12. In this logion, it seems that the authority and status of James outstrips even that of Thomas:

> The disciples said to Jesus, 'We know that you will be going from us: who is going to be our leader?' Jesus said to them, 'Whatever point you come to, you should go to James the righteous. On his account heaven and earth came into existence.'   (*Gos. Thom.* 12)

This is no faint praise for James. Whoever added the Prologue to the collection (assuming again for the moment that he or she did not author other oral sayings in the collection) would have likely done so on his or her understanding of *Gos. Thom.* 13 and 108, which mutually affirm spiritual twinship. But the same editor could hardly have been blamed if, after surveying the collection, it was decided that James was actually the hero of this sayings collection. More to the point, while it cannot be denied that *Gos. Thom.* 13 invites its readers to look on Thomas as a favourable model, if we go so far as to say on account of this saying that there was a self-identified 'Thomas community', there are equally good grounds for supposing that the same collection was somewhere else underwriting a 'James community'.

Conclusion

In order for Riley and DeConick to make their case, and for Pagels in her turn to make hers, it has to be shown from the *Gospel of Thomas* that there was a community so-named as early as the 80s.[28] But in the end the only possible help on this point is *Gos. Thom.* 13. And, as it turns out, even this saying is not much help. Given the obvious symbolic value of assigning the gospel to someone named 'Twin', and given even the more profound reverence accorded to James in the preceding logion (*Gos. Thom.* 12), *Gos. Thom.* 13 (quite apart from the unexamined question as to the proper dating of this logion) affords fairly weak evidence for inferring the existence of a community that swore exclusive loyalty to the historical figure of Thomas. None of this disproves that John wrote his gospel in response to the Thomasine community, but it does show that the basis of the Riley-DeConick-Pagels claim is extremely fragile. Moreover, in all this discussion of apostle wars certain questions have remained

---

[28] At least, they must do so if they wish to avoid the charge of circularity. See the prescient comments in Dunderberg 1997.

unexplored. Why is it, it should be asked, that the collection is implicitly critical of Matthew (*Gos. Thom.* 13) and Simon Peter (*Gos. Thom.* 13 and 114)? Why does the author behind these sayings not pick on other apostles and why, in particular, these two? These questions I will revisit in Chapter 5.

Before leaving off with Pagels, it may be worthwhile briefly to assess the argument of *Beyond Belief* on a theological level, not just a historical level. I suspect that more than a few theologians and laypersons would object to her equating traditional Christian belief with creedal assent, for the New Testament itself makes clear that faith which is no more than adherence to formal propositions is no faith at all (James 2.14). In this respect, if judged by its sources, traditional Christianity has always been interested in getting 'beyond belief'. Along the same lines, I also suspect that many confessing Christians would cry foul to Pagels's contrasting orthodox belief with 'experiential truth', as if Nicene Christianity in principle fails to intersect with experience. Perhaps Pagels's quarrel with orthodoxy and the route she takes in opposition to it arise not just out of her personal experience but out of an impression, made palpable by today's church, that the only viable alternatives before the modern Christian believer are rationalism and mysticism. While I do, as I said, appreciate our author's reuniting faith and history, there is always a danger whereby the latter just becomes a way of personally working out the former. In the end, I wonder if Pagels has made Thomas and John don uniforms and re-enact a particular contemporary western religiocultural conflict, whose mantras and battle cries we know all too well. Because yesterday's Thomas Christians were forced to take a defensive posture and live life on the run, today's Johannine (read: orthodox) Christians must make reparations to today's Thomas Christians. Unfortunately, while there are parallels between then and now, neither uniform quite fits.

Yet Elaine Pagels has successfully made her case on other fronts. First, it is hard to question her conclusion that those who used and profited from the *Gospel of Thomas* saw salvation as proceeding from within. It did not, at any rate, involve belief in Jesus or require any extrinsic reality. Second, there is something to be said for the comparisons between the *Gospel of Thomas* and John and their respective protologies. Finally, there needs to be more discussion of the interapostolic conflict. In the meantime, we must consider the contributions of one more interlocutor.

3

The Thomas community on the way: April D. DeConick

In this chapter we conclude our survey of *Gospel of Thomas* research. If Patterson has been the most influential within the academy, and Pagels has been the most influential amidst the broader public, April D. DeConick, recently appointed Isla Carroll and Percy E. Turner Professor of Biblical Studies at Rice University, is poised, simply on account of her productivity, to have more long-term influence than either. In addition to a number of articles, she has authored four books on the *Gospel of Thomas*, including a commentary fresh off the press.[1]

In her first book, *Seek to See Him: Ascent and Vision Mysticism in the Gospel of Thomas* (1996), DeConick argues against the Gnostic origins of the gospel, affirms its encratite and Hermetic influences, but above all seeks to speak to its early Jewish mystical roots. Here she locates *Thomas* alongside the literature of Merkavah mysticism, whereby the initiate sets out through certain ritualistic practices to ascend unto a vision of the throne (merkavah) of God, and therefore a vision of Godself. Devoting a good portion of this book to a comparison of *Gos. Thom.* 50 with other ascent literature, DeConick envisages the logion as reflecting an interchange taking place at one of the nodal spheres between the angels and the mystic.[2] Inasmuch as the Thomas community was intent on fulfilling a mystical journey, they were ever – even in the eyes of their opponents – a community 'on the way'. Later in the same book, following a discussion of the importance of the transformative vision of the divine, DeConick works out the implications of this theory for understanding *Thomas*'s sources.[3]

Five years later, DeConick published *Voices of the Mystics: Early Christian Discourse in the Gospels of John and Thomas and Other Ancient*

---

[1] Unfortunately, I was not able to obtain DeConick's commentary until the present book was already well into its final stages. I include it, however, in the bibliography.
[2] DeConick 1996: 73.
[3] DeConick 1996: 175–80.

Christian Literature (2001). In this monograph, again with reference to the mystery religions, Hermeticism, and Judaism, DeConick reasserts her case for *Thomas*'s bearing witness to a mystical community. Then, drawing on J. H. Charlesworth's reading that the author of the fourth gospel is very intentionally casting the *dramatis persona* Thomas in a negative light, DeConick reasons that John must be polemicizing against Thomasine mysticism in a roundabout way so as to buttress his message that salvation must come only by faith in Christ.[4] The brand of mysticism to which *Thomas* attests comes to light later on in such Syriac texts as the *Gospel of the Saviour*, the *Apocryphon of James*, and the *Ascension of Isaiah*. I have already dealt with DeConick's thesis, as it is worked out by Pagels, in the previous chapter.[5]

Review

For the purposes of this study, I will focus on a more recent volume which I presume to be the culminating product of her earlier thought: *Recovering the Original Gospel of Thomas: A History of the Gospel and its Growth* (2005). In this book, a full-blown expansion of an earlier article written to explain the compositional origins of the Thomasine gospel,[6] DeConick sets forth an alternative paradigm to the major hypotheses on offer: the 'literate model', the 'oral-literate model', and the 'redaction model'.[7]

The first of these approaches, the literate model, suggests that the author of *Thomas* 'largely used written gospels as sources when composing his own gospel'.[8] According to DeConick, this model struggles 'to explain *why* a single author would choose to include in his composition conflicting sayings and doublets from his written sources'.[9] In addition, the literate model must explain not only why the author selected the sayings he or she did, but also why the author would 'choose to structure the gospel so loosely'.[10] Here we hear echoes of Patterson who, like many others, sees doublets and *Thomas*'s apparent lack of organization as indicative of non-written sources.

The second model is the oral-literate model. According to this theory, which DeConick associates with Koester, the author of *Thomas*

---

[4] Charlesworth 1995. DeConick 2001: 68–85.
[5] DeConick 2001: 133–62.
[6] DeConick 2002.
[7] DeConick 2005: 39–55.
[8] DeConick 2005: 39.
[9] DeConick 2005: 41.
[10] DeConick 2005: 42.

drew on both oral and written traditions. DeConick is critical of Koester's argument for several reasons, not least the fact that his oral-literate model does not solve the problem of differing sayings within the same collection: 'nothing in the text indicates that an author was deliberately setting up conflicting sayings or diverse traditions'.[11] Our author does, however, credit Koester for having emphasized the oral dimension to Thomas's background. For in spite of

> studies in orality and the heroic efforts of a few biblical scholars to align their research with it, scholars of early Christianity in general remain unfamiliar with the compositional process common to cultures dominated by orality or have ignored it. Most continue to impose upon the ancient authors a 'literate imagination,' suggesting that composition occurred by cutting and pasting information from written sources into their new text by editors or redactors.
>
> (DeConick 2005: 47–8)

The importance of the 'oral imagination', as her first chapter, 'The "New" *Traditionsgeschichtliche* [History of Traditions] Approach', makes clear, can hardly be overstated. DeConick wants to adopt a reconstruction of *Thomas* that does justice to the dynamisms inherent in a predominantly oral culture.

The third general approach to *Thomas*, represented by Stephen Patterson and William Arnal, is the redaction model. This is similar to the oral-literate model in that it conceives of the author of the core collection drawing on oral and written sources, but includes the added dimension of subsequent editing, the insertion of sayings or glosses, and other kinds of scribal infringements. Whereas both Patterson and Arnal see *Thomas*, like Q, as consisting of two layers reflecting two separate milieus, DeConick is less enthusiastic about such comparisons. Rejecting an approach to *Thomas* on the model of Q, our author insists that the collection must be understood on its own terms.[12]

In contrast to these three general approaches, DeConick proposes a fourth alternative, one that derives its name from William McKane's description of the compositional process he envisaged taking place behind certain OT prophetic and wisdom materials: 'rolling corpus'. Inspired by McKane's vision of Jeremiah and Proverbs as predominantly orally based collections snowballing and accruing sayings over time, DeConick puts forward her fundamental theory: that the *Gospel of Thomas* underwent an analogous evolution involving additions, deletions and modifications through multiple reperformances in an oral

---

[11] DeConick 2005: 45.
[12] DeConick 2005: 51–4. See Arnal 1995.

medium.[13] While our author does not rule out the possibility that written materials were added to this rolling corpus, this is improbable *a priori*: 'I have come to recognize that this accrual more likely took place during a reperformance or a scribing of that reperformance than as a conscious literary redaction.'[14] According to DeConick, the chief merit of this model over its competitors lies in its ability to explain the doublets and in particular the contradictions that occur in *Thomas*.

In the following portion of the book, DeConick attempts to identify the 'original *Thomas*', the core or Kernel Gospel, as well as various layers of oral tradition, as they aggregated over time. Like a cook peeling an onion, she begins by stripping off layers of sayings that do not seem to cohere with the original kernel. The first sayings to be excised are those in which the disciples pose questions. In these cases, 'the identified unit in its entirety should be considered *secondary*', but in certain cases material is preserved when 'the saying itself does not appear to reflect later Christian interests'.[15] Next, interpretive clauses that may be suspected of reflecting later Christianity are also discarded.[16] Once these unoriginal, secondary, sayings are identified, DeConick proceeds to cull from the remainder any sayings that share themes and vocabulary with the discarded sayings; these too must be presumed to have derived from later stages.[17] Any material judged to be anachronistic (reflecting the concerns of later Christianity) is also removed from the original set of sayings; these include 'topics about leadership, discipleship, Jewish law, Christology, soteriology, or eschatology'.[18] Finally, any sayings that potentially pertain to the deaths of eyewitnesses, Gentile converts or the delay of the eschaton must also be flagged up as late. But 'late' is not very late at all. At the end of the day, DeConick shows us four stages (for lack of a better term). First, there was the Kernel Gospel, dated 30–50 CE; then come accretions relating to relocation and leadership crises, dating to 50–60 CE; next come accretions relating to Gentiles and early eschatological crises, 60–100 CE; and finally, other accretions, 80–120 CE. I will respectively call these Stage 1, Stage 2, Stage 3 and Stage 4.

From here DeConick goes on to discuss Stage 1, the Kernel Gospel. This first oral layer itself has been structured into five speeches, each speech with its own theme. What emerges here is a picture of

---

[13] DeConick 2005: 55–63.
[14] DeConick 2005: 57.
[15] DeConick 2005: 66.
[16] DeConick 2005: 69–71.
[17] DeConick 2005: 71–4.
[18] DeConick 2005: 78.

Jesus as Prophet-Orator, a depiction similar to that found in Jerusa-lemite Christianity: 'This Christology was grounded in Jewish expectation that during the Last days, God would send his Messianic Prophet who would restore God's Law to its original intent, preparing believers for the Final Judgment.'[19] This Christology, DeConick continues, also 'survived and was further developed in communities of Ebionite Christians in eastern Syria, Christians responsible for traditions ultimately recorded in the Pseudo-Clementine corpus.'[20]

Against those who identify *Thomas* as a wisdom text, DeConick emphasizes its apocalyptic dimensions and goes to great pains to locate its apocalyptic imagery within second-temple Judaism.[21] But this is not quite apocalyptic in the sense that it is traditionally conceived:

> Because the apocalyptists were so convinced of the imminent end of history, they understood that they lived in a time when the traditional boundary between earth and heaven was starting to collapse . . . Because the boundary was about to collapse, the heavens had become more permeable in the waning days of the world. As history marched toward its end and the Kingdom of God began replacing the kingdoms of this world, God was becoming immediately accessible to very pious humans who were crossing the threshold into his new world. The vision of the merkavah and Yahweh which previously had been reserved for the prophets and priests of Israel were now becoming available to the elect remnant. (DeConick 2005: 133)

Eventually, the Thomas community became disappointed with Jesus' failure to return and came to terms with this non-event by reinterpreting the kingdom. Rather than being a future, apocalyptic, reality, the kingdom was now seen as occurring within the individual.[22] The shift in perspective from future kingdom to present, interiorized, kingdom was accompanied by the notion that the Thomas Christians were now in a position to experience Eden restored.[23] The final result is a kind of fusion between Judaism and Egyptian Hermeticism:

> By 120 CE, the focus of this theology turned away from the cosmic endings to the human being who, with the aid of the Holy Spirit, conquered his or her body of passions and recreated, in its place, the virtuous body of the prelapsarian Adam. He or she took his or her place in Paradise, preparing for the great transformative visions of Jesus and God through an encratic regime and meditative praxis. By so

---

[19] DeConick 2005: 123.
[20] DeConick 2005: 124.
[21] DeConick 2005: 138–48.
[22] DeConick 2005: Ch. 6.
[23] DeConick 2005: Ch. 7.

doing, the person came face to face with his or her own Image or God-Self, a vision which restored his or her soul to its original glorious Image. (DeConick 2005: 237)

Like Pagels, but unlike Patterson, DeConick is not very interested in using *Thomas* as a witness to Jesus' words. She puts it this way:

The 'historical' Jesus for them [the Thomas Christians] was the 'living' Jesus who was ever-present in their community. As he continued to guide and teach them as their community grew and encountered problems and changing needs, they continued to update their gospel with new sayings which they believed were answers from Jesus himself. (DeConick 2005: 249)

Like the champions of the old Form and Traditions Criticism, DeConick, as a self-styled advocate of a 'New Traditions Criticism', does not have much time for a figure as elusive as the historical Jesus. But, apparently, the early Thomas community did not have time for the historical Jesus either. With echoes of Bultmann, DeConick believes that as long as Jesus was present in spirit among his first followers, they felt little compulsion to inquire after the facts of his life.

Response

In reading April DeConick's writings, I find myself in a state of profound ambivalence. At turns I find myself shouting inside, 'Hurrah!' and 'That makes complete sense!' At other turns, I am flummoxed, unable to explain why she comes to the conclusions she does. I know of no other Thomas scholar with whom I am so deeply in agreement, but at the same time so deeply in disagreement. In Chapter 6 I will speak to the more convincing aspects of her argument and will do so with great satisfaction. At present, however, it is necessary to point out a number of points at which her thesis is vulnerable to rather serious criticisms.

First, when it comes to the question of the historical Jesus and Christian origins, DeConick is equivocal. On the one hand, she is convinced that Jesus was a preacher of eschatological judgment; on the other hand, she sees the life and ministry of Jesus as having no measurable relevance to Christian beginnings:[24]

As for the actual beginning of Christianity, certainly there was never a singular point of origin nor one event that caused everything to swing into motion. Nor was the development linear or romantic as Luke

---

[24] On the former point, see DeConick 2005: 149–50, 238.

would have it. A complex of impulses worked together to bring about the formation of Christianity, social forces being only one of many. Certainly the teachings of Jesus *as they were remembered* played a big role given the reliance of the missionaries on the books of Jesus' speeches. The impulse to give meaning to the troubling death of Jesus was also foundational given the allusions and interpretations of his death across the early literature. This process, fueled largely by exegesis, led to Christological developments very early in the tradition.

(DeConick 2005: 247)

While a good deal of scholarship, not to mention traditional Christianity itself, has come to the conclusion that the origins of Christianity are to be traced to the death and resurrection of Jesus, or at least, more vaguely, to the Christ-event, DeConick flatly says: 'certainly there never was a singular point of origin'. This is fair enough as a statement, but without argumentation as to why Christianity could not have come from a single origin or an alternative explanation as why Christianity did arise, it is almost weightless. Apparently, the 'teachings of Jesus *as they were remembered* played a big role', a point hardly disputable, but DeConick seems to go beyond this by implying that there is no demonstrable relationship between the remembered teachings (purportedly the core sayings of *Thomas*) and the teachings themselves (what Jesus actually said). Nor did the early church care to establish such a relationship, for their highly elastic memory of Jesus was enough. If the mid first-century disciples of Jesus did not bother themselves with remembering the historical Jesus as he really was, neither should twenty-first-century scholars: after all, 'our understanding of the "historical Jesus" is a product of our era'.[25]

The point here is not to chide DeConick for her scepticism regarding the possibility of recovering the historical Jesus, but simply to observe that, in failing to address the identity of Jesus of Nazareth in any substantive way, she has deprived herself of the most readily available explanation for the origins of the community she postulates – and has put nothing in its place. It is not enough to say that Christianity developed as it was buoyed along by exegetical reflection on Jesus' identity and death, because this only begs the question as to why the early Christians felt Jesus' person and death were worth reflecting on (at least more so than earlier and later executed messianic figures) and why, more to the point, anyone came to believe the otherwise preposterous story that Jesus had been raised. While

---

[25] DeConick 2005: 249. Here one can hardly suppress the question as to whether DeConick thinks her understanding of the *Gospel of Thomas* is equally a 'product of our era'.

DeConick may disagree with Jesus-the-sage as he has been purveyed by Koester, Robinson and Patterson, to its credit the Koester school has at least given a plausible account as to why all these Thomasine sayings beginning with the words 'Jesus says' were written down in the first place. If the Thomas community held to a century-long tradition of performing and creating Jesus sayings, as DeConick maintains it did, even the less inquisitive readers among us will wonder how such an enduring institution got its start in the first place. Remarkably enough, this question remains unanswered.

A second problem pertains to the way in which DeConick imagines the writing down of the gospels. She states: 'the gospel texts we possess were not authored by one person but represent traditions that have developed within the memory of the community'.[26] Surely if this were true, it would help her argument, for our gospels could then provide an analogy to what she envisions to have been the case with *Thomas*. But how do we know this is true? There was a day when New Testament critics, deeply influenced by the Bultmannian assumption of community authorship, could make such a statement without batting an eyelid. But that day has come and gone. Since the advent of redaction criticism in the 1950s and narrative criticism in more recent decades, both of which have focused on the contributions of the individual writers, scholars have distanced themselves from unsubstantiated assumptions of authorship-by-committee, even if the mediated traditions were essentially communal in nature. By consigning the individual editors/writers of our gospels to oblivion, DeConick has brought us back to old Form Criticism but in a more radicalized version. While, in their examination of the oral pre-history of the synoptic tradition, Bultman and Dibelius were never so bold as to claim to be giving a full account of the gospels as finished works, DeConick apparently claims to be doing just that for *Thomas*.

Alongside with this insistence on community authorship is an equally unwarranted commitment to the notion that the first Christians preferred their own recollection of Jesus to the written recollection of others: 'we know . . . that the Christians were most confident scribing down their own remembrances than copying written sources because they could guarantee the "truth" of their memories'.[27] While there is undeniably an element of truth here (who wouldn't trust their own memory of, say, a protest rally over what the evening news has to say about it?), this does not mean that Christians, including

---

[26] DeConick 2005: 57.
[27] DeConick 2005: 57.

Christians who never came within a hundred feet of Jesus, were oblivious to the weight of eyewitness testimony. Much less does it mean that early Christians were as a rule indifferent to written sources. The only early Christian gospel writer who speaks explicitly to the issue of sources is Luke, and Luke was – patently contrary to DeConick's assertion – apparently *more* comfortable relying on others' written accounts than simply scribing down his own remembrances (Luke 1.1–4). Nor is Papias's (a church leader writing in the first half of the second century) stated preference for the 'living and abiding voice' over what 'could be gotten from the books' of much help here, for it has been shown that Papias, far from spinning a theory regarding the superiority of 'oral' over 'written', is using an idiom that speaks to the obvious advantage of personally meeting and interacting firsthand with those 'in the know'.[28]

So how were Jesus traditions, the recollections of what Jesus said and did, first passed down? Toward answering this question, DeConick resorts to remarks made by a third-century church father in a text called the *Pseudo-Clementines (Recognitions)*. In commenting on this text, she writes:

> After Clement is instructed about the teachings of the True Prophet by Peter, he makes some fascinating comments about the sequencing of Peter's speeches:
>
>> I shall now call to mind the things which were spoken, in which the order of your discussion greatly helps me; for the way in which the things that you said followed by consequence upon one another, and were arranged in a balanced manner, makes them easily recalled to memory by the lines of their order. For the order of sayings is useful for remembering them: for when you begin to follow them point by point in succession, when anything is wanting, immediately the sense seeks for it; and when it has found it, retains it, or at all events, if it cannot discover it, there will be no reluctance to ask it of the master.
>>
>> (*Rec.* 1.23)
>
> The *Pseudo-Clementines* seem to be preserving a very old memory from the early movement about the process of transmission of the traditions associated with Jesus. It appears that the sayings of Jesus first began to be collected into speeches in which the sayings were arranged rhetorically to provide a memorable interpretation or present an argument to an audience. If the sense of the rhetoric was unclear,

---

[28] Eusebius, *Hist. Eccl.* 3.39.4. On this understanding of Papias, see Alexander 1990; Botha 1993: 751–3.

it was expected that the pupil would inquire after it by asking the teacher. The teacher would expound or justify the saying accordingly.

(DeConick 2005: 34–5)

Seeking to reconstruct the transmission of Jesus traditions on the basis of the above-cited passage from Pseudo-Clement, DeConick asserts that Jesus' sayings were written down into speeches, which were then, for the sake of relevance, subject to various reinterpretations, rearrangements and reperformances.[29]

Certainly, DeConick's reconstruction remains at least theoretically possible. But her 'New History of Traditions' approach not only raises but in fact aggravates the same problems that the old History of Traditions school (classical Form Criticism) never resolved. The reduction of the Jesus tradition into catechetical speeches necessitates the assumption that those who preserved Jesus' memory, while duly impressed with at least some of his words, found nothing about his life or actions worth remembering. And if it is really the case that the memory of Jesus was preserved only in speeches, it remains for DeConick to explain why the Thomas community only preserved the words of Jesus but the canonical gospel writers attributed to Jesus both words *and* actions. Bultmann argued that many of the pericopae in the synoptic gospels were embellishments of discrete free-floating pronouncements, that is, stories created out of whole cloth in order to give a narrative setting to a particular saying. While DeConick seems to be arguing, against Bultmann, that the Jesus tradition was preserved in extended speeches rather than isolated aphorisms, she does not clarify how and why such speeches eventually gave rise to narrative gospels. Short of the very complicated explanation that the early church took hold of these Jesus speeches, diced them into bits, and then *á la* Bultmann constructed stories around these sayings, our author's position virtually entails that the storyline preserved in Mark is entirely mythological.

This would not be completely unprecedented, for Wilhelm Wrede and more recently Burton Mack have adopted similar positions.[30] But even Mack, who among living Jesus scholars is unparalleled in supposing radical discontinuity between the historical Jesus and the early church, leaves room for the synoptic gospels preserving some things about the historical Jesus. In order to explain the synoptic gospels but remain true to her theory of transmission, DeConick must either devise an elaborate explanation for the creation of the synoptic

---

[29] DeConick 2005: 35–7.
[30] Wrede 1971 [1910]; Mack 1988.

narratives or commit herself to a position of scepticism that is off the scale of contemporary Jesus scholarship.

DeConick's use of *Pseudo-Clement* also seems rather precarious. First of all, the emphasis in *Pseudo-Clement* is not so much on rein-terpretation – where DeConick eventually wants to put it – but on the faithful interpretation and the preservation of memory, an earnest inquiry into the very voice of the master and a determination to keep to it. Second, it is extremely problematic to infer the nature of Jesus traditioning on the basis of a single passage from *Pseudo-Clement*, written in a Christian (as opposed to a Jewish) context, occurring several centuries after the fact. If DeConick approves of Jacob Neusner's criticizing the Scandinavian School for anachronistically retrojecting post-70 CE rabbinic memorization practices into Jesus' milieu,[31] she must surely admit the indefensibility of her own reconstruction here. Even if DeConick has read *Pseudo-Clement* right (I don't think she has), the text is almost worthless for reconstructing the process behind the traditioning of Jesus sayings.

DeConick's vision of an orally reperformed *Thomas* not only runs afoul on the mid first-century end for lack of a plausible model, there are additional problems on the tail end of her trajectory as well. She argues – and here, to anticipate my argument in Chapter 6, I think she could not be more right – that Hermeticism made its own contribution to the final stages of the collection's evolution. The problem which a 'pan-oral *Thomas*' view like this encounters here is that Hermeticism was self-consciously a *scribal* movement. If we are to suppose that Hermetic traditions attached themselves to *Thomas* from out of an oral flux, as DeConick wants us to suppose, this contradicts the little we actually do know about Hermetical spirituality, namely, that its secrets were preserved in *books*.[32]

---

[31] See DeConick 2005: 25 n125, where she cites Neusner (1987) with approval. Ironic-ally, while DeConick (25) criticizes 'Riesenfeld's and Gerhardsson's understanding of oral transmission in terms of memorization' as 'insensitive to oral mentalities', mem-orization of tradition appears to be of utmost priority in the very Pseudo-Clementine passage she cites.

[32] See, e.g., *Discourse on the Eighth and Ninth* 54.6–9, 23–25: '"And it is right [for you] to remember the progress that came to you as wisdom in the *books*". . . . "My father, I understand nothing else except the beauty that came to me in the *books*"' (emphasis added). Hermeticism seems to have been strictly a book religion – not surprising considering that Hermes was the god of writing.

DeConick (2005: 224) herself seems to recognize this, but this only raises the question, since she herself finds ten clear instances of Hermetic material (2005: 99–110), whether her paradigm is actually much different from the 'oral-literate' model' she criticizes. It seems to me that one cannot both emphasize *Thomas*'s oral constitution to the degree DeConick does and give any real place to Hermetical influence.

Personally, I have no quarrel with the notion that a good number of sayings in the *Gospel of Thomas* are of oral derivation.[33] Even less do I find fault with the idea that remembered sayings (as opposed to written words staring the compiler in the face) found their way into *Thomas* by the droves. The renewed sensitivity to oral dynamism in New Testament studies has provided a much-needed corrective to an old way of thinking that regarded the transmission of sources to be essentially the same process as cutting and pasting on a word processor. But if Bultmann, as Werner Kelber complains, underestimated the difference oral-consciousness makes,[34] DeConick for her part seems to have gone to the opposite extreme by swapping one vague woolly generalization for another. DeConick states that Jesus' followers adopted 'the compositional process common to cultures dominated by orality'.[35] But if such a one-size-fits-all compositional process indeed exists or did exist almost universally before the Gutenberg revolution, why does DeConick turn to an obscure passage from *Pseudo-Clement* to illustrate the nature of this process as far as Jesus' first followers were concerned? Our author's position that the earliest post-Easter community had little more use for scrolls than they did for doorstops in the end seems to rely rather heavily on unsubstantiated and largely theoretical assumptions.

At this juncture it might be worthwhile to consider DeConick's rationale for preferring an oral, layered, *Thomas* to one written in a single stage. We recall that previous approaches to *Thomas* have, in DeConick's eyes, fallen short in their inability to explain 'contradictory ideologies'. Here, it is to be remembered, she appeals to William McKane, who thought that the varied and sometimes contradictory nature of the biblical proverbs indicated a slow and steady compositional evolution.[36] And so, just as 'we are dealing with "a complicated, untidy accumulation of material, extending over a very long period and to which many people have contributed"' in certain biblical texts, the same phenomenon, DeConick argues, obtains for *Thomas*.[37] Had there been a scribal editor behind the *Gospel of Thomas*, our author surmises, that person would have presumably been a thoughtful and systematic person, rationally ironing out any potential tensions or inconsistencies. Since *Thomas* is patently neither

---

[33] In countering my argument (Perrin 2002), DeConick (2005: 48–9) incorrectly infers otherwise.

[34] Kelber 1983: 2–8.

[35] DeConick 2005: 47–8.

[36] DeConick 2005: 62; cf. McKane 1977: 18.

[37] DeConick 2005: 61–2.

thoughtful nor systematic in this way, it follows that the collection was not the product of editorial design, but must have been reworked (sayings added and deleted) at various points in oral transmission. The oral nature of *Thomas* is betrayed by its tensions and antinomies.

The case, however, is not nearly so cut and dried. While there are certainly both redundancies and tensions in *Thomas* (to these I will return), it is far from clear that the collection is hopelessly self-contradictory. One does not find, at any rate, the kind of formal contradiction that one finds in Proverbs.[38] But even as I grant that *Thomas* is shot through with vexing incongruities, this point by itself hardly indicates oral sources. For, to return to DeConick's analogy with Proverbs, while it is of course possible that the various maxims that make up the biblical wisdom literature came together from different settings, some where bribery was encouraged, others where the practice was frowned upon, it makes much more sense to me – not to mention an increasing number of scholars specializing in this area – that the collocation of contradictory sayings was part of an *editor's* intentional design.[39] Although McKane will certainly go down in history as a major contributor in his field, his understanding of Proverbs (*viz.* that the collection originated as discrete entities only to be patched together through a lengthy process of oral transmission) looks as if it is being – if it has not already been – overturned in favour of a view that Proverbs owes its form to an editor not a compiler of oral traditions.[40] And if this is how McKane's theory has fared since his publications in the 1970s, we cannot invest too much start-up capital in an argument that depends on the same now-outmoded premises.

Moving from the theory of oral origins to the practice of Tradition Criticism, we find ourselves even deeper in the waters of speculation. As our author sorts through the logia, her overarching assumption is that a saying is early (that is, part of the original Kernel Gospel) unless it is demonstrably late. But this assumption is groundless, especially since she connects the Thomas tradition with the *memory*

---

[38] DeConick does not spend much time on the point, but see DeConick 2005: ix.

[39] See the discussion in Snell 1993 and Heim 2001.

[40] Writing near the turn of the millennium, K. M. Heim (2001: 64) notes that seven out of the nine most recent commentaries on Proverbs (not including the then soon-to-be-published commentary by Waltke) espouse a theory of contextual groupings, explaining antinomies and repetition as the products of redaction, not oral snowballing. Quite apart from the analogy to Proverbs, it is unclear how postulating an oral theory of composition actually resolves the problem of internal inconsistencies. It seems to me rather simply to shift the blame somewhere else, in this case on the performer rather than the editor.

of Jesus rather than with Jesus himself. Given the enduring staying power of the memory of Jesus (according to DeConick, the Thomas community orally perpetuated its memory of Jesus for a century or so), there is no reason why the same collection that she provisionally attributes to the first two decades after Jesus' death could not just as easily on her own assumptions be assigned to a date a century later.

But the way in which later accretions are identified is also very suspect. True to classic Form Criticism, DeConick claims that sayings involving the disciples in discussion must be seen as secondary: 'In most cases, the identified unit in its entirety should be considered secondary, especially when . . . the saying itself is anachronistic or mirrors the interests and ideologies of later Christians.'[41] In practice this means that regardless of the form, if the content looks late, it is late. And for our author 'late' includes, among other things, any talk of 'leadership, discipleship, Jewish law, Christology, soteriology, or eschatology'.[42] This is a pretty unusual list, especially if, as DeConick thinks, Jesus was an apocalyptic eschatological prophet. One would think that an apocalyptic eschatological prophet and/or his immediate followers would have at least a few things to say about leadership, discipleship and law – not to mention soteriology and eschatology.

Equally problematic is the inconsistent application of methodology. Quite rightly she argues that sayings containing 'characteristic vocabulary' of the identifiable later stages should as a matter of course be assigned to the same later stage.[43] But why are there so many places where characteristic vocabulary is patently *not* a criterion for assigning sayings to different stages? For example, just as in Matthew contrasts have been identified as characteristically Matthean (as opposed to deriving from one of his sources), so too in the Coptic collection there are contrasts, not least among them a contrast between 'inside' and 'outside'. But, oddly, on DeConick's reckoning, the three occurrences of this inside/outside contrast (*Gos. Thom.* 3.3, 22.4 and 89.2) fall into three different stages (Stage 3, Stage 4 and Stage 1, respectively). The phrase 'one and the same' occurs in *Gos. Thom.* 4.1, 22.5 and 23.2, all of which logia are assigned to the putative last stage. But this makes it hard to explain why the only other use of the phrase (*Gos. Thom.* 4.3) occurs in Stage 1. One might expect the distinctive Thomasine phrase 'There will be days' (*Gos. Thom.* 79.3, 38.2) to have issued from one setting, but for DeConick the phrase belongs to two separate stages. It is clear that the community behind

---

[41] DeConick 2005: 66.
[42] DeConick 2005: 78.
[43] DeConick 2005: 72–4.

Stage 4 was keenly interested in talking about 'entering the kingdom' (*Gos. Thom.* 22.2, 3, 114.3, cf. *Gos. Thom.* 75), but then, inexplicably, other logia containing the very same phrase are assigned to Stage 1 (*Gos. Thom.* 39.2, 99.3) and Stage 3 (*Gos. Thom.* 64.12). The poetic 'taste death' occupies two separate stages of composition (*Gos. Thom.* 18.3 = Stage 3; *Gos. Thom.* 1.1, 19.4, 85.2 = Stage 4); as does the typically Syrian metaphor 'bridal chamber' (*Gos. Thom.* '104.3 = Stage 1; *Gos. Thom.* 75.1 = Stage 4). While Stage 1 is fraught with marcarisms ('Blessed is/are . . .') (*Gos. Thom.* 54.1, 58.1, 68.1, 69.1, 79.1, 2, 103), this does not seem to have dissuaded our author from assigning the very same language to Stage 3 (*Gos. Thom.* 18.3, 69.1) and Stage 4 (*Gos. Thom.* 7.1, 19.1, 49.1). While the language of 'worth' and 'being worthy' (common coin in Hermeticism) is allocated to Stage 4 (*Gos. Thom.* 56.2, 85.1 and 114.1), when the same phraseology turns up in *Gos. Thom.* 55.2 and 62.1, the material is assigned to Stage 1. Finally, one would think that the Thomasine interest in 'rest' arises from one community setting, but DeConick assigns it two (*Gos. Thom.* 86.2, 90.1, 61.1 = Stage 1; *Gos. Thom.* 50.3, 51.1, 60.6 = Stage 3). There are other such instances, but I think the point has been made clear enough. DeConick's parcelling of *Thomas* on the inconsistently applied criterion of language patterns lends the impression that she is leading us where she wants us to go.

As fanciful as the shape and content of Stage 1 are, DeConick proceeds from here to delineate five discourses within this Kernel Gospel – an astounding move for one so keen to emphasize the destabilizing impact of oral consciousness.[44] It is at this point that even the most sympathetic of readers can no longer suspend disbelief. Lacking any sort of foothold in history, highly speculative in both its conceptualization and implementation, DeConick's project simply fails to convince. Instead of persuading the reader of the various stages of *Thomas* history, and five discrete discourses within the first stage, her study seems more effectively to underscore the difficulty of hypothesizing a multiplex *Thomas*.

Finally, a few words are in order regarding DeConick's proposal that Jesus' followers, precisely in their interest *as a philosophical school* to remain faithful to Jesus, thought up sayings and in good conscience attributed them to Jesus. That the Jesus movement appropriated the philosophers' practice of pseudomnity is an interesting proposal that may be worthy of further investigation. However, there are reasons to be cautious. If Lewis R. Donelson is right in maintaining that in

---

[44] DeConick 2005: 113–22.

'no case can it be deduced with certainty that this was done innocently with no intention to deceive', then this prompts the question
as to whether the early Christians also intended to deceive, and, if
they did, how this squared with their insistence on the truth of their
claims (Luke 1.4; Gal. 1.8–9, 20; 1 Thess. 2.3, etc.).[45] It cannot simply
be assumed that the methods and motivations of the Neo-Platonists
and Pythagoreans applied without remainder to the first Christians.

Rather than reflecting far-reaching inventiveness, the earliest
Christian documents show an overall conservative outlook on Jesus'
words. Once Paul received and passed on the words surrounding
the eucharist (1 Cor. 11.23–26), there is no evidence that the words
of institution were ever creatively 'reperformed' or underwent substantive reformulating. Paul backs his instructions with the claim
that the words of institution come directly from the Lord, a claim
whose substance very few scholars are willing to doubt (1 Cor.
11.23). Distinguishing in the same letter between a word of the
Lord and his own word (1 Cor. 7.10, 12), Paul is working from a
categorical distinction between what 'Jesus says' and what 'Paul says'.
Accordingly, there is not one instance, in fact, in which a New Testament writer seeks to buttress his position by appealing to a statement
fallaciously attributed to Jesus. And yet, according to DeConick, this
was standard practice for the Thomas Christians.

The analogy to Greco-Roman philosophical practice also breaks
down when one considers that when philosophical schools used the
name of their venerated master in promulgating their own views,
they did so centuries after the death of their master. It was at least a
long enough period to ensure that there would be no way of check-
ing the authenticity of the quotation. But on DeConick's reconstruction, Jesus was being creatively re-remembered only a few years after
his death. In proposing a radical discontinuity between the Jesus
tradition and the Jesus community, this argument conjures the spectre
of the old Form Criticism.[46] In doing so, it opens up DeConick to the
same criticism that Vincent Taylor laid at the feet of Bultmann, and is
still worth repeating today: how could Jesus' followers so wilfully ignore
facts that were so easily verifiable through eyewitness testimony?[47]

---

[45] Donelson 1986: 10–11. For bibliography where intent to deceive is demonstrable in the
same schools, see Donelson 1986: 7 n2. See also Speyer 1971: 109–68; Rist 1972.

[46] Thus, e.g., the approach of Dunn (2003: 330–5) is only superficially similar.

[47] His remarks (1949: 41) are *à propos*: 'It is on the question of eyewitnesses that form criticism presents a very vulnerable front. If the Form-Critics are right, the disciples must
have been translated to heaven immediately after the Resurrection.' See now especially
Bauckham 2006.

The oddity of what is being proposed is driven home on imagining an analogous situation, say, a meeting at a fictitious Vladimir Lenin Society. Admirers and relatives of the departed Lenin are present; they wait for the ritual to begin. Finally, participants begin to to take turns performing Lenin sayings.

> Lenin says: 'A lie often told becomes truth.'
> Lenin says: 'History will be kind to me, for I intend to write it.'
> Lenin says: 'Military intelligence is a contradiction in terms.'
> Lenin says: 'We have nothing to fear but fear itself.'
> Lenin says: 'Forgive your enemies, but never forget their names.'

You realize full well that Lenin only really said the first saying; the rest you recognize as coming from, in corresponding order, Winston Churchill, Groucho Marx, Franklin Delano Roosevelt and John F. Kennedy. Those who knew Lenin, or knew people who knew Lenin, know that Lenin didn't say any of these things. But they are unperturbed, for they consider each saying to be an appropriate memory of the long-lost leader. Apparently, the society has been meeting like this for decades. Some sayings will drop out, others will be added in. But all of them will reflect faithfully on the community's memory of Lenin and what he stood for.

If I understand her argument correctly, DeConick maintains that a community undertaking this practice or something quite similar to it explains the composition of the *Gospel of Thomas* with all its tensions and duplications. To be fair, whatever was going on in the Thomas community would probably be considered strange by modern sensibilities. Nevertheless, given the choice between textual tensions and the scenario she is proposing, I would take my chances with the textual tensions. At its best, DeConick's reconstruction totters on the bizarre; at its worst, it is the stuff of what only an academic could believe. To be sure, truth is often stranger than fiction, but historians should not make it stranger than it has to be.

Conclusion

Perhaps there is an answer as to why *Thomas* has the tensions it has and why at least some of its sayings, patently not originating with Jesus, are ascribed to Jesus. If there is, I don't think we find it here. The model proposed in *Recovering the Original Gospel of Thomas* raises as many questions as it answers. How did this century-long institution of reperforming Jesus' words get its start? How do we square the Thomas Christians' veneration of Jesus as Prophet-Orator with their almost complete disregard for what he actually said? Is it really credible that Jerusalem-based Thomas Christianity, open as it was to Egyptian pagan influences, and the Jerusalemite church of the New Testament, uncomfortable as it was with Paul's mission to the Gentiles, could *both* identify James as their leader? Other questions remain. In sum, the proposal strains our imagination, lacks any convincing historical analogy, and simply does not match with what we do know about mid first-century Christianity.

We must press on. We must continue to search for a method to Thomas's madness by considering alternative explanations. We must, in other words, find an account of *Thomas* that explains the tensions without sacrificing plausibility. I hope to lay the groundwork for such an account in the next chapter, which begins Part 2 of this book.

Part 2

WHAT SHOULD BE SAID ABOUT THE *GOSPEL OF THOMAS*

4

The Syriac *Gospel of Thomas*

Having canvassed the views of Patterson, Pagels and DeConick regarding the Coptic *Gospel of Thomas*, I will now set forth in Part 2 what I believe needs to be said about our mysterious text. But before doing so, perhaps a few summarizing remarks are in order. What problems surrounding this gospel have been pinpointed and what kind of solutions do we have so far?

Stephen Patterson, it will be remembered from Chapter 1, frames an argument that touches on the formal features of the text as well as its content. As for the former, Patterson finds it particularly interesting that the sayings in *Thomas* do not generally follow the sequence that we encounter in any canonical gospel text. This seems to indicate, short of imagining someone furiously zigzagging back and forth through a copy of Matthew or Mark or Luke, that the sources behind *Thomas* were oral in nature. All sides must admit that there is something compelling about this argument. For the view that *Thomas* is essentially independent of the synoptic gospels, its apparently haphazard order constitutes good evidence in its own right. Those who insist on the Coptic collection's fundamental dependence on the New Testament gospels, on the other hand, must also explain why the order falls the way it does.

Patterson goes on to ground this account of *Thomas*'s formal features (its apparent primitive quality, its pell-mell arrangement, the occasional use of catchwords) in a socio-historic setting that finds its point of origin in Jesus himself. We know that these sayings go back to Jesus, Patterson argues, not simply because the sayings are introduced by the phrase 'Jesus says' or the like, but because the asceticism we find in the Coptic collection matches up with the itinerant lifestyle Jesus enjoins on his followers. While this argument may have an initial attractiveness, in my judgment it does not hold up to scrutiny. The particulars of Thomas's asceticism are borne out neither in the teachings nor in the practices of Jesus.

In Chapter 2, I recounted Elaine Pagels's argument that *Thomas*, or at least the form of spirituality represented and practised by self-proclaimed Thomas Christians, prompted the writing of the fourth gospel. That John was taking his best shot at Thomas while introducing novel Christological claims, in Pagels's view, depends on the observation that the *dramatis persona* Thomas receives shoddy treatment from the pen of the fourth evangelist. This argument, however, I found to be unconvincing. There are moments in which Thomas comes off rather well in the fourth gospel. Moreover, it is not at all obvious, as Pagels seems to think, that John's Christology and soteriology are so desperately at odds with what other, earlier, NT writers have to say.

The other side of Pagels's coin is no shinier: the evidence for the existence of 'Thomas Christians' at the turn of the first century is slight. Those portions of *Thomas* that actually make the gospel about 'Thomas' (Prologue and title) should be dated no earlier than the mid second century. What is more, the one logion within the collection proper that takes a bow in the direction of the *dramatis persona* Thomas (*Gos. Thom.* 13) is positioned alongside another saying (*Gos. Thom.* 12) that gives equal if not higher accolades to James. In order to be consistent then, Pagels would have to surmise that these were not simply Thomas Christians, but Jacobean-Thomasine Christians. The contribution of *Beyond Belief* lies elsewhere. While Pagels has failed to provide convincing argument for the existence of a Thomas community at the close of the first century, she is right to ask why there is talk about the apostolic figures in the first place and why certain creational images discernible in John are also found in *Thomas*.

In Chapter 3 I examined April DeConick's detailed argument for the 'original *Gospel of Thomas*'. Here too the case seems to be wanting. DeConick's premise that *Thomas*'s oral nature is to be inferred from the incongruous content of the individual sayings is predicated on McKane's now *passé* judgment on the oral-based compilation of Proverbs and on – although this is somewhat more debatable – the equally outdated notion that the gospels were authored by communities rather than individuals of some literary talent. DeConick's reconstruction of *Thomas*'s setting relies on certain assumptions regarding the transmission of early Jesus material, assumptions which in turn are based on passing comments culled from an early third-century source bearing neither on Jesus nor on first-century traditioning. Finally, DeConick's Traditions History involves too many unwarranted assumptions and suffers from too many methodological inconsistencies. Her determination to unpeel the successive layers of the oral *Thomas* tradition according to the principles of a New Form Criticism, an exercise that has already been rejected in principle by another self-proclaimed 'New Form Criticism',[1]

---

[1] As set out by Klaus Berger (1984: 10–13).

in the end is simply speculative. At the same time, even if the particular solutions DeConick provides do not seem satisfactory, the questions she poses of the text are ones deserving answers.

And to the questions we shall return. While I believe that each of these three hypotheses under survey falls short of providing a credible reconstruction of the origins of the *Gospel of Thomas*, it would be foolish to ignore the force of some very shrewd observations made along the way – observations crying out for interpretation. If one were to combine the studies I have just reviewed, press them down and shake them together, and then ask, 'What important questions are prompted by the evidence?', one could do worse than come up with the following list:

1 What accounts for the strange sequence of sayings in *Thomas*? Why do the sayings occur in the order that they do? (Patterson)
2 How might we explain the ascetical elements in *Thomas*? What socio-religious movement or movements might account for this renunciation of the world? (Patterson)
3 Why is Thomas so interested in creational themes, that is, in protology? (Pagels)
4 Why is the *Gospel of Thomas* according to *Thomas*? Why not some other apostle? Furthermore, what does this gospel say about the other apostles and why does it say what it does? (Pagels)
5 What accounts for the disparate substance of the sayings? (DeConick)
6 Why are all these sayings connected with Jesus, when Jesus most certainly did not say at least some of things attributed to him? (DeConick)

To this list of six, one might add a seventh, summarizing, question:

7 Is there a single setting which can be hypothesized behind *Thomas* that answers the above six questions in a stroke?

The relevance of this last question, which may not be equally clear to all, comes into clearer focus when one considers an inherent weakness of the current North American view of *Thomas*.

As should be clear by now, all three scholars under review, following the Koester school, conceive of the Coptic gospel as the cumulative result of a long oral-traditioning process. There is of course nothing *a priori* unfeasible about this. However, to state the obvious, what we have in our possession is a whole *Gospel of Thomas*. We do not have anything resembling a *Gospel of Thomas: Phase One*, *Gospel of Thomas: Phase Two*, or a *Gospel of Thomas: Phase Three*, not at least among the hard evidence.[2] The various compositional layers reflecting different periods and different settings are merely hypotheses. When one encounters a self-contained text, which has every appearance of being a literary whole, the natural assumption – unless circumstances patently dictate otherwise – is that the *basic* final form of the text is attributable to one hand.[3] So when source critics wish to make a case for multiple authorship of a document, they must do just that: make a case. The reason why the burden of proof falls on the one proposing multiple stages of composition is that, all things being equal, the simplest explanation for the existence of any document is the one requiring the fewest assumptions.

Consider, for example, a situation in which I awake one morning to find a deplorable sight. The lids to my rubbish bins are on the ground, the plastic bags in the rubbish bins have large gaping holes, and the discarded packaging from last night's pork chops is now strewn about and cleaned of its meaty juices. One explanation for this set of circumstances might go something like this. First, the neighbourhood vandal passed by, knocked off the lids to the rubbish bins and then with his knife tore into the plastic bags. Next, whether hours or moments later, a very hungry homeless person saw the rubbish bins, the holes in the plastic bags and with that the possibility of some edible food. He reached in to grab for the food and in the process had to remove the discarded pork chop packaging. Finding nothing, he went away. Then later a good rain soaked the packaging so as to remove any trace of blood or meat juice. Surely such a chain of events would explain the evidence.

But it is not the best explanation. In this case, the more natural account is that some animal, perhaps a raccoon or fox, knocked the lids off the bins, tore into the bags with its claws or teeth, and then proceeded to help itself to pork chop residuals. This explanation is preferable, because the best answer to any puzzle is the answer that involves the fewest moves, just as the strongest case in court is the one requiring the fewest witnesses. This is precisely why, to give yet another example, M.-E. Boismard's rather elaborate solution to the synoptic problem (how does one explain the literary relationship between the first three gospels?), involving as it does multiple stages

---

[2] The Oxyrhynchus fragments are no exception, precisely because they are *fragments*. Since one of these includes the Prologue, it must be said to witness to the text after it achieved its status as a complete *Gospel of Thomas*.

[3] This is not to say that we are to assume no minor modifications in the transmission process. Such changes are in the nature of the case virtually unavoidable.

and sources, has failed to convince many scholars.[4] Amid the various options for describing the origins of *Thomas*, many of which have involved scripting a rather large cast of characters and historical situations, replete with entrances and exits (here's where Jesus comes in, here later is where inter-apostolic controversy makes its entrance, here later still is where Gnosticism steals the show), any account that can explain *Thomas* as the product of one time, one place and one mind is to be preferred on general grounds. As Occam would say with razor in hand, 'If there is a single explanation involving a single background, which sufficiently speaks to the questions that have been raised in connection with *Thomas*, let's have it.'

I believe that there is a single background. But in piecing it together along with my own answer to these six posed questions, I am reminded that someone once said that when building a house, you should choose your foundation materials carefully. Or, to switch metaphors, when climbing a tree it is normally a good idea to start with the trunk, for there's no use going out on a limb before you're even off the ground. So then, in setting forth my own argument regarding the origins of the *Gospel of Thomas*, I wish to begin with as solid a footing as possible. Rather than planting my first foot on the premise that *Thomas* is inherently primitive in form (Patterson), or that a community that honoured Thomas existed in the first century (Pagels), or that a string of seemingly tensive statements must arise from an oral context (DeConick), I would like to begin with a starting point that is far less disputable and one in fact on which virtually all scholars agree: *Thomas*'s Syriac origins.

The original language of the *Gospel of Thomas*

In determining the provenance of this writing, most scholars have felt it unnecessary to go much further than the opening line: 'These are the words of Didymus Judas Thomas' (*Gos. Thom.* Prologue). The words 'Didymus' and 'Thomas' both mean 'twin', in Greek and Aramaic/Syriac, respectively. And while 'Thomas the Twin' is hardly distinctive (cf. John 11.16), the coupling of the name 'Judas' with 'Thomas' is unique to the Syriac tradition. We find this linkage in such Syriac texts as the Old Syriac of John 14.22 (and in the *Diatessaron*

---

[4] Boismard (1979) argues that Matthew is dependent on an earlier version of itself (which in turn derives from Q and source A), and on intermediate Mark (which also derives from A, but also sources B and C). Mark depends on the earlier form of Matthew, but also draws on intermediate Mark. Luke depends on Proto-Luke (which in turn depends on Q, source C and source B) and intermediate Mark.

on which it is based), the Syriac *Acts of Thomas*, and the *Abgar Legend*. Very clearly, for the early Syrian church, Thomas was a kind of patron saint, and Judas Thomas was the typical way of naming him.

There are other indications of Syrian provenance. For example, in *Gos. Thom.* 100 Jesus is shown a 'gold coin' (Coptic: *noub*), a word reflecting coinage only current in Syria.[5] Likewise, while the term *monachos* ('solitary') eventually came to mean something like 'monk', it was only in Syriac at this stage of the word's development that it meant what it does in *Thomas*, namely, a celibate.[6] Many more such considerations could be adduced, but these would only confirm what already seems to be the case on other grounds: the Syrian provenance of the *Gospel of Thomas*. And toward being more precise, since Edessa was the major centre of thought and learning in eastern Syria, it is to Edessa that *Thomas* has been assigned.[7] The majority of scholars think no differently.

It is at the next step, on the question of *Thomas*'s original language of composition, that scholarship has – as scholarship sometimes does – taken a curious but not completely inexplicable turn. While at least one scholar has argued that the Coptic gospel is represented in its original language, and others suppose a Syriac or Palestinian Aramaic background, most have been of the view that *Thomas* was first set down in Greek.[8] An original Greek *Thomas* commends itself for three reasons. First, the *Gospel of Thomas* is only one book out of a rather large 'library', and there is good reason to think that a large number of texts in this collection were the product of Coptic-speaking scribes copying from Greek texts, which in turn were ultimately copies of Greek originals. The Coptic translations of Plato and the *Sentences of Sextus*, for example, undoubtedly trace themselves back to Greek originals. Second, the fact that our earliest witnesses to *Thomas* (the Oxyrhynchus fragments) are written in Greek also suggests Greek as the original language of composition, just as, were our earliest extant witness in, say, Armenian, we might be justified in surmising Armenian as the original language. Third, Greek was the common language of the ancient world. If you wished to write anything that could be read throughout the Roman empire, Greek

---

[5] Guey 1960.

[6] Adam 1953–54, Beck 1956, Haenchen 1961, Harl 1963.

[7] See the defence of this point in Klijn 1972, in response to Ehlers 1970.

[8] Garitte's (1960) proposal of Coptic has not, to my knowledge, been picked up. The following subscribe to an originally Syriac *Thomas*: Strobel 1963; Quecke 1963; Rudolph 1969; Morard 1980; Guillaumont 1981; Drijvers 1982. Nagel 1969 is unclear whether he means Palestinian Aramaic or Syriac (Eastern Aramaic).

would be the way to go. These considerations have generally swayed scholars to think in terms of an originally Greek *Thomas*.

As weighty as such factors may be, they are far from decisive. In the first place, it is clear to paleographers that there are multiple hands involved in the writing of the Nag Hammadi Coptic texts. One should not, therefore, attach too much significance to the fact that just because certain Nag Hammadi texts are ultimately derived from a Greek original, they must all be ultimately dependent on a Greek original. Indeed, in the *Gospel of Philip*, which immediately follows *Thomas* in the ancient codex, there is a pointed interest in Syriac etymology: 'The eucharist is Jesus. For he is called in Syriac "Pharisatha", which is "the one who is spread out", for Jesus came to crucify the world' (*Gos. Phil.* 63.21–24). This certainly does not prove beyond a shadow of a doubt that the *Gospel of Philip* was first written in Syriac, but the author's statement along with several other factors have given more than a few scholars cause for inferring as much.[9] In short, if *Thomas*'s originally Greek character is deduced from what is presumed to be the first language of its neighbouring texts, it is helpful to remember that this deduction is hardly necessary and depends on a generalization that probably entails exceptions.

Second, we must appropriately assess the implications of the fact that our earliest witnesses to *Thomas*, the Oxyrhynchus fragments, were written in Greek. While the Greek of *P. Oxy. 1, 654* and *655* might induce us to suppose that the autograph ultimately behind these texts was also of Greek letters, this must be a guarded judgment. The three Oxyrhynchus fragments were clearly written by three different hands, on three different documents, and at three different times. During the period in which these texts were being copied down in southern Egypt, the same *Gospel of Thomas* was also drawing the notice of Hippolytus in Rome. All of this means that *Thomas* was not only extremely popular – one Oxyrhynchus copiest could be a crank, but three hands over a matter of decades is a following – but had an international reputation. Were a Greek copy of *Thomas* found holed up in a remote cave somewhere without having any discernible impact outside of its own originating community, we would agree that Greek was probably its first and last language. However, as we have been recently reminded by a certain best-selling thriller which itself involves secret societies and secret communications, when books become internationally popular, they also soon find themselves translated into multiple languages. And the more popular they are, the more quickly

---

[9] E.g. Ménard 1968, 1980; Drijvers 1970: 13, 15, 18–19.

they are translated. Given the obvious popularity of the sayings collection, the assumption of an originally Greek *Thomas* on the basis of early Greek copies is not quite as strong as it seems to be at first blush.

Finally, and most importantly, if *Thomas* was written in Edessa (again, a point virtually indisputable), then one can assume as a matter of course that the text would be very quickly translated into Greek. Edessa was in fact a bilingual city where texts were constantly being translated from Syriac into Greek and vice versa. The *Acts of Thomas*, for example, which bears a small host of resemblances to our *Gospel of Thomas*, seems to have been originally written in Syriac, translated into Greek, and then translated again back into Syriac![10] As Hans Drijvers puts it:

> Edessa was called the Athens of the east because it had a famous school where philosophy and rhetoric were taught to the young. Greek works were most likely read in Greek, but the teaching was mainly in Syriac, so that there existed a continuous process of translation from Greek into Syriac and the other way around. (Drijvers 1992: 126)

Elsewhere, Drijvers writes on Edessean texts in general: 'the question of language is not decisive: almost all writings that originate in that area and date back to the first three centuries AD are handed down in a Syriac and a Greek version, and it is often very difficult to establish which was the original'.[11] Given the remarkable fluidity of texts, whereby texts appearing in Syriac would in short order make their way into Greek, the Greek quality of the Oxyrhynchus fragments offers little resistance to the theory that *Thomas*, much like Bardesanes's *Concerning Fate* or Tatian's *Diatessaron*, was written in Syriac only to be quickly translated into Greek.

To press the point further, that the vast majority of ancient Edessean inscriptions are in Syriac (not Greek) points up the difficulty of asserting, as most scholars have done, that the *Gospel of Thomas* was composed in Edessa and in the language of Greek.[12] It is a point just short of astonishing that on the one hand scholars are so quick to acknowledge the Edessean origins of *Thomas*, but on the other hand have not bothered to contemplate the linguistic implications of this point in light of the archaeological evidence. If it is almost

---

[10] See Klijn 1962: 1–7.

[11] Drijvers 1984: 3.

[12] Drijvers (1972) shows that out of the six dozen or so recoverable inscriptions from that region, only a few were written in Greek. But see also Millar 1971: 1–8; Schmitt 1980: 198–205.

unanimously agreed that *Thomas* was written in Edessa, then there should be equally broad and serious consideration given to the possibility that *Thomas* was first scratched out in Syriac letters.

In my previous book, *Thomas and Tatian: The Relationship between the Gospel of Thomas and the Diatessaron*, I argue this very thing, but not on the grounds of provenance. Building on the work of a number of scholars who detected 'Syriacisms' in the *Gospel of Thomas*, I maintained that there is an extremely strong case to be made for *Thomas*'s Syriac character. Since that case will be vitally relevant to my own argument, I rehearse part of it here.

Enter the *Diatessaron*

The connection between *Thomas* and a Syriac-speaking background is nothing new. Not too many years after the publication of the *Gospel of Thomas*, the Dutch scholar Gilles Quispel pointed out that there were numerous parallels between the wording of the Coptic gospel and what we suppose was in the so-called *Diatessaron*, a Syriac gospel harmony composed by a man named Tatian. History tells us that Tatian was a philosophically inclined 'seeker' who set out from his native Syria and, after experimenting with various philosophies and mystery cults, converted to Christianity at some point towards the middle of the second century. Eventually, he came to study under the famed apologist Justin Martyr in Rome, where a Syriac-speaking community had already been established. Following Justin's martyrdom, Tatian apparently returned to his native land and soon took it upon himself to write what would come to be known as the *Diatessaron*. The *Diatessaron* (literally meaning 'through four') was not only the first Syriac gospel record but one of the first gospel harmonies ever to be written. Probably drawing on a model used by his mentor Justin, Tatian decided to convey the four-fold gospel (Matthew, Mark, Luke and John) to his people in one gospel, that is, as one continuous chronological narrative, involving bits and pieces of all four, but also a dose of Tatian's own cache of materials and editing predilections. Understandably, this *Diatessaron*, which we can date to around 173 CE, became an instant success among Syriac-speaking Christians.[13] Its prominence endured well into late antiquity when Bishop Rabbula, uncomfortable with its theological tendencies and its displacement of the four 'separated gospels', ordered its removal from his see. Unfortunately, we have no extant copies of the Syriac

---

[13] See Petersen 1994: 119, 427; 2005.

Diatessaron, but we are able to reconstruct its basic sequence of gospel pericopae and, in many cases, the precise wording of the original. Just as Tatian was destined to have considerable influence in the eastern church (even though the west tended to see him as having turned to heresy), textual critics tell us that his gospel harmony even outstripped its author in terms of influence. The impress of the *Diatessaron* would range far and wide, providing the paradigm for numerous other very old gospel harmonies and influencing the wording of countless translations of the canonical gospels throughout Asia and Europe.[14]

Quispel was not the only scholar to notice connections between Thomas and Tatian, for there are others.[15] One of them, August Strobel, draws interesting comparisons between *Gos. Thom.* 86 and the parallel text in Matthew and Luke, which are identical.[16] He lays out the comparisons as in Table 1.[17]

The correspondences between *Gos. Thom.* 86 and the *Diatessaron*, as reconstructed by Strobel, are fascinating. We see that Thomas and Tatian have the possessive adjective ('*their* holes'), where the synoptic tradition has none. Against the synoptic record, both Thomas and Tatian omit the phrase 'of the air' and include the verb 'to have' before the 'nests'. Matthew and Luke, on the other hand, lack the verb 'to have' and have 'nests' instead of 'nest'. Thomas and Tatian agree in saying that the son of man has 'no place to lay his head and rest.' Matthew and Luke read differently, for they say: 'the son of man has *nowhere* to lay *the* head.'

Strobel's observations are significant for two reasons. First, the level of detailed correspondence between *Thomas* and the *Diatessaron* against the synoptic tradition at this point prevents a dismissive explaining away of the text-critical data as the product of chance. Second, as important as it is that Thomas and Tatian share so many similarities, what is extraordinary is that the two traditions are in fact *identical*. Were we to translate *Gos. Thom.* 86 back into the original language of the *Diatessaron*, Syriac, we would in the same act be reconstructing the very (Syriac) words of the *Diatessaron*.

The multiple Diatessaronisms in *Gos. Thom.* 86 are no isolated phenomenon. In comparing the *Gospel of Thomas* against our best reconstruction of textual variants in the *Diatessaron*, Gilles Quispel finds

---

[14] See Petersen 1994: *passim.*

[15] See, e.g. Schippers 1960; Baker 1965b; Ménard 1975a, 1975b; Drijvers 1982; Baarda 1991.

[16] Strobel 1963.

[17] This table originally appeared in Perrin 2006: 69.

Table 1

Matt. 8.20 = Luke 9.50	Gos. Thom. 86	Diatessaron par. Matt. 8.20 = Luke 9.50
Foxes have	Foxes have	Foxes have
holes	**their** holes	**their** holes
and the birds	and ___ birds	and ___ birds
of the air	___	___
	have	**have**
nests,	**their nest,**	**their nest,**
but the son of man	but the son of man	but the son of man
has nowhere	has **no place**	has **no place**
to lay the head.	to lay **his** head	to lay **his** head
	and rest.	**and rest.**

over 160 textual variants shared by *Thomas* and the Diatessaronic tradition.[18] These variants occur throughout the *Gospel of Thomas* and, more importantly, on examining Thomasine sayings that parallel the synoptic gospels (roughly half of the entire collection of 114 sayings) one finds that there are only a few logia that do not bear the marks of Diatessaronic influence. (It should be pointed out that a good portion of the *Diatessaron* cannot be distinguished from the received Greek text.)[19]

In light of the data, Quispel suggested that there was a common oral Aramaic source on which Thomas and Tatian ultimately and independently drew. But in asserting this, he rules out without cause the possibility that Thomas used Tatian or vice versa. What makes Quispel's inference particularly difficult is the fact that *Gos. Thom.* 86 and its Diatessaronic parallel share precise wording. Just as identical wording between the synoptic gospels suggests (in those places) written dependence of one sort or another, the very close similarities between Thomas and Tatian also imply (in those places) either that one used the other or that they both drew on the same written source. In other words, in portraying the relationship between Thomas

---

[18] Quispel 1975. Quispel has an extensive bibliography on this subject.
[19] Quispel 1975: 174–90.

and Tatian, if one is prepared to exclude written sources from the picture, then one must by the same logic also reject the notion that the synoptic writers were aware of one another's work. These days the number of scholars who hold to such a position on the synoptic problem are few indeed. In sum, there are actually three reasonable possibilities: (1) Thomas knew and used Tatian, (2) Tatian knew and used Thomas, or (3) they both drew on a common *written* source.

Given this framing of the problem, the original language of composition behind Coptic *Thomas* also becomes relevant. If Tatian wrote in Syriac (which we assume), and if Thomas also wrote in Syriac (which we theorize), this would have made it fairly easy for Thomas to have used Tatian, or vice versa. Or, given the same conditions, perhaps both authors drew on the same Syriac text. Discerning the linguistic character of *Thomas* is valuable in that it holds promise of shedding some light on how we might conceive of its relationship to the *Diatessaron*.

Syriac senses and sounds

As I have mentioned, a number of scholars have argued that there are indications that *Thomas* was first composed in Syriac or at least that it passed through a Syriac-speaking stage of transmission.[20] Unfortunately, in modern Thomasine scholarship such voices are seldom heeded; the implications of their observations are barely considered. In my own work I have attempted to rehabilitate this view. I begin by showing how certain difficulties in *Thomas* can be explained as a misunderstanding of a Syriac original. For example, in *Gos. Thom.* 61, Salome asks Jesus:[21]

> 'Who are you, man, that *as from one* you have come up on my couch and have eaten from my table?'   (*Gos. Thom.* 61)

The words describing the manner in which Jesus comes up on the couch are nonsensical in the Coptic. Some, unsuccessfully in my view, have tried to emend the putative Greek original.[22] I propose the awkward wording of the Coptic is best explained by postulating that the original source read in Syriac: *min-ḥdā*. This Syriac phrase

---

[20] Cf., in addition to scholars noted above, Quispel 1981, who believes Thomas passed through an Aramaic stage. Like several other scholars of the period, Quispel does not distinguish Western Aramaic from its sister dialect, Eastern Aramaic, that is, Syriac.

[21] This example is taken from Perrin 2002: 45–6.

[22] See Layton 1989: 74.

literally means 'from one', but also 'suddenly'. Thus, in the original saying, Salome exclaims: 'Who are you, man, that you have *suddenly* come on to my couch?' In this case, while the translator correctly translated into Coptic on a word-by-word-equivalence basis, he or she essentially mistranslated by writing: *hōs ebol hen-oua* ('as from one'). There are other instances of this sort whereby curiosities in the Nag Hammadi text can be explained by tracing the text's steps backwards to a Syriac original.[23]

None of this proves of course that the entire *Gospel of Thomas* was written in Syriac. But given that Thomas is said to have been composed in a city where Syriac is the primary language, and given the fact that scholars (not just myself) have detected more than a few Syriacisms, the question can hardly be avoided: was *Thomas* as a whole first set down in Syriac?

I believe so. And I believe that the Syriac composition of *Thomas* can be demonstrated by a close examination of the collection's catchwords. We recall Patterson's discussion in which he finds catchwords the primary organizing principle of the sayings contained in *Thomas*. I quite agree. This becomes clear right from the beginning:

> These are the secret *sayings* which Jesus the living one spoke and Didymus Judas Thomas wrote down.
> And he said, 'Whoever finds the interpretation of these *sayings* will not taste death.'   (*Gos. Thom.* Prologue and 1)

The repetition of the word 'sayings' in the first two sayings is intentional. Whoever chose to perform or write these two sayings consecutively did so for a reason, for there are many more such word pairings where that came from. However this collection came together, whether through oral performance or written composition, catchwords are certainly an important factor in determining the order of the sayings.

But if catchwords involve not just repetition of sense, but the repetition of sound (we are constantly being reminded of the oral/aural quality of ancient texts), then one way to explore the question of *Thomas*'s original language of composition is through its use of catchwords. Surely, if the collection was first set down in Greek, there would be verbal linkages unique to Greek and completely undetectable in Coptic or Syriac. Likewise, if *Thomas* was first written in Syriac, then we might expect verbal connections that would not surface in Coptic or Greek (or English!) translation.

---

[23] See Perrin 2002: 43–6.

In my own study, I worked with the extant Coptic text, a reconstructed Greek text (using the Oxyrhynchus fragments and several Greek retroversions already published), and a reconstructed Syriac text. While there is inevitably some guesswork in reconstructing the Syriac, thankfully I was able to make use of some controls. When Thomas parallelled the NT scriptures, I supplied the word-for-word equivalent of the oldest extant Syriac copy of those scriptures (Old Syriac). (Next to the *Diatessaron*, the Old Syriac is the oldest Syriac version of the gospel; it drew on the *Diatessaron* at countless points.) Of course it was not of first importance to replicate the original grammar of each Thomasine saying. The question in each case is, 'What is the best Greek or Syriac equivalent for the corresponding Coptic word at hand?' Fortunately, Syriac word usage is fairly predictable. More often than not, the best option is fairly clear.

My study of catchwords in a hypothetical Syriac *Thomas*, a reconstructed Greek text, and the extant Coptic text contained revealing results. In Coptic *Thomas*, I find that out of 114 sayings, there are 269 words that may be linked to at least one other word either in the immediately preceding or in the immediately following logion. In a reconstructed Greek version, I find a slightly lower number: 263. This is odd, because if *Thomas* were originally written in Greek, and if catchwords generally were predicated as much on sound connections as on semantic connections, one would expect the number of Greek catchwords to be considerably higher than what we find in the Coptic.[24] Instead the number of catchwords in Greek and Coptic are roughly the same. But we find that if we examine a Syriac version of *Thomas*, we find that the number of catchwords almost doubles: 502.[25] This is considerable.

But it's not just the sheer number of catchwords that is remarkable. The distribution of these putative catchwords is also a factor. How broadly spread out are these catchwords, on the various linguistic options? One way to measure distribution is by determining the number of sayings that are (1) connected to either the immediately preceding or the immediately following logion, (2) connected to both the preceding and the following logion, and (3) completely isolated, that is, lacking a catchword connection altogether. On any translation of the *Gospel of Thomas*, the number of sayings containing

---

[24] Of course, it is possible that catchwords were introduced at the Coptic stage of transmission. However, if this were the case, one would also expect the number of Coptic catchwords to be considerably higher than the number of Greek catchwords. I am willing to be shown differently, but I find no substantial difference.

[25] Perrin 2002: 57–155.

catchwords is impressive. In the reconstructed Greek and extant Coptic versions, I find that about half the sayings are verbally linked in two directions, forwards and backwards. The statistics for the Greek and Coptic are again roughly similar for the percentage of sayings that show a catchword connection on one side, that is, with either the preceding or the subsequent logion, but not both. But, interestingly, the numbers for the Syriac reconstruction are quite different. In the Syriac, I find that 11 per cent of the sayings are connected on one side only while 89 per cent of the logia are connected on both sides, that is, to the preceding and subsequent logia. Given these numbers, it would be fair to say that the Syriac shows twice as much interconnectedness as the Coptic and Greek versions.[26]

But there is one observation that is the most significant of all: that in a Syriac *Gospel of Thomas* and only there do we find no isolated sayings. Neither Greek nor Coptic comes close. This strongly suggests that the whole collection was written not in Greek, as is widely supposed, nor in Coptic, but in Syriac. Not only so, but if the *Gospel of Thomas* was written in Syriac, then it was also very likely a compositional unity. Again, neither Coptic nor Greek *Thomas* approaches this thoroughgoing unity.

Before taking this any further, we must face head on the possibility that all these results suggesting Syriac composition are nothing but a blend of speculation and luck. Of course, on any reconstruction, there would be a natural temptation to make the data do certain things. The technical term for this is 'fudging'. However, in the final analysis the charge of tendentious retro-translating does not wash and that is because of the *patterns* of catchwording we see in Syriac *Thomas*. For example, in *Gos. Thom.* 10 we find the word 'fire', while the following logion contains the word 'light': in Syriac, the two words 'fire' and 'light', *nurā* and *nuhrā*, would have been almost indistinguishable to the ear. Coincidence? Perhaps. But then we must reckon with the fact that precisely the same word pairing occurs again in *Gos. Thom.* 82.1 and 83.1 (2x), 2. And again we have a third occurrence of 'fire' in *Gos. Thom.* 16.2, this time linked to 17 not with 'light' per se, but – through a more indirect wordplay – 'eyes', a standard metaphor for 'light' (Matt. 6.22–23). Words for 'fire' occur four times in the collection (*Gos. Thom.* 10; 13.8; 16.2; 82.1); 'light' is found in seven sayings (11.3; 24.3 [4x]; 33.3; 50.1 [2x]; 61.5; 77.1; 83.1 [2x], 2). The statistical probability that these pairings are incidental is 6.8 per cent.[27]

---

[26] Perrin 2002: 57–155.

[27] Stephen Carlson and Andris Abakuks have kindly confirmed these statistics.

There are other catchword patterns. The word 'wealth' (Coptic *ᵉmmᵉntrᵉmmao* = Syriac *'etar*) occurs twice in the sayings collection (29.3, 85.1); both times in conjunction with the like-sounding word 'place' (Coptic *ma* = Syriac *'atar*) (30.1, 2; 86.2). Coptic words for 'place' (*ma*, *topos*) occur in *Gos. Thom.* 4.1; 18.2; 22.6 [4x]; 24.1; 30.1, 2; 33.2; 50.1; 60.6; 64.12; 67; 68.2; 86.2. Of course it is possible that the collocation of 'wealth' with 'place' was a matter of random chance. But such randomness is rather unlikely: there is a 3.8 per cent chance that its repeated connection with *ᵉmm ᵉntr ᵉmmao* is fortuitous.

Consider another example. The word 'women' (= Syriac *nešše*) is found in only three logia in the collection (*Gos. Thom.* 15; 46.1; 114.1). Each of these logia, interestingly, also falls next to a saying which, when on the basis of the Old Syriac is translated back into Syriac, contains the word *naš*, i.e. 'someone' (*Gos. Thom.* 14.5; 47.1; 113.4). Whether *naš* can be presumed beyond these three sayings is questionable. Given the limited use of both terms, their recurring collocation strongly suggests that *nešše* ('women') and *naš* ('someone') are intended to be phonologically linked. Again, we cannot deny the theoretical possibility that these collocations of 'women' and 'someone' are merely a matter of chance. But 'theoretical possibility' shades off into the incredible: the likelihood that these sayings with these words simply *happened* to be next to each other is .0085 per cent. In light of these Syriac-only 'catchword patterns' and the strong statistical evidence that these patterns were intentional, it is hard to doubt the unity and Syriac quality of the first text of *Thomas*.

Comparing Coptic (*NHC* II,2) and Greek (*P. Oxy.* 1, 654, 655) Thomas

Further corroborating evidence comes when we compare the extant Coptic *Thomas* against the Greek fragments. The differences between the Greek Oxyrhynchus fragments and their Coptic parallels have piqued the curiosity of scholars. No one suggestion has proven completely convincing. Elsewhere I have explained how certain differences between our Coptic and Greek texts can be explained by the supposition of a common Syriac original.[28] By way of example, we might compare the following:

'Where there are three, they are atheists (*atheoi*).'   (*P. Oxy.* 1.23–24)

'Where there are three gods, they are gods (*hennoute*).'

(*Gos. Thom.* 31)

---

[28] Perrin 2004.

Guillaumont sheds light on the unusual assertion by proposing that what is in view here is the Jewish practice whereby a quorum of three elders is necessary to settle interpretive disputes.[29] In this case, those envisaged are serving not as gods, but as judges. This coheres with a Syriac context, for in Syriac the word *alāhē* means both 'gods' and 'judges'. But still there are problems: the Greek and Coptic texts seem to say almost opposite things. But if we take Guillaumont's solution a step further, we can without too much difficulty imagine that the Syriac rending would involve something like this: 'Where there are three judges (*alāhē*), they are indeed judges (*l-alāhē*).'[30] If so, it is easy to see how a scribe, with faulty hearing of the Syriac original, may have generated a separate line of transmission. One scribe thought he heard, 'Where there are three, they are atheists (*lā-alāhē*),' generating the Greek *atheoi*; another scribe hearing the same Syriac words thought he heard, 'Where there are three, they are gods (*l-alāhē*),' yielding in the Coptic line of transmission, *hennoute*. Here is one instance in which differences between the extant Greek and Coptic may be explained by positing a common Syriac source.

Another instance may be found by comparing the following:

'And my soul *is concerned* (*ponei*) for the sons of men . . .'

> (*P. Oxy.* 1.17–18)

'And my soul *was in pain* (*ti tkas*) for the sons of men.'

> (*Gos. Thom.* 28.3)

While 'to be concerned' and 'to be in pain' share some conceptual overlap, the senses are in fact distinct. How do we explain the difference in meaning between the Greek and Coptic? Again, the Syriac theory comes to the rescue. If the lector, reading *Thomas* for the copyists, uttered the Syriac Qal form *'nā* in order to describe the condition of Jesus' soul, then the Greek translation ('to be concerned') has it right. But if the lector actually used the very similar sounding Aphel stem of the same verb, i.e. *ā'nā*, then the Coptic has it right. Whether the Greek line or the Coptic line got it right, we cannot be sure. But it seems that the original saying contained either *'nā* or *ā'nā* and, again, one line of transmission preserved the sense of the original, while the other line, on account of faulty hearing, did not. Since I give five further examples of the same phenomena elsewhere

---

[29] Guillaumont 1958: 114–16.

[30] The inclusion of the *lamedh* in the predicate is appropriate, given the determinative sense. Hebrew has an analogous construction.

(including examples that suggest Syriac as opposed to Western Aramaic provenance), there is no need to repeat myself further.[31]

Syriac catchwords and redaction

An added strength of the Syriac theory is that it explains certain redactional changes the editor seems to have made to his material. If the compiler of the Thomasine collection put a high priority on establishing catchword connections between the sayings, one might suspect that when catchword linkages did not naturally present themselves, the editor would look for ways to create them. I suggest this is precisely what we do find, but again, only in Syriac:

'When you go into each land *and walk about the districts*, if they receive you, eat what is set before you.' (*Gos. Thom.* 14.4)

'When you enter into a town and they receive you, eat what is set before you.' (Luke 10.8)

Among the differences between *Gos. Thom.* 14.4 and Luke 10.8, the most obvious is the inclusion of the clause 'and walk about the districts' in the Thomasine text. While a form-critical approach might seek to reconstruct the Traditions History of this saying apart from its context in the collection, here I suggest context is everything. Consider this comparison between *Gos. Thom.* 14.4 and material in the previous logion:

'When Thomas *returned* (*panni*) to his friends they asked him . . .' (*Gos. Thom.* 13.7)

'When you go into each land and walk about the *districts (penayim)*, if they receive you, eat what is set before you.' (*Gos. Thom.* 14.4)

If *Gos. Thom.* 13.7 originally contained the verb *panni* ('return'), a likely supposition in the case of a Syriac original, then there could hardly be a more effective way of repeating this rare combination of syllables in the next logion than by adding the word 'districts' (*penayim*). Of course there may have been theological reasons for the editor to have added 'and walk about the districts', but none that we can make out. We can, however, explain the presence of this clause by supposing a Syriac original.

Gos. Thom. 17 has provoked the spilling of much ink among *Thomas* scholars.[32] In respect to this logion ('I shall give you what no eye has

---

[31] Perrin 2004: 144–51. Other studies (e.g. Baarda 1991: 386–7) also show why Syriac is to be preferred over Western Aramaic.

[32] Most recently, see Onuki 1991, Dunderberg 1997, and Sevrin 1999.

seen and what no ear has heard and what no hand has touched and what has never entered into the human heart'), I am interested in why – against all extant parallels – the phrase 'what no hand has touched' was included. In light of a Syriac original, the answer becomes clear. While it is difficult to ascertain what precise inflection of the verb 'to know' would have occurred in a Syriac version of *Gos. Thom.* 16 and 18, it is almost certain that the root word in question would have been *ida'*. Recognizing this, the astute editor realizes that all that needs to be done to link *Gos. Thom.* 16 to *Gos. Thom.* 17, and *Gos. Thom.* 17 in turn to *Gos. Thom.* 18, is insert one word in the middle saying: 'hand' (Syriac: *ida'*). Of course, he could not just add the word by itself, it would have to be in a phrase that flowed appropriately with the context: 'I shall give you what no eye has seen and what no ear has heard *and what no <u>hand</u> has touched* . . .'. The otherwise unexplainable addition of 'what no hand has touched' can be chalked up to the premise that the collection was written in Syriac by an editor who was very keen to keep a catch-word chain going.[33]

To the modern reader, all this may seem rather odd. But to the ancient Syrian this kind of linking of semantic and phonological entities would have been entirely familiar. Early Syriac literature is replete with this kind of trope, as can be seen on examination of Ephraem, Narsai, Jacob of Serug, *Acts of Thomas* and the *Odes of Solomon*.[34] Several examples of the play on words that we find in the *Odes* (among the earliest extant Syriac texts) are even discernible in *Thomas*.[35] Stylistically, a highly paronomastic Syriac *Gospel of Thomas* coheres with what we know about early Syriac literature.

The Original Language of the *Gospel of Thomas*: Conclusions

I freely grant that none of this *proves* that *Thomas* was written in Syriac. But to insist on 'proof' is to misunderstand the nature of history. History very seldom if ever 'proves' anything. Rather, what

---

[33] Whether or not it is credible that the editor of *Thomas* would go to such limits to sustain his game is of course a matter of judgment. However, it is difficult to overestimate the significance of word play in antiquity. As Frederick Ahl (1985: 322) writes: 'The ancient text, be it philosophical or poetical, is a texture not only of sounds and words, but of soundplay and wordplay . . . [These] are not, I suggest, an occasional ornament of the writer's art: they *are* his art.'

[34] See Perrin 2002: 157–69. We even see an interest in wordplay in Edessa's material culture; see Segal 1970: 34.

[35] Perrin 2002: 160–64.

historians seek to do is to reconstruct the model that best explains the available data. In my view, an originally Syriac *Gospel of Thomas* makes the most sense on a number of counts. The reader who studies this evidence and yet chooses to demur must be prepared to explain: (1) why an Edessean text should be believed to have been written in Greek instead of Syriac; (2) why the number of catchwords in a reconstructed Greek *Thomas* (the putative original language) is no greater than what we find in the Coptic copy; (3) why the number of catchwords in a Syriac copy of *Thomas* roughly equals the number of catchwords in a Greek and Coptic *Thomas put together*; (4) why there are seven points of divergence between the Coptic and Greek recensions of *Thomas* that can all be explained by postulating shared dependence on a Syriac original; (5) why phrases like 'walk about in the districts' (*Gos. Thom.* 14.4) and 'what no hand has touched' (*Gos. Thom.* 17), among others, have been added; (6) why several of the same paronomastic word pairings that occur in a Syriac *Thomas* also show up in the second-century Syriac *Odes of Solomon*; and (7) why certain Thomasine word pairings repeat themselves in such a way that if asked to regard them as merely random, we would be asked to believe the statistically impossible. Until these points are sufficiently addressed, I think that a Syriac *Gospel of Thomas* carries far more explanatory power than any other model on offer.

Of course, the case would be stronger still were there the proverbial smoking gun, a Syriac *Gospel of Thomas* turning up in a monastery somewhere, or a newly discovered letter of Eusebius in which he writes, 'Oh, by the way, the *Gospel of Thomas* was first composed in Syriac.' But we make countless inferences on a day-to-day basis without being bothered in the least by the absence of a smoking gun. Returning to my open rubbish bins with the scattered pork chop packaging, what if I were to call my brother-in-law the zoologist and he were to affirm the presence of fox hairs and fox scat around the garbage bins, what conclusion would I draw?

'It must be a fox then,' I say to my neighbour.

'A fox? Why do you say a fox?' says my neighbour.

'Well, the lids are overturned, there are holes ripped into the plastic bags, the packaging has been removed and licked clean of its juices. There are also fox hairs and fox faecal matter right around the rubbish bins. We can safely say then that foxes have been here.'

'Ah, yes, but did you see the fox?' my sceptical neighbour retorts.

'No, but the circumstantial evidence can hardly show otherwise.'

'Nonsense. Show me the fox. Then and only then will I believe you. Until then I intend to write a letter to the editor of the local paper regarding our vandal problem.'

'You wouldn't happen to be a New Testament scholar, would you?' I ask.

Apparently, I have a few neighbours who, as far as the *Gospel of Thomas* is concerned, are essentially saying: 'Show me the fox.'[36] Like the Red Queen in *Through the Looking-Glass*, NT scholars sometimes force themselves to believe the impossible, if by so doing they can avoid having to believe the obvious. If there are ample clues to suggest that a fox has been at work, then a fox it is. If there are ample clues to suggest Syriac as the original language of the *Gospel of Thomas*, there is no reason to doubt this.

Back to the *Diatessaron*

At this point I shall assume that *Thomas* was in fact first penned in Syriac. The burden of evidence, I submit, is now on those who insist on thinking otherwise. But if this is true, then another inference almost ineluctably follows, namely, that the *Gospel of Thomas* was not a slowly snowballing oral collection, drawing from different oral strata. Instead, it was a carefully worked piece of literature, brought together at one place and at one time by an industrious Syriac-speaking editor. This is evident on two considerations.

First, the consistency of the catchword pattern indicates a literary as opposed to an oral background. Even for Bultmann, who was loath to attribute synoptic material to the editorial activity of the gospel writers, long chains of sayings indicated the presence of an editor who worked hard to put those sayings together.[37] Or consider the judgment of Stephen Patterson in his discussion of the significance of catchwords in *Thomas*:

> The significance of such a pattern in Thomas may be assessed variously. For example, an editor might have organized the collection in this way to facilitate its memorization. The utility of this for the street preacher, who would compose his or her speeches *ad hoc* in the busy colonnades of the agora, is obvious. Alternatively, one could well imagine an editor assembling these sayings simply as he or she remembered them, catchwords triggering the recollection of each new saying. In this case the catchwords will not have been part of any conscious design on the part of the editor, but simply the result of his or her own process of remembering. *The occasional gaps where no catchwords are to be found suggest the latter.*[38]

---

[36] Luomanen 2006: 149 n74.

[37] Bultmann 1963[1921]: 322.

[38] Patterson 1993: 102. Italics added.

Patterson considers the dilemma: catchwords could point in the direction either of editorial design or of more spontaneous oral traditioning. He chooses the latter and he does so because he finds occasional gaps in catchwording, that is, he finds that some sayings in *Thomas* are isolated. But if *Thomas* was written in Syriac and if, as at least my reconstruction suggests, a Syriac *Thomas* has no gaps at all, then by the same logic Patterson would have to agree that the evidence suggests the conscious design of an editor.

A second reason for inferring editorial activity on the part of Thomas, as opposed to envisaging one who merely assembled stray oral traditions, is the complexity of the catchword associations. As one might suspect, given that I have found over 500 Syriac catchwords in a collection of 114 sayings, a number of sayings have multiple catchword connections sprouting out in two directions at once. Designing this is no easy task, but requires the kind of patience and ingenuity that characterize those who create crossword puzzles. Or, less anachronistically, this requires a similar process that seems to have gone into the composition of Proverbs, that is, if Heim and Weeks (among many other scholars) are correct in their assessment. Regarding catchwords in the biblical book of Proverbs, Heim writes approvingly of Weeks's judgment:

> Finally, the high number of linked sayings calls for an explanation. Why should the editors of the collection have taken so much trouble to connect them? Here is Weeks' explanation, together with his rejection of another standard attempt to explain the phenomenon:
>
> > In the majority of cases, a saying shares with at least one of its neighbours an initial letter, a catchword, or a form. The effect of this is to give a sort of flow to the reading or recitation of the material, the motivation for which was probably aesthetic: the links are too varied and irregular to have served as a mnemonic device. (Weeks, *Wisdom*, 33)
>
> Opponents of the existence or significance of groups need to provide an explanation for the many links between sayings, and the standard one is that they were aids to memory. Weeks, correctly in my opinion, showed that this explanation is not adequate . . . The most natural explanation, that the editor(s) wanted to create some kind of textual coherence, remains a viable option.[39]

Heim's concluding sentence is accurate if not somewhat understated when weighed against the remainder of his monograph. Given the complex chain of connections that comes to surface on the Syriac theory, *Thomas*'s editorial unity can hardly be doubted.

---

[39] Heim 2001: 17–18.

If this be so, the question then arises as to the nature of this author's sources, especially in regard to that material paralleled in the synoptics. What do we have so far? We have a Syriac *Thomas* with synoptic-like material that bears uncanny resemblances to Tatian's *Diatessaron*, also written in Syriac. I have already spoken against the general possibility of a strictly indirect oral relationship between the two texts, given the sometimes tightly shared parallels. But we have something else: we have now the supposition that the order reflected in the Coptic text more or less preserves the order we would expect to find in its hypothesized Syriac parent text. This insight helps us with the question of sources. Whereas it is regularly claimed that the sayings in *Thomas* do not reflect the sequence of the canonical gospels and this in turn often becomes, as it does for Patterson, the basis for arguing for the collection's independence, it must be said (as Patterson concedes) that this claim is not completely true. At points the *Gospel of Thomas* does follow the order of both the synoptics and the *Diatessaron*: Gos. Thom. 8–9, 32–33, 42/43–44, 47, 65–66, 68–69, 92–93 and 93–94.

If Thomas were imitating the sequence of Matthew 12 this would explain *Gos. Thom.* 44 and 45.2–4, but would not explain the insertion of 45.1 (= Matt. 7.16). Luke as a source would explain the wording of *Gos. Thom.* 45, but would not explain the collocation of *Gos. Thom.* 44 and 45, as Matthew 12 does. The case for Thomas's dependence on Matthew or on Luke has its merits as well as its problems. The best explanation is that the hand behind *Gos. Thom.* 44—45 drew on a harmonization of Matthew and Luke as reflected in the *Diatessaron*, where judging by the eastern witness of Ephraem and the western witness of the Middle Dutch harmony, the words of Matthew 12.32–35 seem to have attached themselves precisely at this point of the Sermon on the Mount.

In addition to these examples, there is a particularly interesting instance involving *Gos. Thom.* 44 and 45. The parallels may be laid out as shown in Table 2 (overleaf).

Given the fact that my reconstructed Syriac *Gospel of Thomas* shows no isolated sayings, we find it unlikely that sayings were added to the collection in stages. Just as if we were to find an intricately woven tapestry and rightly suppose that it was created on one loom, so too we are best served by thinking of *Thomas* being wrought on a single verbal loom: *Thomas* shows every sign of being a compositional unity. Thus if *Thomas* is a compositional unity and reflects the order of the *Diatessaron* at nine places (eight of which also follow the sequence of Matthew and/or Luke), this Diatessaronic order could not have been the product of a later scribe. Since it is extremely unlikely

Table 2

Gospel of Thomas	Matthew	Luke
Gos. Thom. 44.1 Jesus said, 'Whoever speaks against the father will be forgiven, 2 and whoever speaks against the son will be forgiven.	**Matthew 12.32** And whoever says a word against the Son of man will be forgiven;	**Luke 12.10** And every one who speaks a word against the Son of man will be forgiven;
3 However, whoever speaks against the holy spirit will not be forgiven, neither on earth nor in heaven.'	but whoever speaks against the Holy Spirit will not be forgiven, either in this age or in the age to come.	but he who blasphemes against the Holy Spirit will not be forgiven.
Gos. Thom. 45.1 Jesus said, 'Grapes are not harvested from thornbushes, nor are figs gathered from thistles, for they do not give forth fruit.	**Matthew 7.16** You will know them by their fruits. Are grapes gathered from thorns, or figs from thistles?	**Luke 6.44** . . . for each tree is known by its own fruit. For figs are not gathered from thorns, nor are grapes picked from a bramble bush.
2 A good man brings forth good from his storehouse; 3 an evil man brings forth evil things from his evil storehouse which is in his heart. He also says evil things. 4 For out of the fullness of the heart he brings forth evil things.'	**Matthew 12.35** The good man out of his good treasure brings forth good, and the evil man out of his evil treasure brings forth evil. **Matthew 12.34b** For out of the abundance of the heart the mouth speaks.	**Luke 6.45** The good man out of the good treasure of his heart produces good, and the evil man out of his evil treasure produces evil; for out of the abundance of the heart his mouth speaks.

that Tatian's order was inspired by Thomas, I am of the conviction that Thomas in fact had access to a copy of the *Diatessaron* or drew on his memory of hearing it directly.[40]

---

[40] Tatian's use of *Thomas* is unsustainable. This amounts to saying that although Tatian was indebted to the four gospels for almost his entire harmony, at these more than half-dozen places he inexplicably left off from the canonical gospels and depended instead on *Thomas*, but only where *Thomas* happened to match the order of the synoptic gospels!

The attractiveness of this account is two-fold. First, very simply, it explains why the vast majority of Thomasine sayings that parallel the synoptics contain Diatessaronisms. Second, and here we get to the first of the seven questions posed at the beginning of this chapter, this reconstruction explains what Patterson asked to be explained: the rhyme and reason of Thomas's order. On the whole, the author of *Thomas* showed little interest in following the order of his sources. He was much more concerned with thematic groupings and above all with linking sayings together by catchwords. The editor's obsession with catchwords, however, only clearly emerges in the Syriac. Nonetheless, at nine points Thomas betrays his primary source: Tatian's *Diatessaron*. He certainly had other sources, both oral and written. But alongside these he also had a working knowledge of the first gospel to be written in Syriac. This means that the *Gospel of Thomas* was written some time after 173 CE, the dating of the *Diatessaron* itself. By duly appreciating the importance of catchwords, much more noticeable in the Syriac, and by allowing for Thomas's use of Tatian, we provide the best explanation for the sequence of Thomasine sayings precisely as they are preserved in the Coptic text.

Objections considered

The theory that Thomas knew and used Tatian is not without vulnerability. It has been objected that if *Thomas* was indeed written in Syriac at some time after the composition of the *Diatessaron* in the 170s, this leaves precious little time for it to have been translated into Greek, circulated and brought down to Egypt, where it could have been found as early as 200 CE.[41] Doesn't this scenario require, in other words, a speed of transmission and promulgation that makes it immediately implausible?

I think not. In the first place, as I have already pointed out, we know that Syriac writings from Edessa were very routinely and very quickly translated into Greek. Thus, the time required between the first public circulation of the Syriac *Thomas* and its being copied into Greek may have been as little as a few weeks. Second, we also know that the *Gospel of Thomas* was extremely popular. If it became popular almost immediately (it's harder to imagine the text languishing in obscurity and then suddenly catching on), then it was presumably also copied numerous times, with more copies being made of the copies,

---

[41] So, e.g. DeConick 2005: 48–9.

and so on. Third, since the road to and from Edessa was a well-travelled one, and since there seems to have been heavy traffic between Syria and Egypt, it hardly beggars belief that a copy of *Thomas* eventually found its way, after 20 or 30 years, to Oxyrhynchus.[42] If it was possible for Irenaeus, writing in southern France in the 180s, to have authored a text that would then be copied and brought to southern Egypt within two decades, surely it involves no extraordinary supposition to suggest that *Thomas* made the same pilgrimage over a much shorter distance with an extra ten or more years to spare.[43]

My argument assumes, uncontroversially, a date of roughly 200 CE for the earliest of the Greek fragments of *Thomas*. More than once I have either read or been told that *P. Oxy.* 1, 654 and 655 should be dated to the year 200 CE or *before*.[44] This is incorrect. The three fragments have all been dated to the first half of the third century – the latest of the three (*P. Oxy.* 654 and 655) anywhere up to 250 CE.[45] The earliest of the three, *P. Oxy.* 1, may, according to Attridge in the standard critical edition, be plausibly dated 'shortly *after* 200 CE'.[46] How far after we cannot be sure. Hippolytus, writing in the 220s or 230s, speaks of *Thomas* as if it was in broad circulation; Origen makes similar noises not much later.[47] So it may well be that the Oxyrhynchus fragments were representative of this early third-century broad circulation. Again, we cannot be sure. But we should not be *too* dogmatic about the date 200 CE. Scribal styles change over time, but they do not change suddenly or dramatically (as anyone who has kept a lifetime's worth of handwritten letters can testify). Thus, when we think of the conventional dating of the Oxyrhynchus fragments, we may think plus or minus *some* years, but again, for the sake of argument I am

---

[42] On the interchange between Edessa and the rest of the Roman world, see Drijvers 1992: 124–5.

[43] On the Irenaeus text in Egypt, see Roberts 1979: 14, 24.

[44] So DeConick (2005: 48): 'The Greek fragment P. Oxy. 1 is dated by B. Grenfell and A. Hunt to a date *no later than 200* CE. This date has been accepted by scholars as the *terminus ad quem* for the manuscript copy because the paleographic analysis of the manuscript places it at 200 CE' (italics original). The first statement is not quite right: according to the nineteenth-century discoverers, 'the papyrus itself was written not much later than the beginning of the third century' (Grenfell and Hunt, 1897: 16). Grenfell and Hunt's 'not much later than the beginning of the third century' does not mean 'no later than 200 CE.' The second statement is a non sequitur. How can a document simultaneously be dated to 200 CE and have (consequently?) a *terminus ad quem* of 200 CE?

[45] Attridge 1989: 97–9.

[46] Attridge 1989: 97.

[47] See Introduction, pp. 8–9.

conservatively assuming that *P. Oxy.* 1 was penned in the year 200 CE. While this tentative assumption means that things did move along quickly between Edessa and Egypt, it certainly presents no insuperable difficulty. Things had to have moved fast if, after no mention of *Thomas* in the second century, we suddenly find that by 230 CE church fathers in both the east and the west were chattering away about it.

Thomas and asceticism

My argument to this point has touched on only one of the questions raised by Patterson: the question as to why the *Gospel of Thomas* has the unusual sequence it does. On my understanding, the order of the Thomasine sayings appears to have been driven by catchwords much more than has been heretofore realized, and a Syriac *Thomas* explains the order satisfactorily. But there is another issue which, I believe, we are now prepared to address: Thomasine asceticism. In doing so, I will not depend on the case I have made so far, but will attempt to set out a fresh argument from a different angle as to why a late second-century *Thomas* makes most sense.

We recall that Patterson delineated various ascetical practices shared by Thomas Christians. I would like to focus on three. First, the community members seem to have divested themselves of their earthly possessions, for their Jesus instructed them to 'fast in regard to the world' (*Gos. Thom.* 27.1). The one who had become wealthy was called to renounce wealth (*Gos. Thom.* 110, cf. *Gos. Thom.* 86), business dealings (*Gos. Thom.* 64.12), and even family ties (*Gos. Thom.* 101). Second, there are indications that Thomas Christians kept to a spare, meatless, diet. For them the 'days when you ate what is dead' (*Gos. Thom.* 11.3), the carcasses of slaughtered animals, were bygone days, presumably before they associated themselves with the Thomas community. The body that nurtured itself on body was wretched indeed, as was the soul of the same meat-eating body (*Gos. Thom.* 87, 112). Third, Thomas Christians idealized celibacy. It was the 'solitaries' (*monachoi*) who were the elect; they and they alone would find the kingdom (*Gos. Thom.* 49). While many would position themselves by the door of salvation, only the sexually continent would enter the true, spiritual, bridal chamber (*Gos. Thom.* 75). Life with the Thomas Christians involved commitments to poverty, vegetarianism and sexual abstinence.

In clarifying the historical linkage between Tatian and Thomas, we observe that the practices of the Thomas community also marked Tatian's life as well. According to Irenaeus, whose report has some verisimilitude, Tatian became increasingly radical after the death of his mentor Justin Martyr.[48] As Tatian sees it in his *Oration to the Greeks*, written five or so years after the *Diatessaron*, the world and everything in it were 'madness'.[49] As a result, it was necessary to die to the world and restore the body as a fit dwelling place for the Spirit of God. Passions had to be transcended; the things of this world were to be despised.[50] In the *Diatessaron*, which most scholars believe Tatian edited in order to promulgate his views, we see a similar discomfort with possessions.[51] Tatian also goes on record for condemning the eating of meat.[52] Jerome, who found this viewpoint downright scandalous, maintained that Tatian came to this position by taking up the Nazirite vows.[53] Whether or not Jerome understood and accurately reported Tatian's motives is difficult to say. But we need not doubt the substance of the report.

Finally, once more like Thomas, Tatian was opposed to marriage. Those who had intercourse, conjugal or otherwise, received 'corruption in the flesh'.[54] This is corroborated by Irenaeus who reports that Tatian considered all sexual relations as *porneia* (sexual immorality).[55] According to Clement of Alexandria, who possessed Tatian's writings, Tatian admitted that scripture made concessions for marriage (1 Corinthians 7), but such concessions were no moral justification.[56] But on this point there is no need to turn to the witness of others: the *Oration* − not to mention the *Diatessaron* − bears this out, for there Tatian puts marriage on a par with paedophilia.[57]

In considering the asceticism of Tatian against the backdrop of early Syriac Christianity, it is difficult to determine whether he primarily came to his views on his own (as the church fathers report) or whether his outlook after Justin's death was much like what he knew when he was in Syria as a younger man. Allowing for the

---

[48] *Adv. Haer.* 1.28.1. While Irenaeus and others after him may have condemned Tatian in part because they misunderstood him and his native culture, there may well have been a sense in which Justin's remaining alive tethered Tatian's evolving convictions (we see the same dynamic between Luther and his protégé Melanchthon). Petersen (2005: 151) is on the mark when he writes 'that Irenaeus' . . . allegations against Tatian appear well founded'.

[49] *Oratio* 11.2. For a discussion of the dating of the *Oration*, see Grant 1953 and criticisms in Hunt 2003: 21–36.

[50] *Oratio* 11.2.

[51] E.g. Vööbus 1958: 39–45; Elze 1960: 124–6; Petersen 1994: 76–83. But see the cautions of Hunt (2003: 145–55) and Petersen (2005: 144–9).

[52] *Oratio* 23.2.

[53] Jerome, *Jo. Hier.* 1.3. See also Vööbus 1958: 35. On the Nazirite vow, see Num. 6.1–21.

[54] Jerome, *Comm Gal.* 6.8.

[55] Irenaeus, *Adv. Haer.* 3.23.8.

[56] Clement of Alexandria, *Stromateis* 3.12.86.

[57] *Oratio*, 8.1–2.

sake of argument that Thomas preceded Tatian, there is a third possibility put forward by Quispel: that Tatian inherited his views from
Thomas.[58] Toward resolving this issue without prejudging Thomas's
relationship to Tatian, it needs to be pointed out that when ascetical
ideas do come to surface in the Syriac literature, these are consistently in the post-Tatianic period and closely allied with concepts
occurring both in Tatian and in Thomas. For example, the ethos of
Gos. Thom. 27 ('If you do not fast in regards to the world') makes its
way into the early third-century Syriac *Acts of Thomas*, where it is
clear that fasting also relates to the renunciation of one's personal
property.[59] This perspective is no less Tatian's than Thomas's. In our
Thomasine collection the bridal chamber is used as a metaphor
for spiritual union and salvation (*Gos. Thom.* 75, 104). The same image,
with which Tatian would be quite happy, becomes a stock metaphor
in Syriac literature of a slightly later period.[60] In *Thomas* there is
an inordinately frequent use of the verb 'to stand' (*Gos. Thom.* 16.4,
18.3, 23.2, 28.1, 75, 99.1). The language of 'standing' is also very
common in early Syriac Christian literature, as it capitalizes on a
pun between *qum* ('to stand') and *qeyama* ('covenant'): those who took
their *stand* with vows of celibacy were 'sons of the *covenant*'.[61] All
this means that if there was a time in Syriac Christianity when precisely these ascetical elements were demonstrably 'in the air', it is
in the decades after Tatian. *Thomas* by virtue of its ascetic emphases
fits snugly in that same period.

Given the way in which early Syriac Christianity begins to take
its distinctive shape only after Tatian, it may be tempting to trace the
entire movement lock-stock-and-barrel back to Tatian himself. This
seems to be the viewpoint of Irenaeus, Epiphanius and Eusebius,
as well as more than a few modern-day scholars. But to have had
such a singlehanded, powerful influence on Syriac Christianity would
have been quite a feat. Moreover, there seems to be significance in
the fact that while the extant criticisms against Tatian come almost
exclusively from the western wing of the church (Clement of
Alexandria is admittedly an exception), there is no evidence that Syrian
Christians joined in this chorus of condemnation. Had Tatian been so
radically innovative in what he enjoined, would he have had enjoyed
such a favourable and enduring reception among his fellow Syrians?
It seems doubtful.

---

[58] Quispel 1985: 55.
[59] See discussion in Vööbus 1958: 84–6 with references.
[60] *Acts Thom.* 12, 14, 124, etc. *Gos. Phil.* 69, 81, 82.
[61] See Vööbus 1958: 97–103; Murray 1975: 13–14, with bibliography.

Certain elements of Tatian's programme are already discernible in the religious life of pre-Tatianic Syria. In his homeland Tatian would have been accustomed to the sight of fasting Jews, Marcionites and even Hermeticists. The cult of Orpheus, which was active in second-century Syria, also abstained from meat. If Jewish-style celibacy was, as Vööbus argues, part and parcel of the Jewish-Christian mission to Syria, then this too would probably have been nothing new to Tatian.[62]

Yet Tatian was a catalyst. By all accounts he was a highly influential figure and there must be some significance in the fact that it is only after Tatian − bracketing still the historical relevance of *Thomas* − that a Tatianic-style asceticism or Encratism (teaching against marriage, meat and wine) is observable in Syriac Christianity.[63] Perhaps the best course then is to surmise tentatively that Tatian, having returned to Syria, taught a form of Christianity which in its ascetical practices already had isolated parallel in the Syriac culture but which in its inner logic or structure brought something that proved to be new and influential. Much as NT scholars are accustomed to talk about 'Pauline Christianity' as something which the apostle to the Gentiles both inherited and conceived, perhaps on analogy Tatian too saw himself building on an existing structure of belief and practice, but nonetheless giving it fresh coherence and underpinnings.

Unfortunately, our sources are too few and far between to illuminate in any thorough detail what practices and beliefs Tatian (re-)encountered in returning to Syria. Careful comparisons between Tatian and pre-Tatianic Christianity would be hard to make. If the Syrians were strangers to asceticism, then Tatian's acquired fame could be explained by his having imported a complete novelty. But since this is not the case, since Syrians of various religious stripes (Jewish, pagan or Christian) already seem to have been practising an asceticism of one kind or another, it is unlikely that Tatian made a name for himself primarily by what he practised and told others to practise. Among those who for religious reasons were already averse to either sex, or steak, or Sauvignon, Tatian would have likely earned his reputation precisely because he brought all these practices together and brought to bear on them a well-formed biblical-theological rationale.[64] It was Tatian's teaching then that became the spark which enflamed

---

[62] Vööbus 1958: 3−30.

[63] On Encratism see Gasparro 1985; Brown 1988: 90−102.

[64] This allows for the possibility that Jewish ascetical and Marcionite elements preceded Tatian, just as Orpheism, which swore off meat, almost certainly did.

early Syriac Christianity. And as the flame spread, so too presumably did the nature of that fire.

But none of this rules out the possibility of a *Gospel of Thomas* written *c.* 70 CE (Patterson), or *c.* 100 CE (Pagels), or over the course of a century, *c.* 30–130 CE (DeConick). After all, it is certainly possible that Tatian, even as the dominant shaper of late second- and third-century Syrian Christianity, drew his inspiration from *Thomas* and the Thomas community that preceded him. True, this is possible. There is, however, a conspicuous weakness in this supposition: if the *Gospel of Thomas* attests to a particular Syrian Christian asceticism in the late first century/early second century, and this asceticism only resurfaces again two or three generations later but in precisely the same form, how do we explain the pregnant silence of those intervening two or three generations? Again, to be clear, it cannot be ruled out that an ascetically oriented Christianity appeared in the form of *Thomas* in Syria around 100 CE, went underground for seven to ten decades leaving no literary remains, and then at the end of that period reappeared in the likes of the *Acts of Thomas* and *Odes of Solomon*. But history abhors a vacuum and is not too fond of discontinuities either. If Tatian's career coincided with the Encratistic transformation of Syrian Christianity and if *Thomas*, whose dating is unknown, shares those same Encratistic elements, what are we to infer?

One possibility, which my interlocutors are implicitly or explicitly advancing, is that the *Gospel of Thomas* witnesses to a late first-century/early second-century community that underwent no discernible change and remained silent for almost a hundred years before becoming the primary impetus behind Tatian's asceticism as well as that of the early third-century author of the *Acts of Thomas*. But then if Thomas influenced Tatian rather than vice versa, when did this point of contact take place? We know that Tatian did not convert to Christianity until after he left Syria, whereupon he finally came to Rome at some time in the mid second century. Unless one is prepared to argue that Thomas Christians or the *Gospel of Thomas* influenced Tatian while he was in Rome (a rather difficult point, I think), it can only be on his return to Syria in the early 170s that such influence could have occurred. But since Tatian's *Diatessaron* reflects the impress of this very same asceticism, and since the *Diatessaron* is dated to around 173 CE, it is only within the space of a few years at most, between Tatian's homecoming and his writing of the *Diatessaron* (itself a project that must have taken months) that Thomas Christianity could have revolutionized the thinking of Tatian. This is a rather small window, I think, to allow for the theological transformation of someone whose intellectual calibre and grounding had earned him his own school in Rome.

In my view, it is most reasonable to suppose that the *Gospel of Thomas*, on the one hand, and the *Acts of Thomas* and the *Odes of Solomon*, on the other, do not witness to two opposite poles of a century-long historical trajectory. Instead Thomas and these other Syriac texts occupy the same general location on a trajectory given new impetus through Tatian himself. *Thomas*, in other words, belongs to the constellation of texts that finds its pole star in the author of the *Diatessaron*. We cannot completely exclude the possibility of Tatian's dependence on Thomas, but the view entails too many difficulties for the imagination.

But whence came Tatian's beliefs and practices? Emily J. Hunt convincingly argues that Tatian's views, including his asceticism, were largely formed through his contact not with Syriac Christianity, but through his mentor Justin Martyr in Rome.[65] She builds on Ugo Bianchi's suggestion that Encratism as it developed in the second-century world derived from the influence of the Jewish philosopher Philo (*c.* 20–*c.* 50 CE).[66] While we cannot be certain that Justin, Tatian's instructor, leaned on Philo, a number of scholars are prepared to accept some kind of Philonic influence on the apologist.[67] On this assumption, some of these have traced Philonic themes pushing their way though Justin and on to Tatian.[68] While Quispel, like Bianchi and myself, is convinced of Encratism's Alexandrian roots, he connects Tatian's Encratism with his exposure to Egyptian devotees as they settled in Mesopotamia.[69] But Hunt's account of Philo's influence on Tatian via Justin is far preferable in that it explains why Tatian hit the Syrian ground running with his Encratistic theology. Having learned at Justin's feet to synthesize Philo and Christianity, and having recognized the apologetic value of affirming his own culture's ascetical practices, Tatian with a very intentional missionary focus introduced Philonic concepts to his Syrian setting, not least through his *Diatessaron*.[70] In doing this, Tatian injected new life and coherence into

---

[65] Hunt 2003: 52–73.

[66] Hunt 2003: 115; Bianchi 1985b: 296.

[67] On the debate, see Runia 1993: 97–105. Perhaps influenced by Martín 1987, Runia himself seems to have moved from rejecting Philo's influence on Justin (1993: 104–5) to embracing it (1995: 195).

[68] Elze 1960: 80–92; Martín 1987, 1988; Hunt 2003.

[69] Quispel 1985: 60.

[70] Tatian's creating a Syriac gospel for his people is of course itself a missionary gesture. This is not to rule out the possibility that Philo had already reached the Syrians through the Neo-Pythagorean philosopher Numenius (cf. Runia 1995: 195–8), but Tatian's Justin offers the best explanation for the sudden Philonic flavour of early Syrian theology.

a trajectory of ascetical practice that bore, among the first of its fruits, the *Gospel of Thomas*.

This argument has the added value of explaining texts like *Gos. Thom.* 82: 'Whoever is near me is near the fire.' As has been pointed out elsewhere, Justin was very interested in describing Christ through the image of fire; for him there was cash value in the metaphor, which he ultimately derived from Philo, as a way of explaining his *Logos* theology (i.e. theology of the word).[71] Following in the footsteps of his master, Tatian too picks up on this metaphor.[72] From Philo to Justin to Tatian, we finally find the same theological imagery in *Thomas*.[73]

That Thomas was one of the first heirs and interpreters of the Tatianic legacy is all the more plausible on consideration of the strong possibility that Tatian, upon his return to his native Syria, settled in Edessa, the provenance of *Thomas* itself. Harnack and Zahn argue precisely this scenario in their own reconstructions of Syriac Christianity.[74] For Harnack as well as for Zahn (the one man whose criticism Harnack feared), Tatian's return to Edessa as opposed to some other locale makes most sense given the city's strategic importance as a centre of learning. I am inclined to agree. If Tatian was interested in maintaining a school like the one he had begun in Rome and re-exerting his broad influence, he could do no better than Edessa.

In this case, we might imagine the scenario as follows. Having been exposed to Philonic Encratism while under Justin at Rome, Tatian arrives in Edessa in the early 170s and soon thereafter sets himself to composing the *Diatessaron*. Once the gospel harmony is completed, circulated and copied, Tatianic thought begins to assert itself very quickly in Edessa. Next, our author Thomas, belonging to an Edessean Christian community that no doubt knew Tatian and had been availing itself of his *Diatessaron* and its articulation of Encratistic sentiments, takes up his pen and composes the *Gospel of Thomas* in the mid to late 170s. While preserving its own set of theological distinctives against Tatian, including (as we shall see in the

---

[71] Hunt 2003: 120; Siegert 1988.

[72] *Oratio* 5.1–3.

[73] Interestingly, almost a hundred years ago, Tatian's linking Christ with fire prompted J. Rendell Harris to suppose that the author of the line, 'Whoever is near me is near the fire,' in the *Srboyn*, an Armenian text ostensibly first written in Syriac near the close of the second century, was Tatian himself. He may be right, but this is impossible to prove. Harris, of course, never knew of our Coptic *Gospel of Thomas*, and so never knew that the very same phrasing occurs in *Thomas*.

[74] Harnack 1958[1897]: 1.289; Zahn 1881: 282.

next chapter) its denial of the resurrection, the Thomas community does follow suit in its views on sexuality, meat-eating and mammon. Such views as those of Tatian and Thomas lay at the root of an emerging regional praxis.

Conclusion

I have sought in this relatively lengthy chapter to resolve two questions: (1) Why does *Thomas* not follow the synoptic gospels in its ordering of the sayings? and (2) How do we explain its ascetical elements? Toward answering the first question, I have proposed that our sayings collection has been misunderstood largely because we have failed to appreciate its original language of composition. If *Thomas* is recognized as having been first set down in Syriac, for starters, the order of the sayings – precisely as we have it in the Coptic – makes perfect sense.

But there are other things that begin to fall into place too. In the case of Syriac composition, *Thomas* also appears to be a compositional unity following the order of the *Diatessaron* at a number of places. This situates the autograph at some time in the last quarter of the second century. Historically, a late second-century *Thomas* makes much more sense than a late first-century or early second-century text, simply because the only other texts we have that attest to an ascetically inclined Syriac Christianity are texts that issue from this late second-century or early third-century period. Within this mix a Tatian-to-Thomas direction of influence is more likely than the reverse. Thomas-style asceticism finds its point of origin at the confluence of two rivers: second-century Syriac ascetical practices undertaken in a broad religious milieu, and Philonic Encratism, as it was mediated through Justin Martyr and Tatian. I will take a closer look at the theological rationale for this asceticism and the controversy this eventually spawned with proto-orthodox Syrian believers in the next chapter.

5

Challenging the apostolic line

Controversy has a way of leaving its own paper trail. When communities live in harmonious agreement on what they perceive to be the important and self-defining issues, there is generally little need to talk about 'the other'. When everyone agrees, for all intents and purposes there is no 'other'. But once pressures from without or internal conflicts from within disrupt theological accord, suddenly people start talking, and then writing, and then writing with very pointed words. Sometimes, the most pointed polemic of all is that which is cast not in explicit but in symbolic terms.

This seems to be just the case when we consider a logion we have already encountered in Chapter 2. It is a saying that involves a small but interesting cast of characters:

> Jesus said to his disciples, 'Compare me to someone else and tell me whom I am like.' Simon Peter said to him, 'You are like a righteous angel.' Matthew said to him, 'You are like a wise philosopher.' Thomas said to him, 'Teacher, my mouth is entirely incapable of saying whom you are like.' Jesus said, 'I am not your teacher. Since you have imbibed, you have become drunk on the bubbling spring which I have dug.'[1] And he took him, withdrew and told him three words. When Thomas came back to his friends, they asked him, 'What did Jesus say to you?' Thomas said to them, 'Were I to tell you even one of the things which he told me, you would pick up stones and throw them at me. Then a fire would come out of the stones and consume you.'
> (*Gos. Thom.* 13)

This logion, one of the few that mentions the disciples by name,[2] gives rise to several observations. First, Jesus invites three disciples to compare him to someone else. 'Whom am I like?' Jesus asks. 'Identify

---

[1] Clarysse (1994) examines the phrase in *Gos. Thom.* 13 conventionally translated as 'the bubbling well which I myself have measured'. While this translation is viable on grammatical grounds, Clarysse opts for the above translation.

[2] Thomas appears in the Prologue, James is highly honoured in *Gos. Thom.* 12, Salome addresses Jesus in *Gos. Thom.* 61.2, and in *Gos. Thom.* 114.1 Simon Peter requests that 'Mary leave us'. Thomas's praise of James may have something to do with the fact that he is held up as an ideal ascetic in early Christian tradition, cf. Eusebius, *Hist. Eccl.* 2.23.5.

me, if you will, with some social or historical role.' In obliging their
master, the three disciples give three different answers; their responses
show that each disciple has interpreted Jesus differently. Second,
Thomas's answer is different from that of Matthew and Simon Peter
in that it emphasizes the ineffability of Jesus' person. While the first
two apostles to respond are able to summarize Jesus with a phrase,
Thomas's only words are to the effect that words are insufficient.
Of these three respondents, Thomas is the only one to merit Jesus'
approval, as is evident by what follows when Thomas is given an
'inside track'. Jesus takes him aside, gives him three 'words' of private
instruction (providing much fodder for future scholars wondering
what the 'three words' are), and even places Thomas on a par with
himself: 'I am not your teacher.' Third, and most interesting, the
special knowledge that Thomas acquires in private conversation with
Jesus places him not only in a category separate from the other disciples, but also in some sense in opposition to them as well. 'Were
I to tell you what Jesus told me,' Thomas says, 'you would stone
me.' Stoning of course was the punishment reserved especially for
blasphemers. Somehow Thomas has laid hold of some insight that
puts him beyond the pale of what Matthew and Peter considered
right belief.[3] And yet if the disciples were to attempt such a stoning,
the stones themselves would shoot out fire that would consume
them, and Thomas would remain alive, vindicated at the last.

What we have here, it seems to me, is not a historic account of
an actual conversation that took place among three disciples. Rather,
we have in *Gos. Thom.* 13 a fanciful but deeply symbolic scene in
which Matthew and Simon Peter, as representative of a particular community or communities, are made to play second fiddle to Thomas,
who is also representative of a community. This is no small matter
that divides them. Thomas possesses a knowledge to which neither
Matthew nor Peter has access; it is also a knowledge which, if
communicated to those on the outside, would engender serious but
ultimately wrongheaded persecution. While Matthew and Peter each
have their own way of talking about Jesus, these two disciples are
in their understanding far closer to each other, the logion suggests,
than they are to Thomas. Because of Thomas's success in recognizing
Jesus, which in turn has earned him an even more profound, and
even dangerous, insight into Jesus' person, Thomas must henceforth
keep his secrets, or else face the prospect of persecution at the hands

---

[3] The point, a crucial one, is picked up by Walls (1960–1: 269), but seems underappre-
ciated by Trevijano Etcheverría 1992 and Wayment 2004.

of those who (falsely) claim to know the truth. If this much is true, then this only prompts two obvious questions: (1) Who are Matthew and Simon Peter and/or what do they stand for? and (2) Who is Thomas or what does he stand for?

The Voices behind Matthew and Simon Peter

At first glance, it may be tempting to suggest that Matthew and Peter represent a segment within Jewish Christianity, if not Jewish Christianity itself. The so-called school of Saint Matthew, assuming such a school existed in the first place, seems to have consisted mostly of Jews.[4] Simon Peter, as Galatians 2 reminds us, was also closely associated with the Jewish wing of the church. Given Thomas's anti-Jewish stance elsewhere (*Gos. Thom.* 6, 39, 52), a case may be made that the author of this logion is taking to task a Jewish trajectory within the first-century church, perhaps the church at Jerusalem.

While this is plausible, we do not get any sense from *Gos. Thom.* 13 itself that the point of contention revolved around Jewish issues, not directly anyway. In getting back to why Matthew and Simon Peter are so very wrong, rather than starting with what we think these figures represented in the early church, perhaps it is best first to focus on the responses they give. Then and only then do we begin to think about how these figures were understood.

First we encounter Simon Peter, who says to Jesus, 'You are like a righteous angel/messenger.'[5] This may be significant. The Gospel of Mark, which early church tradition claims to have been written at Peter's dictation, begins with a quote from Malachi 3.1: 'Behold, I send my messenger before thy face, who shall prepare thy way' (Mark 1.2).[6] According to Malachi, this messenger is indeed the prophet Elijah (Mal. 4.5), a prophecy on which Mark is particularly eager to capitalize in his own account of both John the Baptist and Jesus. At times, it appears as if John the Baptist is Elijah (Mark 9.11–13); at times Jesus appears to be the promised messenger (Mark 11.12–17; cf. Mal. 3.1). Apparently, Mark had little problem holding both to be true simultaneously. In any event, the modelling of Jesus on Elijah is important to Mark (Mark 1.3) and fundamentally shaped his

---

[4] Stendahl 1968: 33–5.
[5] In Coptic as in Greek (and as in Syriac), the same word is used for 'angel' and 'messenger'.
[6] The earliest testimony to Peter's behind-the-scenes authorship comes from Papias, as preserved in Eusebius (*Adv. Haer.* 3.39.15), who also vouches for the Marcan–Petrine connection.

characterization of Jesus.[7] If the first hearers of Mark took for granted Peter's role in the writing of the second gospel (history suggests that they did), and if these same hearers shared an appreciation for Mark's casting Jesus in the role of an Elijahan 'righteous messenger', then Simon Peter's summarizing statement, 'You are a righteous messenger,' is suggestive of the second gospel itself.

The suggestion is only confirmed when we turn to Matthew's statement about Jesus: 'You are a wise philosopher.' In this phrase there are indications that this time the Gospel of Matthew is in view. If Mark settled on Elijah as being a manifold type of Christ, Matthew saw Jesus first and foremost – and more so than any other gospel – as the new Moses.[8] Whatever Moses' accomplishments on Israel's behalf, second-temple Judaism would come to see the patriarch above all as a law-giver, and then, as it represented itself to a dominant Hellenistic culture, as a wise philosopher.[9] Justin Martyr saw Moses in these terms, as did his student Tatian:

> But now it seems proper for me to demonstrate that our philosophy is older than the system of the Greeks. Moses and Homer shall be our limits, each of them being of great antiquity; the one being the oldest of poets and historians, the other the founder of all barbarian wisdom.[10]
> (*Oratio* 30.1)

Tatian later continues:

> Therefore, from what has been said it is evident that Moses was older than the ancient heroes, wars, and demons. And we ought rather to believe him, who stands before them in point of age, than the Greeks, who, without being aware of it, drew his doctrines from a fountain. For many of the sophists among them, stimulated by curiosity, endeavoured to adulterate whatever they learned from Moses, and from those who have philosophized like him.
> (*Oratio* 40.1–2)

I suggest then that the author of *Gos. Thom.* 13 is alluding to the fact that in Matthew's gospel Jesus is portrayed as a type of Moses and

---

[7] As Joynes (1998: 19) puts it (in connection with Mark): 'the Elijah motive is not exhaustively fulfilled in John the Baptist; it is carried over to interpret the character and fate of Jesus too.' For the parallels between Elijah and Jesus in Mark, see Gundry 1993: 62.

[8] This becomes apparent from very early on in the gospel, where Jesus' narrowly escaping from Herod (Matt. 2.13–18) is set against the background of Moses' miraculous delivery from Pharaoh's infanticide (Exod. 2.1–10). For fuller exploration of Jesus as Moses, see, e.g., Allison 1993.

[9] See Liermann 2004: 258–94; also Goulet 1987; Mack 1985.

[10] Justin (1 *Apol.* 44, 60) was eager to show Plato's dependence on Moses' doctrine.

that Moses is the pre-eminent 'wise philosopher'. If Jesus is the new Moses, he is also 'a wise philosopher'.

Clearly, the author of *Gos. Thom.* 13 is not simply giving privilege to Thomas, as representative head of a particular socio-religious entity, over and against Matthew and Simon Peter, as representative heads of a particular socio-religious entity or entities; he is first and foremost denigrating the erstwhile fisherman and tax-collector in their respective accounts of Jesus, the Gospel of Mark and the Gospel of Matthew. But before considering exactly why our author discounts the first two canonical gospels, a few remarks may be in order regarding what this means for locating *Gos. Thom.* 13 historically. The earliest extant testimony that attributes one set of Jesus 'oracles' to Matthew and another set to Mark, under the auspices of Peter, comes from the second-century figure Papias.[11] Papias is notoriously difficult to date, but even if we go with a fairly early dating within the first quarter of the second century, most scholars are inclined to feel that Papias is not referring to our canonical Matthew and that the first gospel was in fact formally anonymous until some time in the middle of the second century. In this case, *Gos. Thom.* 13 should be assumed to have been written some point after the same time.

This *terminus a quo* is confirmed in light of Willy Clarysse's translation of the phrase typically translated 'which I have measured out' (*Gos. Thom.* 13.5). Clarysse convincingly argues that the traditional translation of *Thomas* at this juncture is less preferable than another possibility: 'which I have dug'.[12] If Clarysse is right – and as my translation shows, I believe he is – then this line from *Thomas* suddenly brings to mind a verse from another Syriac text that may have been written around Tatian's time, if not slightly later: the *Odes of Solomon*.

> And speaking waters touched my lips from the fountain of the Lord generously.
> And so I drank and became intoxicated, from the living water that does not die.
> And my intoxication did not cause ignorance, but I abandoned vanity,
> And turned toward the Most High, my God, and was enriched by His favours.   (*Odes Sol.* 11.6–9)

For the poet this intoxication did not lead to acts that would be regretted by morning. On the contrary, here we have the provocative image of being intoxicated on God's living waters, which leads to

---

[11] Eusebius, *Hist. Eccl.* 3.39.15–16.
[12] Clarysse 1994.

truth. Thus the writer of the ode and Thomas use the same image in the same way, and here we may also include the Gnostic *Pistis Sophia*.[13] The image itself seems to derive from Jesus' words to the Samaritan woman, as recorded in the fourth gospel (John 4.14). This only confirms that *Gos. Thom.* 13 has a *terminus a quo* in the middle of the second century, before which time the fourth evangelist does not seem to have enjoyed a broad reception. All this suggests that our logion was composed not only in dependence on John, but also in the second half of the second century.

Philo and the hermeneutical divide: from Justin to Tatian to Thomas

But I believe we can be even more precise in dating *Gos. Thom.* 13, and, in doing so, establish a third line of argument for a late second-century *Thomas*.[14] We recall that Thomas very humbly says: 'My mouth is entirely incapable of saying what you are like.' Apparently, this is the response that Jesus was looking for: against Matthew and Peter who in their gospels represent Jesus along the lines of a well-known Jewish figure, Moses and Elijah, respectively, Thomas declares that the right description of Jesus, in essence, is no description at all. While the canonical writings themselves sometimes take the *via negativa* in talking about God (e.g. 1 Tim. 1.17), and similar tendencies can be found in Judaism as well as second-century Middle Platonism, we also find the same hesitancy to name divinity in Justin Martyr, who, precisely in his articulation of negative theology, again seems to have been influenced by Philo.[15] The apophatic theology in *Gos. Thom.* 13 would certainly be hard to tie back to Philo via Justin, were it not for the fact that we already apparently find a Philonic stream of influence reaching Tatian through the channel of Justin Martyr, in terms of the latter's *Logos* ('Word') theology.[16] If a Philo–Justin–Tatian avenue of influence is discernible here, it is certainly possible that Philo's views on revelation beat the same path via Justin to Tatian's door, and then from there on to Thomas's.

---

[13] *Pist. Sophia* 4.141.

[14] In Chapter 4, I argued (1) that a unified, Syriac *Thomas* must necessarily follow the *Diatessaron* (*c.* 173 CE), and, on different grounds, (2) that Thomas's asceticism was likely inherited from Tatian.

[15] So, classically, Goodenough 1968: 127–73. More recently, see Trakatellis 1976: 46. By negative or apophatic theology, I mean discourse that seeks to describe God more in terms of what God is not than in terms of what God is. Such theology tends to see positive, propositional, language about God as inherently misleading.

[16] Martín 1988.

Of course possibility is not the same as probability. But the case for Thomas's finding his ultimate source in Philo is strengthened when we consider the similarities between Tatian and Philo. First, although Tatian obviously thought enough of the 'representability' of God to compose a gospel harmony, the author of the *Diatessaron* and the *Oration to the Greeks* nonetheless emphasizes the incomprehensibility of God and our inability to describe or represent him.[17] Structurally, the fourth chapter of Tatian's *Oration*, precisely where he discusses this theme, provides the thesis statement for the remainder of the *Oration*.[18] While God's unknowability stands close to the heart of Tatian's theology, it is with a certain concrete aim that Tatian voices his fundamental insistence that God should not be portrayed as 'indigent'.[19] Language about God was unfitting if it entailed divine self-disclosure in particular (socio-historically situated) rather than in universal terms. The same warning comes to the surface in the writings of Justin's school.[20]

Both Tatian and the broad Justinian school seem to be working out the same concern that preoccupied Philo in his dialogue with Hellenistic philosophy. Under Stoic influences, Hellenistic thought valorized Natural Law (which was the same as the rational Law of Nature or Reason) over and against written law. Maintaining that the Mosaic Law was closely tied to the unified Law of Nature, Philo himself argued that Mosaic Law was superior to the laws of the nations.[21] But this integration of Natural Law into his own theology does not solve all the difficulties. Hindy Najman's comments are helpful:

> To put the problem in its general form: the Law of Nature is surely of universal significance for all peoples, but the Law of Moses appears to be concerned, for the most part, with the obligations of a particular people arising from its particular history and relationship with God. How, then, could the particular Law of Moses be, as Philo claims, the perfect copy of the universal Law of Nature?[22]

---

[17] 'Nor even ought the ineffable God to be presented with gifts; for He who is in want of nothing is not to be misrepresented by us as though He were indigent' (Tatian, *Oratio* 4.3).

[18] The fourth chapter closes, 'But I will set forth our views more distinctly'; the remainder of the *Oration* follows.

[19] Tatian, *Oratio* 4.3.

[20] See Justin, *Oratio ad Graecos*, 16–21. Justin's authorship of this text is often doubted; it is much more likely a product of his school, of which Tatian was naturally a member.

[21] Philo, *Mos.* 2.11–12.

[22] Najman 2003: 76.

Toward resolving this, Philo finds the normative force of scripture in the lives of the patriarchs it represents. For Philo, Abraham was 'a law and an unwritten statute'; Moses, the philosopher-king, was himself the embodiment of 'life and reason', reason being one and the same as Natural Law.[23] On this account, while written revelation remains at a remove from the higher Law of Reason it represents, the lives of the patriarchs (as represented in scripture) were more appropriate and direct vehicles for conveying Natural Law, the highest law.[24] Those subject to the patriarchs, who were also philosopher-kings, could only aspire to obey the highest law of natural reason by *mimesis*, the imitation of the philosopher-king who was in turn imitating divine Reason. Although Philo scholars debate whether this renders the Mosaic Law completely superfluous in Philo's thought, it is clear that for Philo written revelation is *to some degree* a shabby substitute for the lived life revelation depicts. In the end, the authority of the Mosaic Law is undercut by its own particularism.[25]

I suggest that *Gos. Thom.* 13 is operating by the same Philonic logic, and, as with Tatian, it is a logic with a polemically sharpened edge.[26] Behind *Gos. Thom.* 13 and the entire collection stands one who has appropriated Tatian's insistence on God's ineffability and 'non-indigence', but radicalized it. In doing so, our author Thomas recoils against the portraits of the first two gospels, perhaps partly because they are *Jewish* portraits but more so because they are, quite simply, *portraits*.[27] The Jesus of the *Gospel of Thomas* is a Jesus who transcends the constraints not only of Jewish particularism, but of any manifold, perspectival attempt to represent that which can only

---

[23] Philo, *Abr.* 5; *Mos.* 1.162, 2.2.

[24] Najman 2003: 76–100; Martens 2003: 105–10.

[25] For bibliography, see Martens 2003: xvi n1.

[26] The polemical thrust of Thomas seems to have been generally overlooked by Pagels and DeConick. One reason for this may have to do with their view that John is responding to Thomas. If John is made out to be the aggressor and Thomas the hapless victim of his assault, I suppose it doesn't help the picture much to contemplate how Thomas seems to be nursing a few (much more easily defined) inter-apostolic grudges of his own.

[27] It should not be ruled out that the transition to a more radically Philonic stance took place not in Thomas but in Tatian. Two considerations might support this. First, the church fathers declare that Tatian, after Justin's death, changed his theological position on at least a few significant points – a claim confirmed by the post-Justinian church at Rome excommunicating him. Second, it may have been Tatian's insistence against the particularity of revelation that induced him to compose his one gospel out of four. Philo was certain that truth was found in unity, and one gospel is naturally more unified than four. Cf. Baarda 1989.

ultimately be represented without words. Perspectivalism stands at odds with the Greek insistence on truth's universality. Thomas Christians, who were certain that Jesus' self-disclosure was meant only to serve as a model to be imitated, must have been deeply disturbed by other Christians who saw the gospels themselves – not just the person of Jesus – as normative. Thus, between Thomas on the one side and Matthew and Simon Peter on the other, there were deep epistemo-logical and therefore hermeneutical differences.

Thomas versus the proto-Palutians ('the Great Church')

Unless the prospect of Thomas being stoned in *Gos. Thom.* 13 is com-plete hyperbole, we must imagine that there was considerable pres-sure on the Thomas Christians to believe differently than they did. The Thomas Christians were, as Pagels emphasizes, a people per-secuted for their belief-system. So then the question becomes, 'Who was it who were setting themselves against the Thomas community?'

In order to answer this, we are best served by returning to Matthew and Simon Peter so as to inquire what community or communities these two *dramatis personae* represent. Irenaeus mentions that the Ebionites used Matthew's gospel by itself and the docetists used only Mark.[28] So it is possible that Thomas Christianity was fighting its battle on two separate fronts, against two separate groups who held to two separate belief-systems.

But what makes this unlikely is *Gos. Thom.* 13's speaking of Matthew and Peter as a collectivity and unified force. 'Were I to tell you even one of these words,' Thomas says, 'you both would stone me.' It is the first two canonical gospels *together* that stand opposed to Thomas. This narrows the possibilities. The most prominent body, of which we are aware, that affirmed the authority of both these gospels and established itself on the witness of the Old Testament scriptures is the proto-orthodox community, or what the anti-Christian Celsus calls 'the Great Church'. In this context of second-century Syriac Christianity, we might also call this community the proto-Palutians.

Palut, the fourth-century *Doctrina Addai* tells us, was consecrated first Bishop of Edessa by Bishop Serapion of Antioch near the end of the second century.[29] And while this legend-laden Syriac text is highly suspect as a historical source, since Ephraem mentions this

---

[28] *Adv. Haer.* 3.11.7.
[29] *Doctrina Addai* 32b.

same Palut and his followers without any of the proto-orthodox triumphalism that scholars like Walter Bauer first sniff out and then historically snuff out, the datum should not be disallowed.[30] The *Chronicle of Edessa* speaks of a flood in 201 wiping out the 'church of the Christians', and archaeology has left us indication of Syrians being buried in the early 200s with a distinct hope in bodily resurrection.[31] Christianity in its proto-orthodox form was alive and well, if not somewhat beleaguered, in late second-century Syria. While their numbers may have been small in comparison to the competing sects, the official organization of a 'church' under Palut is not quite the smoke and mirrors that Bauer would have us believe.[32]

But Palut's ordination toward the end of the second century was an event long in coming. We do not know when Christianity came to Edessa and its environs, but perhaps Vööbus's carefully reasoned argument is right in setting a date near the end of the first century.[33] In this case, it is unlikely that Palut's being established as Bishop of Edessa, and thereby acquiring a connectional status with other bishops in the region, was a sudden or unexpected decision. The community that would one day sit at Palut's feet already had a long history by the close of the second century and the ordination of its first bishop would have been no light matter. Informal relationships with nearby sees were probably already well established.

If so, then we would also expect the nearby Bishop Serapion of Antioch to have had a good deal of shared theological understanding with the Edessean community. Among the accomplishments for which Serapion was to be remembered was his removal of the *Gospel of Peter* from the church at Rhossus, on the north-east corner of the Mediterranean Sea. Initially, Serapion allowed the churches in his see to use the *Gospel of Peter*, but when its docetic content (implying that Christ was only apparently human) was pointed out to him, he retracted and ensured that this and presumably all similar such illegitimate gospels were banned from the churches. In defending his position, Serapion appealed to the apostolic lineage, including

---

[30] W. Bauer's (1971: 21) statement that 'Palut was the leader of those people in Edessa who confessed what later developed into orthodoxy in a sense acceptable to Ephraem' implies that 'Palutian-style orthodoxy' would have been unacceptable to Ephraem's views. The historical data testifies otherwise, cf. Ephraem, *Contra haer.* 22.6. That the Palutians knew nothing of Tatian, as Bauer suggests (1971: 32), seems equally implausible.

[31] See Segal 1970: 20, 24 (on the *Chronicle of Edessa*), Plate XLIII (on mosaic showing Christian resurrection imagery).

[32] Bauer 1971: 1–33.

[33] Vööbus 1958: 6.

the first among them, Peter.[34] Assuming that Syrian members of the Great Church shared Serapion's convictions, their presence in Edessa might well have been troubling to the Thomas community – troubling enough to induce the writing of *Gos. Thom.* 13.

Even if we don't know whether the *Gospel of Thomas* ever made it on to Serapion's list of banned books, *Thomas* did make it on to a few other 'banned book' lists in other parts of the world, as I have already pointed out.[35] Although, frustratingly, history has left us little direct evidence of how *Thomas* was received by the proto-orthodox in Syria, perhaps *Gos. Thom.* 13 can provide evidence of its own. In the first place, if western Syrian proto-orthodoxy, as it was taking shape at the end of the second century under Serapion, was beginning to settle on four gospels (whether in the form of four 'separated gospels' or one gospel harmony) and beginning also to justify the use of these four and only these four on the basis of certain Christological commitments, there is every reason to suspect that Thomas Christians would be threatened by other Christians contemplating formal connections with Serapion – and vice versa. The normative claims of the canonical gospels are of a very different order from what we find in *Thomas*. According to Matthew, Mark, Luke and John, Jesus is the one to whom the believer must consistently turn for truth and salvation. In the *Gospel of Thomas*, salvation comes from within as the believer imitates Jesus. Thomas's Jesus says, 'I am not your teacher': the Jesus of the four canonical gospels for ever remains the teacher. The canonical Jesus is far more totalizing.

We will come back to the disparate Christologies and soteriologies of Thomas Christianity and the Edessean 'Great Church', but for now it needs to be emphasized that the first two disciples mentioned in *Gos. Thom.* 13 are not meant to represent two isolated and erroneous opinions as to who Jesus was. Rather, Matthew and Simon Peter are representative of their gospels, Matthew and Mark, which in turn are metonymies for the emerging four-fold gospel canon and the people who were not ashamed of the particular (as opposed to universal) character of this canon. Not too long after Tatian brought these four gospels to his native Syria and transposed them into one continuous gospel harmony, Serapion began to forbid the use of certain gospels on material grounds. Thomas Christians

---

[34] Eusebius, *Hist. Eccl.* 6.12.2–6. Eusebius mentions possessing a copy of Serapion's correspondence with one Dominimus, who purportedly fell 'from faith in Christ to will worship (*ethelothrēskia*)' (*Hist. Eccl.* 6.12.1). This implies some kind of connection with the same heresy condemned in Col. 2.23.

[35] See Introduction, pp. 8–9.

understood the implications. The delimitation of authorized accounts of Jesus within the proto-orthodox camp, which entailed what Thomas Christians perceived to be philosophically unacceptable notions, ensured a falling out.

Despite the protests of Thomas Christians, those who would soon be called the Palutians pressed on. By the close of the second century, Palut would indeed be consecrated. His see would thereby consider itself spiritually and historically connected with the apostles. But again a different kind of connectionalism, of an informal sort, already lay at the heart of the proto-orthodox ecclesiology and hermeneutics. When Justin's contemporary Hegesippus and after him Irenaeus appeal to an unbroken succession of bishops going back to the apostles, they are attempting to secure pure doctrine and the church's unchallengeable authority to maintain that doctrine.[36] Their hermeneutics (how do we interpret the scriptures?) is made to rest on their ecclesiology (who is authorized to tell us how to interpret the scriptures?). Undoubtedly, as can be seen in Serapion's remarks as recorded by Eusebius, the church of Syria was taking a similar stand around the same time.[37]

In response, those who were not in communion with the Great Church sought to subvert this claim, either by disparaging Peter and the Twelve, with whom the proto-orthodox communities identified themselves, or by providing an account of a secret interchange between Jesus and one or more of his disciples, often Peter. In the Nag Hammadi text the *Letter of Peter to Philip* (*NHC VIII.2*), Jesus prepares to repeat certain teachings which apparently did not register the first time with the disciples on account of their unbelief.[38] The community behind this tractate seeks to authorize itself over and against non-gnostic beliefs by appealing to certain secret teachings that Jesus gave while he was alive. If some, namely the non-gnostics, did not remember these particular teachings, this only witnesses to their hardness of heart. Another Nag Hammadi text, the *Wisdom of Jesus Christ* (*NHC III.4*), has a similar narrative device. Here Jesus reveals the truth provisionally; only after the resurrection and fuller instruction are the true disciples enlightened regarding the nature of the cosmos.

---

[36] Eusebius, *Hist. Eccl.* 4.22.1–3; Irenaeus, *Adv. Haer.* 3.3.3.

[37] Serapion appeals both to the Christology of the *Gospel of Peter* ('we have been able to read it through, and we find many things in accordance with the true doctrine of the Saviour, but some things added to that doctrine' [Eusebius, *Hist. Eccl.* 6.12.6]) as well as to the notion of succession ('For we, brethren, receive both Peter and the other apostles as Christ; but we reject intelligently the writings falsely ascribed to them, knowing that such were not handed down to us' [Eusebius, *Hist. Eccl.* 6.12.3]).

[38] *Peter to Philip* 135.5–8.

Still another Nag Hammadi text, the *Apocryphon of John*, has the same schema. In this text John the son of Zebedee retires to the desert in order to reflect on a few important questions. John realizes that Jesus' teaching before his death was incomplete, but Christ eventually appears to John and makes known to him – and him alone – the secret truth. From then on it would only be those who learned these secrets from John, the 'fellow spirits', who would also be heirs to truth. In each of these cases, the Gnostic writer is hoping to challenge the proto-orthodox claim of having an unbroken line of succession tracing itself back to the apostles. In order to neutralize this claim, the Gnostics made their own version of the very same argument.

We see then that the *Gospel of Thomas* employs a device that is used by other tractates that sit alongside *Thomas* in the Nag Hammadi library. Like one of any number of Gnostic gospels, Thomas seeks to validate its own assertions against competing claims by making a narrativized appeal to a privileged, apostolic, line. It is of course possible that this clash of belief-systems between, on the one side, Thomas Christians and, on the other side, those who prefer the gospel texts or gospel harmony as the final authority, was a kind of intra-mural hermeneutical disagreement and nothing more. But in the case of the Edessean milieu, I am more inclined to believe that by the time *Gos. Thom.* 13 was written, Thomas Christians had already separated themselves (perhaps with some help!) from the community that was on its way to celebrating Palut's consecration.

In second-century Christian tradition, bishops were a visible expression and extension of the apostles themselves.[39] That the community at Edessa was now by the end of the second century on the brink of establishing an episcopacy undoubtedly gave it a new sense of legitimacy and connection with the apostles. Seeing that the claim of their opponents had, at the very least, an increasing appearance of validity, Thomas Christians would be sure to fight fire with fire. By refusing to speak unworthily of Jesus Christ, Thomas shows himself worthy of being made privy to hidden knowledge. It is precisely with this hidden knowledge that Thomas Christians sought to undermine the proto-orthodox, proto-Palutian claim to ecclesiological and hermeneutical authority.

Christology and soteriology in Tatian and Thomas

Given the choice of twelve possible names, the author of *Gos. Thom.* 13 settled on three when it came to writing this interlude: Simon

---

[39] Ignatius, *Mag.* 3, 6; *Phil.* 1. etc.

Peter, Matthew and Thomas. The first two disciples to appear on the scene were no arbitrary selections: they were chosen as representatives of a hermeneutic, an emerging canonical tradition and, finally, the people who perpetuated that hermeneutic and tradition on the basis of apostolic succession. Both the people and their teaching the author of our collection rejects. The better path, so it is suggested, is the path of Thomas. While I have fleetingly treated the significance of 'Thomas' as twin, this needs to be filled out. What do we learn about the Thomas community through its representative *dramatis persona*, Thomas?

Toward explaining this, we must again begin with Tatian and his thought. So far I have emphasized that Tatian maintains a blurry position within early Syriac Christianity. I am not of the view that Tatian was the founder of Encratism, nor do I believe that Tatian was the founder of early Syriac Christianity.[40] Nevertheless, he was a theological innovator in his own way. His contribution to Syriac Christianity lay in his giving its practices and heretofore theologically unformed intuitions a firm, not to mention philosophically sophisticated, foundation.

We have already dealt with Tatian and Thomas's shared practices, but what about the doctrine or narrative undergirding that practice? We can put together a fairly accurate picture from the *Oration*. As Tatian saw it, both angels and humans have free will. Ignoring God's prohibitions against evil, Adam chose the path of disobedience and in so doing forfeited his immortality and the indwelling spirit, which contained God's image and likeness. Though now mortal and bereft of the image of God, Adam at least retained his soul. This soul was the glue that held the body together even as the body contained the soul. The goal for the individual, according to Tatian, was to reclaim the spirit by preparing the soul and body complex to be a worthy temple. If the temple is purified (by abstention from sexual activity, meat and alcohol) and passions are forsaken, the spirit of God condescends to dwell in it. Tatian calls this coupling of soul and spirit 'union', as in marriage union; it is the same as salvation. Salvation in essence is returning to one's true self as it was found in Adam.

Fortunately, the servant of the suffering God, who is also the Logos, provides a model which the individual may imitate in the hope of salvation, union, and restoration to one's original Adamic condition.

---

[40] Following the western fathers, F. Bolgiani (1956–7) holds to the former position; F. C. Burkitt (1904), believing Tatian to be one and the same as the mythical Addai, holds the latter.

Adam's original condition was asexual or bisexual; it was only after the fall, which in Tatian's mind was precipitated by the sexual act, that humanity was cursed with a sexual drive. No longer would they say in this paradise regained that 'Men are from Mars and women are from Venus.' True salvation was the point in which neither male nor female would be 'other', but both would come together in Edenic harmony. Notions of 'mannishness' and 'womanishness' would be but a dim and ugly memory of post-lapsarian existence. In returning to paradise, the Tatianic saint would finally put an end to the battle of the sexes and to sexual attraction. Perhaps Tatian reckoned you couldn't extinguish the one without the other.

Having exercised his free will in accordance with the divine will, Christ can now come and dwell in a human body, a *single* body no less. By his celibacy and obedience, Christ demonstrates that he is the original Adam. He calls all men and women everywhere to leave their families, which are simply repopulating this world of corruption, and through self-control to work their way back to paradise – in this life. But attaining the right understanding, which was salvation, came only by imitating Jesus. Immortality was lost by free will; immortality was to be regained by the same free will.

Tatian's thought clearly had some influence, for in the early third-century Syriac text the *Acts of Thomas* we see his ideas developed in narrative form. Like the *Gospel of Thomas*, the *Acts of Thomas* focuses on Judas Thomas, Jesus' twin. Judas's task is largely to find young brides in order to talk them out of consummating their marriages. The young couples respond positively to Judas's exhortation; they thereby become 'pure temples' and are restored to their original state.[41] By refusing to engage in sexual activity as a married couple, each spouse has found his or her true Bridegroom, the Spirit. The true wedding is the union of soul and spirit. The similarities between Tatian and the *Acts of Thomas* are striking and have been described more fully elsewhere.[42]

No less striking are the comparisons between Tatianic thought and the *Gospel of Thomas*. Like Tatian, Thomas also counts Adam among the reprobate: 'Adam came into being from great power and great wealth. Still he was not worthy of you. For if he had been worthy, he would not have tasted death' (*Gos. Thom.* 85). For both Tatian and Thomas, the ultimate goal is the recovery of the spirit which entails

---

[41] *Acts of Thomas* 9.85.
[42] See now Hunt 2003: 155–63.

the image and likeness of God: 'When you see your likeness, you are glad. But when you see your images which came into being before you, and which neither die nor are revealed, how much you will have to bear!' (*Gos. Thom.* 84) At that point, the individual is restored to his or her androgynous self:

> Jesus said to them, 'When you make the two into one, and when you make the inside to be like the outside and the outside like the inside, and the above like the below, and when you make the male and the female one and the same, with the result that the male is no longer male nor the female female . . .' (*Gos. Thom.* 22.4–5)

The final saying of *Thomas* famously goes as follows:

> Simon Peter said to them, 'Let Mary leave us, for women are not worthy of the life.' Jesus said, 'See, I myself shall lead her so as to make her male, so that she herself will become a living spirit who is like you males. For every woman who will make herself male will enter the kingdom of heaven.' (*Gos. Thom.* 114)

On that day, when male and female coalesce, the disciples will undress and not be afraid (*Gos. Thom.* 37.2). But in order to attain this state, the soul and flesh are insufficient ('Woe to the flesh that depends on the soul. And woe to the soul that depends on the flesh' [*Gos. Thom.* 112]): what is necessary is the spirit. The spirit comes only by becoming like Jesus: 'The one who drinks from my mouth will become like me. I myself will become he, and certain things which are hidden will be revealed to him' (*Gos. Thom.* 108). Thomas, like Tatian before him, sees celibacy as the process of becoming like Jesus who contained in himself both male and female.

In rounding off this discussion regarding the similarities between Tatian and Thomas, it is worth giving particular attention to Thomas's use of special terms used to designate this state. Leaving aside the uses of the Coptic *oua ouôt* ('single one', *Gos. Thom.* 11, 22, 23, 106), we confine ourselves to *monachos* ('solitary).

> Jesus said, 'Perhaps men think that it is peace which I have come to cast upon the world. They do not know that it is division I have come to cast upon the earth: fire, sword, and war. For there will be five in a house, and it will be a matter of three against two, and two against three, father against son, and son against father. And they will stand as a solitary (*monachos*).' (*Gos. Thom.* 16)

> Jesus said, 'Blessed are the solitaries (*monachos*) and the elect, because you will find the kingdom. Indeed, you are from it, and you will return to it.' (*Gos. Thom.* 49)

Jesus said, 'There are many who are standing at the door. But it is the solitaries (*monachos*) who will enter the bridal chamber.'

(*Gos. Thom.* 75)

For a point of comparison, we can refer to another Nag Hammadi text, the *Dialogue of the Saviour*. Here we have an account of Jesus speaking to his disciples:

'But when I came, I opened the path and I taught them about the passage which they will traverse, the elect and solitary (*monachos*), who have known the Father, having believed the truth and all the praises while you offered praise ... You are the thinking and the entire serenity of the solitary (*monachos*). Once more, hear us just as you heard your elect. (*Dial. Sav.* 120.24–25; 121.19)

In *Thomas*, as in the *Dialogue of the Saviour*, one's elective status is tied to the station of being 'solitary'. It is only the solitary who will see the kingdom and only the solitary who will enter the bridal chamber. But is the bridal chamber the same bridal chamber Tatian has in mind, namely, one in which spirit and soul come together in perfect, original, union? Happily, the *Gospel of Philip* sheds some light:

The true race is renowned in the world ... that the sons of the bridal chamber dwell. Whereas in this world the union is one of husband with wife – a case of strength complemented by weakness – in the eternal realm (aeon) the form of the union is different, although we refer to them by the same names. (*Gos. Phil.* 76.4–9)

Other portions of the *Gospel of Philip* (68.23–26; 69.1–14; 70.9–33) also make clear that the bridal chamber is not a literal bridal chamber, but a metaphor for spiritual reintegration and salvation. Tatian's influence seems to have extended to the *Gospel of Philip* as well.

The concept of the Greek and Coptic *monachos* finds its best Syriac equivalent in *ihidāyā*. It was an important concept in early Syriac Christianity and I believe this very term originally stood in the *Gospel of Thomas*. As Robert Murray nicely summarizes, to become *ihidāyā* was to forsake family, to become circumcised in heart (cf. *Gos. Thom.* 53), and to put on the singleness of Christ.[43] As Tatian and the early Syrian Christians saw it, following Jesus meant taking up a life that said 'No' to procreation, in order to say, 'Yes' to new creation. If in Chapter 4 I show how Thomas and Tatian shared similar practices, here we see that those shared practices were driven by the same theological reasoning.

---

[43] Murray 1975: 16.

Conclusion

It is time to return to our seven questions. In her study of the *Gospel of Thomas*, Pagels raises the following two issues:

1 Why is Thomas so interested in creational themes, that is, in protology?
2 Why is the *Gospel of Thomas* according to *Thomas*? Why not some other apostle? Furthermore, what does this gospel say about the other apostles and why does it say what it does?

The two questions are in fact related. Thomas is so interested in protology because his eschatology (doctrine of last things) is in essence also his doctrine of beginnings, for, as Thomas himself puts it through the mouthpiece of Jesus: 'For the place where the beginning is, there will the end be as well' (*Gos. Thom.* 18.2). It is not the case, as Pagels proposes, that Thomas and John drew on the same pool of creational images and ideas at some time in the first century. Thomas uses a number of Johannine images, because he is indebted – *mutatis mutandi* – to Tatian's late second-century *Logos* theology. The creational images that we find in the first chapter of John (light, life, Word, etc.), all provide the theological staples for Tatian and, after him, Thomas as well.

Finally, it is Thomas's notion of creation that also explains why this text is called the *Gospel of Thomas*, and not, say, the *Gospel of Harold*. Jesus, as the recapitulation of the androgynous Adam, has come to call us to a world that knew no sin, knew no passions, knew no carnivorous existence, and knew no sex. By becoming Jesus' twin, by imitating Jesus and becoming mystically and experientially one with him, the Thomasine believer sought to recreate Edenic paradise on earth. For Thomas it is only in the experience of paradise, the reuniting of the spirit and soul in the metaphorical bridal chamber, that knowledge of God could be had. Jesus according to Matthew, Mark, Luke and John – this was Jesus according to the Great Church. But this was not the Jesus of Thomas.

6

The Jesus of the *Gospel of Thomas*:
An extreme makeover

If Patterson and Pagels have together raised four important questions regarding the origins of the *Gospel of Thomas*, I believe that the account I have offered provides the best solution to all of them. There remain, however, two more unresolved issues, which April DeConick has brought to the fore: (1) What explains the disparate content of the Thomasine sayings?, and (2) Why are these sayings generally attributed to Jesus who certainly was not responsible for at least some of them?

Towards answering these questions, I will ultimately suggest that one could do no better than to turn to the writings of DeConick herself, where she provides a scholarly yet accessible discussion of the influence of Hermeticism on the *Gospel of Thomas*.[1] As DeConick points out, Hermeticism was an ancient religious movement which was modelled on the mythological Egyptian genius Hermes Trismegistus, who in turn was identified with Thoth, the Egyptian god of wisdom: 'Hermes Trismegistos was the thrice-great revealer of God's mysteries to worthy humans seeking immortalization, seeking "to become god" (*C. H.* 1.18–19; 20–26; 10.6–7; 11.20; Lat. *Asc.* 5–6; 20).'[2] She continues:

> In the lodges of the Hermetics, religious seekers of many ancient faiths, including Jews who brought with them the Genesis story and speculations about the heavenly *Anthropos* (*C. H.* 1), would gather to receive initiation into the mysteries of God, overcoming the tyranny of Fate and the planets in the process. The journey began with an individual awakening from indifference and ignorance to an

---

[1] DeConick 1996: 8–11 and *passim*; 2001: 44–9; 2005: 206–37. See also Quispel 1981: 259–66. On the relationship between Hermeticism and the related *Book of Thomas the Contender*, see Turner 1975: 120–2. On ancient Hermeticism, see Broeck 2006.

[2] DeConick 2005: 207. While the name Hermes is very ancient, Hermetic philosophical writings did not start attracting attention outside their own circles until the second century CE. The original texts that have survived may be dated as early as the late first century CE up until the third century CE, but most falling in the second century. See Mahé 1976; 1978: 2.25 n 139; 1991: 349. Fowden 1985: 4–11.

awareness that God exists and wishes to be known (*C. H.* 1.31). This
is characterized by the Hermetic as a state of '*nous*' or 'mindfulness,'
the stirring of the conscious from drunkenness or sleep (*Prayer of
Thanksgiving* 64.8–15).   (DeConick 2005: 208)

Perhaps something like the modern-day Masons, the secret Hermetic
societies adapted themselves easily enough to a variety of religious
belief-systems. As a result, many early Syriac Christians apparently
had no problems identifying themselves as Christians and simultaneously as devotees of Hermes; certainly, the Hermetic philosophy
fitted hand-in-glove with Tatian and Thomas's view of salvation as an
interior experience.[3]

DeConick is one of the few *Thomas* scholars, along with Gilles
Quispel, who have illuminated the thought world of *Thomas* by casting the sayings collection against the background of Hermeticism.
Considering the fact that both our recensions of *Thomas*, the Greek
and the Coptic, derive from troves that both include a good number
of Hermetic texts, it is little short of remarkable that more has not
been made of the Hermetic element up to this point. Since good
groundwork has already been laid elsewhere, I will do no more than
make a few cursory comparisons, which may not only be helpful to
the reader, but also add a few drops of fuel to a fire that has long
needed stoking.

For starters, we find similar images in *Thomas* and Hermeticism. For
example, in *Gos. Thom.* 28 we read as follows:

> Jesus said, 'I took my stand in the midst of the world and I appeared
> to them in flesh. I found that they were all *drunk*; I did not find any
> of them thirsty. And my soul became distressed for the sons of men
> because *in their hearts they are blind* and they do not see. For they were
> empty as they came into the world, and they are still empty as they
> are seeking to leave the world. But as for now they are *drunk*. When
> they *shake off their wine*, then they will repent.'

Interestingly, the metaphor of intoxication/sobering coupled with an
unseeing heart occurs in the Hermetica:[4]

> Where are you heading in your *drunkenness*, you people? Have you
> swallowed the doctrine of ignorance undiluted, vomiting it up already
> because you cannot hold it? Stop and *sober yourselves up*! Look up

---

[3] Likewise, Hermeticism puts 'special emphasis on piety in determining one's relationship
to the divine man'; this piety amounted to possession of 'the mind' (*nous*) (Gasparro 1972:
60). See also Quispel 1981: 263; Luck 1985.
[4] All translations are from Copenhaver 1992.

with the *eyes of your heart* – if not all of you, at least those of you
who have the power.   (*C. H.* 7.1)

By themselves, the images of drunkenness and blind hearts are frequent enough in ancient literature. However, the coming together of
both these metaphors in one and the same passage, both in *Thomas*
and in the Hermetica, seems to point to an interchange of some
kind. This is only one instance to show that at least in some of its
imagery, *Thomas* draws on the Hermetic teachings.[5]

Comparisons may be drawn in terms of form as well. The many
dialogues in the *Gospel of Thomas* are a source of mild embarrassment
for the view that the Coptic gospel reaches back to Jesus. Such
dialogue, form criticism tells us (rightly or wrongly), shows a later
stage in the traditioning process. Here again in order to make sense
of *Thomas* as a first-century text, we must appeal to a theory of multiple stages. A much simpler explanation presents itself when we realize
that this combining of dialogues and pronouncements is standard
fare in the second-century Hermetic literature. In another chapter
of the *Corpus Hermeticum*, the initiate is in conversation with the
revealer Poimandres, who says:

> 'Truly you have understood. But why is it that "he who has under-
> stood himself advances toward god," as god's discourse has it?'
> 'Because,' I said, 'the father of all things was constituted of light and
> life, and from him the man came to be.'
> 'You say your speech well. Life and light are god and father, from
> whom the man came to be. So if you learn that you are from light
> and life and that you happen to come from them, you shall advance
> to life once again.'   (*C. H.* 1.21)

As in *Thomas*, the dialogue here is merely a literary device used
for explicating the revealer's hidden wisdom. There are also, once
again, further comparisons of content. First, here we find the Platonic
notion, characteristic of the Hermetic literature, of salvation on the
basis of self-knowledge;[6] it is a notion that also finds its way into
Thomas (*Gos. Thom.* 67, 70) and certainly coheres with Tatianic thought.
Another point of comparison arises from the observation that the
Hermetic god is equated with light and is also the creator of humanity. The initiate, perhaps Hermes himself, is to learn that he as a human
is 'from light' and will one day go to life and light again. Again, this
is precisely what we find in *Thomas*:

------

[5] Quispel (1985: 265) identifies *Gos. Thom.* 3, 7, 50, 56, 80, 87, 111 and 112 as Hermetical
in origin.
[6] Cf. *C. H.* 10.15.

Jesus said, 'If they say to you, "Where did you come from?" say to them, "We came from the light, from the place where the light came into existence by itself, became established, and was revealed through their image." If they say to you, "Are you the ones?" say, "We are its children, the elect of the living father." If they ask you, "What then is the sign of your father in you?" say to them, "It is agitation and rest."'

(*Gos. Thom.* 50)

Like Hermes, the Thomas Christians are to say, perhaps to their Hermetic guides (cf. *Gos. Thom.* 3), 'We came from the light.' In *Gos. Thom.* 77.1, Jesus says, 'It is I who am the light which is above all of them. It is I who am the all. From me the all came forth and unto me the all has reached.' Like the god of Hermes, Jesus is identified with light and – against classic Gnosticism – with the creator to whom all the elect return.[7] Finally, both texts, *Thomas* and the *Corpus Hermeticum*, are deeply interested in the interrelationship between motion and rest.[8] The material similarities between Thomasine thought and Hermetic thought are too significant to be ignored. On this point, DeConick is absolutely right: Thomas Christians synthesized their own faith with Hermetic philosophy. *Thomas* scholars will remain in her debt for giving Hermeticism in *Thomas* its due exposure.

My only qualm is with her explanation as to how and when Hermetic traditions came to enter the Thomasine tradition. Following the lead of Quispel, DeConick holds that the Thomas community incorporated Alexandrian Hermetic tradition 'when the End did not come', that is, when the community felt it necessary to resolve their disappointment with Jesus' failure to return in the first century.[9] This certainly has the appearance of being a workable account. But what DeConick does not explain is why we should believe Hermeticism came to influence the early Jesus movement at such

---

[7] Again, Thomas is widely but, in my view, mistakenly taken to be Gnostic. The god of Thomas appears to be the highest god who is also the creator God, not a demiurge (i.e. lower-level cosmic craftsman).

[8] *C. H.* 2.4, 11; 6.1; 9.9; 10.6 etc. So too DeConick 1996: 93–6. David T. Runia (1995: 196–201) provides an excellent summary of the important Philonic themes of 'rest' and 'standing', and their influence on the Syrian Platonist Numenius, a contemporary of Tatian. 'Standing outside oneself', or simply 'standing', were ways of describing the rest that occurred upon spiritual union with the One. Given Thomas's interest in 'standing' (*Gos. Thom.* 16.4, 18.3, 23.2, 28.1, 75, 99.1), we may be seeing Numenius's impress here in our collection. This would not necessarily be inconsistent with a Hermetic background (which freely helped itself to Platonism) nor the development of 'standing' as thematic in early Syriac Christian literature.

[9] DeConick 2005: 211.

an early stage. First of all, this scenario depends on the assumption, made popular in the early twentieth century through the History of Religions School, that early Christianity drew its central concepts and terminology from Greco-Roman cultic religiosity. Obviously, this is not the place to settle such a looming question, so it will have to suffice to assert rather than argue my own viewpoint: that primitive Christianity took root in a fundamentally Jewish soil that was conceptually self-contained and resistant to the intrusion of pagan practices and theories.[10] The second difficulty with this scenario bears on the fact that we have no evidence that Hermeticism ever made its way out of Egypt before the latter half of the second century CE.[11] The first allusion to Hermeticism in other sources is found in the late second-century writings of Athenagoras and Tertullian, again, the period in which the movement seems to have begun its heyday and precisely the period in which I propose *Thomas* to have been written.[12] Before this time, Hermeticism as a religio-philosophical movement shows no sign of having been exported or assimilated to non-Egyptian religions. Therefore, unless we are prepared to envision early Syrio-Palestinian Christians making pilgrimage to pagan Alexandria for inspiration not terribly long after Paul and Timothy oversaw the burning of invaluable magical scrolls in Ephesus (Acts 19), this is a hard row to hoe.

The role of Hermeticism in *Thomas*

In my judgment, Hermeticism's impact on the Thomas tradition can be best explained not by summoning Egypt, but by focusing again on Edessa and its environs. In the 1950s, J. B. Segal investigated the ruins of seven ancient temples surrounding a mountain located

---

[10] As N. T. Wright (1996: 213) asks in relation to Burton Mack's study of Jesus: 'Are we seriously being invited to think that Jesus, rather than being a prophet in the mould of the great Hebrew prophets, was in fact more like the Alexandrian allegorist Philo, or that his characteristic sayings really resembled the generalized ascetic teachings of the second-century AD pagan moralist 'Sextus'? . . . I am reminded of Schweitzer's comment on those who try to explain Paul's very Jewish thought on the basis of Hellenism: they are, he says, "like a man who should bring water from a long distance in leaky watering-cans in order to water a garden lying beside a stream"' (Schweitzer 1968 [1930]: 140). In this case, DeConick's leaky – and, for all we know, non-existent – watering-can is a displaced Jerusalem-based Christianity that, within decades of the death of James (62 CE), had exchanged its extremely conservative Jewish roots for pagan syncretism. The stream that better explains Thomas's thought is the highly syncretistic ferment that patently characterized late second-century Edessa.

[11] See Fowden 1985: 11 and the bibliography there; Löw 2002: 8–12.

[12] Athenagoras *Leg.* 28.6; Tertullian *Ann.* 33.2; 28.1. See Löw 2002: 41–64.

about 40 miles southeast of Edessa.[13] These temples, representing the seven planets, can be firmly dated to 165 CE and fairly confidently connected with a brand of Hermeticism. Bardaisan (154–222), a prominent figure in the court of the Edessean Abgar VIII ('the Great'), seems to have been aware of this Hermetic religion and in fact draws approvingly on its writings, 'the books of the Egyptians', in his *Book of the Laws of Countries*.[14] The Edessean Bardaisan was contemporary with Tatian and, as I have been arguing, Thomas as well. Thus, whereas arguments that connect Hermeticism with early first-century Thomas Christianity, fail for lack of evidence, the late second-century, Edessean, provenance of *Thomas* explains the data splendidly. Hermeticism as a philosophical system had made at least a partial convert out of the first known Syriac theologian, Bardaisan.[15] It is indisputable, therefore, that if Thomas was written shortly after the *Diatessaron*, it was written at a time when Hermetical ideas were not just in the air in Edessa but were in fashion.

Whereas DeConick increasingly sees the Hermetical elements as incidental to the theological makeup of *Thomas*, I am inclined to see Hermetical thought as being foundational for explaining why the gospel is the way it is. In order to demonstrate the importance of Hermeticism, however, I need first to lay the groundwork by considering two ends of the theological trajectory to which Tatian and Thomas belong. On the earlier end, there is Justin Martyr, Tatian's mentor; on the latter end, we have fourth-century Manichaeism, as represented by Augustine's opponent Faustus. (It was the Manichaeans, practitioners of the heavily dualistic religion that originated in the third century due southeast of Edessa, who came to preserve the Thomasine writings.[16]) In between these are situated Tatian and Thomas.

True to his philosophical sensibilities, Justin compares Christ to the Greek Hermes: both were 'the messenger-like word who was with God'.[17] Justin's comparison is nothing entirely new. Much earlier, in the second century BCE, the Alexandrian Jewish romancer Artapanus penned a biography of Moses in which the Hebrew patriarch is remembered for – among other things – inventing hieroglyphs, allocating the priests their land, and explaining the wonders of shipbuilding.

---

[13] Segal 1970: 45–8.
[14] So Drijvers 1966.
[15] Drijvers 1970.
[16] The Manichaeans' use of the *Gospel of Thomas* is well documented: see, among other patristic writers, Cyril of Jerusalem, *Cat.* 4.36, 6.3. On the theological continuity between Thomas Christianity and Manichaeism, see Drijvers 1982: 161–75; Funk 2002.
[17] Justin, *1 Apol.* 22.2.

Of course, scripture has no record of Moses doing any such things. But these are precisely the very activities predicated of Hermes Trismegistus. Artapanus fuses Moses with the Egyptian demigod of wisdom as a kind of apologetic: that which the Egyptian pagans honoured in their revealer Hermes came to fuller expression in the Jewish giver of the law.[18]

Other early church fathers after Justin were equally ready to grant credence to Hermes. But more fascinating than the fact that the early Christian writers respected Hermes is *why* these Christian writers were so impressed with the Egyptian legend. With Augustine's admiring approval, Cyprian of Carthage praised Hermes because he 'speaks of one God, and confesses that He is incomprehensible, and past our powers of estimation'.[19] Along these lines, a writing ascribed to Justin, but perhaps belonging instead to one of Justin's disciples, speaks of Hermes' wisdom in speaking of the ineffability of the divine.[20] While there is no reason to believe that this writing actually goes back to Tatian himself, we have good grounds for suggesting that Tatian, simply as Justin's disciple, belonged to this cadre of apologists who appealed to Hermes as part of their Christian apologetic. As Hermeticism was just becoming a philosophical force in the mid second-century world, Justin's school was not opposed to co-opting Hermes as a mouthpiece for Christ, if not a type of Christ. It is more likely than not, then, that Tatian was among this number who, like Paul who became Greek to the Greeks (1 Cor. 9.21), saw the apologetic value of casting Jesus as Hermes. Why? Because Tatian, and so too Thomas after him, were interested in contextualizing Jesus for all those Syrians who were more than ready to give Hermes or Hermes lookalikes due consideration.

Two centuries later, we find Augustine's Manichaean opponent, Faustus, taking a very similar line. If Augustine portrays Faustus's viewpoint accurately, the Manichaean thinker saw the prophets of the Hebrew Bible as irrelevant when it came to preaching to Gentiles. In order to earn the intellectual respect of a Gentile audience, it was important to draw on Gentile philosophers:

> Again, I say, the Christian Church, which consists more of Gentiles than of Jews, can owe nothing to Hebrew witnesses. If, as is said, any prophecies of Christ are to be found in the Sibyll, called Trismegistus,

---

[18] Mussies 1982.

[19] Cyprian, *De idol. vanit.* 6; Augustine, *Contra Faustum*, 44.

[20] Justin, *Oratio ad Graecos*, 38. The author appeals 'to Hermes, who says plainly and clearly, "that it is hard to comprehend God, and that it is impossible even for the man who can comprehend Him to speak of Him to others"'.

or Orpheus, or any heathen poet, they might aid the faith of those who, like us, are converts from heathenism to Christianity. But the testimony of the Hebrews is useless to us before conversion, for then we cannot believe them; and superfluous after, for we believe without them.   (Augustine, *Contra Faustum*, 13)

Faustus takes his place in a community that used the *Gospel of Thomas* and saw itself as standing in continuity with the Thomasine tradition. While certainly there must have been important differences between fourth-century Manichaeism and second-century Thomas Christianity, there would assuredly also be important threads of continuity.

Both the Thomas community and the later Manichaean community are equally determined to set aside the Jewish setting of the Christian message. In *Gos. Thom.* 52, Jesus' disciples approach him and say, 'Twenty-four prophets spoke in Israel, and they all spoke through you.' In response to the mistaken disciples, Jesus only has this to say: 'You have neglected the one living in your presence and have merely spoken of the dead.' This need not be interpreted as a blanket anti-Jewish statement. Rather, Jesus' words are simply saying, as Faustus would say later, that 'the testimony of the Hebrews is useless'.[21] What the Gentiles need are Gentile means of persuasion. And what better proof for the Gentile Greek than the proof issuing from the mouth of the thrice-great Hermes? While I grant that much water passed beneath the bridge between the end of the second century and the time of Faustus, it is also true that when certain ideas give rise to a new movement, those same ideas typically die hard.

It is in light of these observations that we can return to our two remaining questions: (1) What explains the disparate content of the Thomasine sayings?, and (2) Why are these sayings generally attributed to Jesus who certainly was not responsible for at least some of them? I submit that both these questions can be resolved on the following scenario. Justin, well aware that a Hermes cult was developing in the mid second-century world, used the legendary figure as a way of illustrating the truth of Christianity. In turn, Tatian, duly impressed with this apologetic move, went back to his native Syria and, even more convinced of Hermeticism's popularity there, strove to uses Hermes as a bridge for his gospel. The Thomas community, already well indebted to Tatian's theology, took this further. For Thomas Christians, the similarities between Jesus and Hermes were irresistible: both were mediating figures sent to interpret divine

---

[21] So too Moreland 2006.

will on behalf of humanity; both too secured immortality through self-purification, but remained among the chosen in order to show the way. Thus, in order to make their message more palpable to a culture already familiar and comfortable with Hermetic categories, it made excellent sense to the Thomas Christians to tailor their gospel accordingly. As such the *Gospel of Thomas* may be as much a foundational document as an apologetic tract, specially crafted to convey the community's beliefs in an idiom that would resonate with its intended audience.

In this case, *Thomas* can be compared to another Manichaean favourite, the *Sibylline Oracles.* This text, a collection of diverse affirmations and propositions spoken through the prophesying Sibyll, seems to have fooled a large number of ancient readers (including some we might expect to know better) into thinking that the words of the Sibyll were truly her words. In reality, the statements were drawn from a vast variety of sources, from Genesis to Homer to eager Christian interpolators. Here we find many sentiments and ideas, often linked together with acrostic patterns and other rhetorical devices, but none contributing to a cohesive or unitary statement of theology.[22] In Syrian Hermeticism this tradition of delivering the diverse opinions of philosophers and alchemists through one authoritative voice continued as late the sixth century.[23] To the Hermetic author, it mattered little whether Hermes or Poimandres actually spoke the words attributed to them: what mattered is that they were true. And if they were true, then ultimately they did trace themselves back to the source of all wisdom. The same may be said of Thomas's Jesus. Thomas knew full well that not all that he had ascribed to Jesus actually and historically went back to Jesus. But as Thomas saw it, if Jesus said it, it was true. And conversely, if it was true, then Jesus said it – or might as well have done.[24]

---

[22] As Löw (2002: 22) remarks, the fundamental difficulty of pinpointing a particular hermeneutical synthesis in the Hermetica can be credited to the fact that 'in the Hermetica very many different traditions are taken up in varying degrees of intensity' and are all 'passed down under the name of Hermes Trismegistos'. This difficulty finds analogy in our understanding of *Thomas*: after years of study, no reconstruction of any one philosophical or religious system behind the Coptic text comes close to explaining the whole text.

[23] Brock 1983; 1984.

[24] As Nock (1962: 83) writes regarding Asclepius: 'Thoughts of whatever origin, Platonic, Stoic, or Jewish, appear [*sc.* in the Hermetic writings] as revelation. But it is never necessary, and perhaps never plausible to suppose that the thoughts have any measure of originality.' As for Asclepius, so too for *Thomas*.

Conclusion

It is now time to look back on the path we have taken through this thick wooded glen called *Thomas* studies. After reviewing three major scholars (Chapters 1–3), I have attempted to marshal four arguments for a post-Tatian *Thomas*. No one argument presupposes another; independently they all point back to the author of the *Diatessaron* and the *Oration* as the inspiration behind *Thomas*. When one considers the best evidence for *Thomas's* original language of composition (Chapter 4), ascetical practices (Chapter 4), hermeneutical reflections vis-à-vis Matthean and Petrine Christians (Chapter 5), and Hermeticism (Chapter 6) – all roads lead to late second-century Edessa. In my judgment, no other paradigm makes more sense.

Along the way, I have maintained seven points regarding the Coptic *Gospel of Thomas*. First, the difference between the sequence of sayings in *Thomas* and the sequence of pericopae in the synoptic gospels is best explained by the assumption that the former was written in Syriac and in dependence on – among other texts and traditions – the *Diatessaron*. In this case, the fact that *Thomas* does not follow the order of the synoptic gospels comes as no surprise. It is Tatian's harmony that lies behind *Thomas*, not the discrete Greek gospels that constitute the harmony. But the much more important factor in explaining why the *Thomas* sayings fall the way they do has to do with the editor's commitment to catchwords. If Thomas was interested enough in establishing catchword connections, we could certainly imagine his rearranging sayings as necessary in order to sustain the verbal linkages. On surveying the evidence, there is every indication that the mind behind *Thomas* was indeed 'interested enough'. The Syriac character of *Thomas* is confirmed by redactional activity, differences between the Coptic and Greek recensions, and, most importantly of all, repeated catchword pairs that only work in Syriac. I submit that the burden of proof rests on anyone seeking to refute the notion of a unified, Syriac, *Gospel of Thomas*.

Second, I have sought to explain why the Coptic sayings collection lays so much emphasis on asceticism. The authors of the *Diatessaron* and *Gospel of Thomas* share and commend identical ascetical practices: avoidance of sexual intimacy (outside or inside of marriage), renunciation of personal possessions, and strict vegetarianism. The difficulty with linking *Thomas* to Jesus or his movement lies in the fact that Jesus' followers enjoyed natural marital relationship (1 Cor. 7.10–11, 9.5; Acts 18.26; etc.), possessions (Luke 8.3, 10.38; John 21.1–3; etc.), and an occasional fattened calf (Luke 15.23, 27; Acts 10.9–15; Rom. 14.6; etc.). Jesus himself approved of marriage (Mark

10.7–9) and possessions (Luke 16.9). He was a regular dinner guest at the home of everyday and (presumably) meat-eating Jews, and after his resurrection fish was a favourite (Luke 24.42; John 21.11–15). The inferable practices of the Thomas community fit Tatian to a tee, and far better than we find in Judaism as a whole or in Jesus.[25]

If, on the other hand, it was Tatian who inherited his theological views from Thomas, how and when did that interchange take place? Tatian was converted outside of his native Syria and did not return until just months before undertaking his *Diatessaron*, replete with Tatianic theology. One would expect that if Tatian was master of his own school, he would be well formed and not easily swayed by those to whom he brought his gospel harmony. Could Thomas really have revolutionized the thinking of a man of Tatian's stature and done so in such a short time? I think it is unlikely. The better solution is that it was Tatian who preceded Thomas.

My third point is this: that Thomas's use of creational images, noticed by Pagels, can be best explained by an eschatology initially introduced by Tatian. For Jews of every era and early Christians as well, eschatology was in a sense also protology. Just about everyone (from Isaiah to Paul to Tatian himself) was seeking to get back to Eden, that is, the new creation. But while Isaiah saw new creation in terms of Yahweh's promise of future restoration, and while Paul saw new creation breaking through in the resurrection of Jesus Christ, which manifested its power through the church, Thomas Christians saw things differently. For Thomas Christians the new creation was not something objectively secured through Christ, but rather something subjectively realized through the individual's imitation of Jesus. Only after becoming like Jesus, the Adamic single one *par excellence*, could one expect the Spirit to come and dwell in the temple of the body. And when the Spirit did so, new creation began to take place, but only in the sphere of individual experience. Thus, there are two broad differences between salvation as it has traditionally been envisaged in orthodoxy and salvation according to Thomas. For orthodox believers, new creation has always been an objective and corporate reality, manifest in the present but awaiting fuller and final consummation in the future. Thomas Christians, by contrast, understood new creation to be fully available in the present. They could believe in a here-and-now paradise restored in the face of an imperfect world, because they also believed that new creation was to be apprehended strictly as a subjective experience.

---

[25] Despite the fact that, as DeConick (2005: 176–80) points out, certain strands of mystical Judaism placed value on sexual abstinence.

Fourth, this experience of new creation came only by one's successful imitation of Jesus, that is, by becoming Jesus' twin. The Thomasine Christian community thus seized on the traditional connection between Thomas and Edessa (that Thomas was actually the first apostle to come to Edessa is possible but uncertain) and put it to work for their theology. Thomas Christians taught that by becoming a 'Thomas', a twin, one could have hope of paradise in this life. All this makes for interesting comparisons and contrasts. Like other Christians throughout the second-century world, Thomas Christians regarded Jesus as divine. But in their minds participation in the divine was not something that could be 'taught' (as through the gospels) so much as 'caught' (through personal imitation of Jesus). Against this viewpoint, the Great Church seems to have settled on two notions: first, that Jesus Christ was divine in a unique and inimitable sense, and, second, that it was both possible and appropriate to communicate the nature of Jesus' divinity through the gospel stories. In their Christology and in their sources for establishing that Christology, Thomas Christianity would have undoubtedly stood at odds with the cherished views of Serapion and the Edessene Christians connected with him. Perceiving themselves to be like cats in a dog-only family, Thomas Christians sought to explain their marginalization by claiming to be privy to special knowledge.

Fifth, the diversity of the *Thomas* material can be explained on analogy with the Sibylline Oracles and specifically Hermetic literature. Just as the confluence of different ideas from different settings in the mouth of the seer only contributes to the breadth and authority of the revealer figure, so too it was in Thomas's best interests to make Jesus the mouthpiece of all manner of wisdom. If Jesus was the new Hermes, his pronouncements would have to reflect the same philosophical variety that characterized Hermeticism.

Sixth, since the Hermetic cataloguing of sayings was undertaken with very little worry regarding the authenticity of the source of those sayings, we also have an explanation for why patently non-dominical sayings are attributed to the master Jesus. True, the Thomas community puts words into the mouth of their Jesus. But their Jesus is by no means the historical Jesus or even the memory of the historical Jesus: their Jesus is at once the Jewish Adam and the Egyptian Thoth. The very fact that Tatian himself was eager to give the Syrians a gospel in their own language, which implies, I think, a certain mission-mindedness, makes his appropriation of Justin's notion of Christ as Hermes utterly plausible – in fact, the best explanation.

Seventh, and finally, my explanation for the *Gospel of Thomas* requires no complex periodization, no multiple stages of authorship, and no layers of communities. The *Gospel of Thomas* was a Syriac text written in the last quarter of the second century by a careful editor who arranged his material largely on the basis of catchword connections. As far as his sources, Thomas drew primarily on Tatian's *Diatessaron*, but also undoubtedly drew on his memory of a number of oral and written traditions. It cannot be ruled out that *Thomas* preserves authentic sayings of Jesus; it is simply that, given a span of 140-plus years, this would be extremely hard to prove.

Our author Thomas was inspired not only by Tatian's gospel harmony but also by Tatian's Encratitic theology, which saw Jesus not as the Saviour, but as the one who can show us how to be saved. Through abstinence and vegetarianism, the moral soul could aspire to be reunited to the divine Spirit. While in its sum and substance Thomas theology was radically individualistic, there is a communal aspect to this gospel: its intended use for Hermetical gatherings. As they are known to have done with other texts, the Hermetic initiates probably read *Thomas* to each other with a view to meditating on it and aspiring through it to a higher wisdom.

By so clothing Jesus in a deeply Encratitic and Hermetic guise, the Thomas community no doubt incurred the displeasure of the Edessean proto-orthodox Christians, who were on the cusp of formalizing their connection with Serapion of Antioch. While accepted by some *soi-disant* Christians, the *Gospel of Thomas* was rejected by many others, but not before attaining international status and popularity. It continued to be used predominantly among the Syrian-based Manichaeans who were sympathetic to its stripping away of the Jewish elements of Christianity.

Interestingly enough, Thomas and the Manichaean Faustus also bear some parallel to the twentieth-century giant Bultmann in that all three figures were eager to demythologize the Jewish elements from the Christian message. Just as Thomas and Faustus sought a less Jewish Jesus, one more in keeping with Hellenistic tastes, Bultmann too sought to extract Jesus from his Jewish context. In the process all three gave us a Jesus who could be imitated in certain respects but who in the final analysis could neither be known as human nor make known the divine. 'Why speak of the dead Jewish historical Jesus,' Bultmann or Thomas might ask, 'when you have the living one, the existential Christ of faith, in your very presence?' Given the varying degrees to which my three interlocutors – not to mention Koester and Robinson – align themselves with a Bultmannian understanding of early Christianity, it is no surprise that a Jesus according to Thomas is the Jesus with whom they are most satisfied. Perhaps the broad sense among North American scholars that Christian origins finds a significant point of departure in Thomas speaks less to first-century realities than it does to the truism that history repeats itself. Long after the deaths of Thomas and Faustus, their project of re-presenting Jesus existentially, apart from his Jewish particularity with its concrete demands, remains very much alive.

There are also a number of questions that remain very much alive. When Muhammed Ali and his brothers broke open the cisterns containing the Nag Hammadi codices some sixty years ago, they wondered whether their raised mattock would unleash a legion of genies. When the mattock fell, although keenly disappointed not to see gold coins spilling out, they must have been very relieved to find no evidence of a bedevilling spirit. Little did they know that the *Gospel of Thomas* contained in that jar would mean both riches and bedevilment for those who would gaze on this Coptic text far later. We have been enriched through the discovery of this gospel: as a result of this text we have all the better understanding of the nature of early Syriac Christianity and the trajectories to which it gave birth. But we have also been bedevilled and perplexed. My purpose in writing this book is to work toward demystifying the genie of *Thomas* and to cash out its value as a historical text. The continuity between Tatian and Thomas, their place in early Syriac Christianity, the social context for their respective theologies – whatever down payment this book has made, much more is due on these topics.

There are other questions too, theological questions that Thomas seems to be asking even from the grave. One question is two-fold: 'Who was Jesus and how do we proclaim him?' In the west, for the better part of the past 250 years, this question has been taken up with renewed force and shows no signs of dying down. To be sure, one reason why the *Gospel of Thomas* is so important is that Jesus and who he was is so important. If *Thomas* can correct our picture of the historical Jesus, that's a very important thing to know. But then we ask too, 'What does it mean to communicate the nature of God through Christ?' What is the relationship between ontological divine realities and the language that we use to describe those realities? What is the relationship between the central content of Jesus' message and the first-century Judaism in which he took on flesh? Are these arbitrary and effaceable relationships, or is language about God ultimately inseparable from God himself? In the post-liberal, post-conservative western church, these are no insignificant issues.

It is not my intention to speak to these questions. Rather, my intention has been to describe how the *Gospel of Thomas* fits into the puzzle of Christian origins. It is another gospel, but is it, after all, the 'other gospel' that we have been missing all these years? My point has been that in order to answer that question we must first get the puzzle-pieces of *Thomas* matched to the right box-top. If we look at the epistemological and hermeneutical struggle leading from Philo to Justin to Tatian we have, I believe, the notional roots of Thomas Christianity. In his desire to accommodate the gospel to his homeland, Tatian composed a gospel harmony in Syriac. But he also fashioned a theology that was tailored according to the cultural beliefs and practices of his fatherland. Tatian's fellow Syrian, the one whom we have been calling Thomas, took his project a step further by reinventing Jesus, not as a sage or apocalyptic preacher or messiah, but as the ultimate Hermes. 'Come to me,' this Hermes-Jesus says, 'not for salvation, for I am not your teacher. Come to me in order to learn how to recognize yourself. When you have recognized yourself and have been reintegrated in your inner being and in your mind, then you will rule over all – whatever the circumstances of hearth or history.'

Is this the Other Gospel we have been waiting for? Somehow, I suspect, we have heard this message before. Somehow we have met this Jesus before. The *Gospel of Thomas* invites us to imagine a Jesus who says, 'I am not your saviour, but the one who can put you in touch with your true self. Free yourself from your gender, your body, and any concerns you might have for the outside world. Work for it and self-realization, salvation, will be yours – in this life.' Imagine such a Jesus? One need hardly work very hard. This is precisely the Jesus we know too well, the existential Jesus that so many western evangelical and liberal churches already preach.

If the *Gospel of Thomas* is good news for anybody, it is good news to those who are either intent on escaping the world or are already quite content with the way things are. So perhaps history is repeating itself. Perhaps the original Thomas community was pleased to have a Jesus who could be divested of his Jewish story and domesticated to their way of seeing things. In this case, Thomas's spiritual heirs are alive and well today. Perhaps too the early church fathers rejected this sayings collection because they had little patience for anyone or anything that might confuse their hope of new creation with something approaching a Christianized self-help philosophy. In other words, perhaps the Great Church rejected the *Gospel of Thomas* not because it was 'other', but because it was not 'other' enough. In retrospect, the Jesus of Matthew and Simon Peter, the Jesus of Serapion and Palut, was much more counter-cultural than the one whose words Judas Didymus Thomas claims to preserve.

References

Adam, A. (1953–4), 'Grundbegriffe des Mönchtums in sprachlicher Sicht', *ZKG* 65: 209–39.

Ahl, F. (1985), *Metaformations: Soundplay and Wordplay in Ovid and Other Classical Poets* (Ithaca, N.Y.: Cornell University Press).

Alexander, L. (1990), 'The Living Voice: Scepticism towards the Written Word in Early Christian and in Graeco-Roman Texts', in D. J. A. Clines, S. E. Fowl and S. E. Porter (eds.), *The Bible in Three Dimensions: Essays in Celebration of Forty Years of Biblical Studies in the University of Sheffield* (JSOTSup 87; Sheffield: Sheffield University Press): 221–47.

Allison, D. C. (1993), *A New Moses: A Matthean Typology* (Minneapolis: Fortress Press).

Anderson, P. N. (2006), *The Fourth Gospel and the Quest for Jesus: Modern Foundations Reconsidered* (LNTS; London: T. & T. Clark).

Arens, E. (1997), *Kommunikatives Handeln und christlicher Glaube: Ein theologischer Diskurs mit Jürgen Habermas* (Paderborn: Schöningh).

Arnal, W. E. (1995), 'The Rhetoric of Marginality: Apocalypticism, Gnosticism, and Sayings Gospels', *HTR* 88: 471–94.

Asgeirsson, J. M., A. D. DeConick and R. Uro (2006), *Thomasine Traditions in Antiquity: The Social and Cultural World of the Gospel of Thomas* (NHS 59; Leiden: Brill).

Attridge, H. W. (1989), 'Appendix: The Greek Fragments', in B. Layton (ed.), *Nag Hammadi Codex II,2–7: Together with XIII,2* Brit. Lib. Or. 4926(1), and P.Oxy 1, 654, 655: Vol. 1: Gospel According to Thomas, Gospel According to Philip, Hypostasis of the Archons, and Indexes* (NHS 20; Leiden: Brill): 95–128.

Baarda, T. (1989), 'ΔΙΑΦΟΝΙΑ–ΣΨΜΦΟΝΙΑ: Factors in the Harmonization of the Gospels, Especially in the Diatessaron of Tatian', in B. Aland and W. L. Petersen (eds.), *Gospel Traditions in the Second Century: Origins, Recensions, Text and Transmission* (CJA 3; Notre Dame, Ind.: University of Notre Dame): 133–54.

—— (1991), ' "Chose" or "Collected": Concerning an Aramaism in Logion 8 of the Gospel of Thomas and the Question of Independence', *HTR* 84: 373–97.

—— (1993), 'Clement of Alexandria and the Parable of the Fisherman: Mt 13,47–48 or Independent Tradition?' in C. Focant (ed.), *Synoptic Gospels: Source Criticism and the New Literary Criticism* (BETL 110; Louvain: Louvain University Press; Louvain: Peeters): 582–98.

—— (1995), ' "The Cornerstone": An Aramaism in the Diatessaron and the Gospel of Thomas?' *NovT* 37: 285–300.

—— (1997a), ' "Blessed are the poor . . .": John Dominic Crossan on Logion 54', *GTT* 97: 127–32.

—— (1997b), '"Vader – Zoon – Heilige Geest": Logion 44 van "Thomas": ("Father – Son – Holy Spirit": Logion 44 of "Thomas")', *NedTT* 51: 13–30.

Baker, A. (1965a), 'Fasting to the World', *JBL* 84: 291–4.

—— (1965b), 'Gospel of Thomas and the Diatessaron', *JTS* 16: 449–54.

Bauckham, R. (1998), 'John for Readers of Mark' in R. Bauckham (ed.), *The Gospels for All Christians: Rethinking the Gospel Audiences* (Grand Rapids: Eerdmans): 147–71.

—— (2006), *Jesus and the Eyewitnesses: The Gospels as Eyewitness Testimony* (Grand Rapids: Eerdmans).

Bauer, W. (1971 [1935]), *Orthodoxy and Heresy in Earliest Christianity*, ed. R. A. Kraft and G. Krodel (Mifflintown, Pa.: Sigler).

Bauer, J. B. (1994), 'Nag Hammadi und das Thomas-Evangelium', in J. B. Bauer and H. D. Galter (eds.), *Gnosis: Vorträge der Veranstaltungsfolge des steirischen Herbstes und der Österreichischen URANIA für Steiermark vom Oktober und November 1993* (GTS 16; Graz: Universität Graz): 21–44.

Beasley-Murray, G. R. (1987), *John* (WBC 36; Waco, Tex.: Word Books).

Beck, E. (1956), 'Ein Beitrag zur Terminologie des ältesten syrischen Mönchtums', *SA* 38: 254–67.

Benoit, P. (1973), *Jesus and the Gospel* (New York: Herder and Herder).

Berger, K. (1984), *Formgeschichte des Neuen Testaments* (Heidelberg: Quelle & Meyer).

Betz, H.-D. (1970), 'Delphic Maxim *Gnōthi Sauton* in Hermetic Interpretation', *HTR* 63: 465–84.

Bianchi, U. (ed.) (1985), *Tradizione dell'enkrateia: Motivazioni ontologiche e pro-tologiche* (Rome: Edizione dell'Ateneo).

—— (1985b), 'La tradition de l'enkrateia: Motivations ontologiques et pro-tologiques', in U. Bianchi (ed.), *Tradizione dell'enkrateia: Motivazioni onto-logiche e protologiche* (Rome: Edizione dell'Ateneo): 293–315.

Boismard, M.-É. (1979), 'The Two-Source Theory at an Impasse', *NTS* 26: 1–17.

Bolgiani, F. (1956–7), 'La tradizione eresiologica sull'encratismo', *Atpub* 91: 1–77

Botha, P. J. J. (1993), 'Living Voice and Lifeless Letters: Reserve towards Writing in the Graeco-Roman World,' *HvTSt* 26: 742–59.

Brock, S. (1983), 'A Syriac Collection of Prophecies of the Pagan Philosophers,' *OLP* 14: 203–46.

—— (1984), 'Some Syriac Excerpts from Greek Collections of Pagan Prophecies,' *VC* 38: 77–90.

Brodie, T. L. (1993), *The Quest for the Origin of John's Gospel: A Source-Oriented Approach* (New York: Oxford University Press).

Broeck, R. van der (2006), 'Hermes Trismegistus I: Antiquity', in W. J. Hanegraaff et al. (eds), *Dictionary of Gnosis and Western Esotericism* (2 vols; Leiden: Brill): 474–99.

Brown, P. R. L. (1988), *The Body and Society: Men, Women, and Sexual Renunciation in Early Christianity* (New York: Columbia University Press).

Bultmann, R. (1963 [1921]), *The History of the Synoptic Tradition* (New York: Harper & Row).

Burkitt, F. C. (1904), *Early Eastern Christianity: St. Margaret's Lectures, 1904, On the Syriac-Speaking Church* (London: Murray).

Cameron, R. (1982), *The Other Gospels: Non-canonical Gospel Texts* (Philadelphia: Westminster).

Cerfaux, L. (1957), 'Les paraboles du royaume dans l'Évangile de Thomas', *Mus* 70: 307–27.

Charlesworth, J. H. (1995), *The Beloved Disciple: Whose Witness Validates the Gospel of John?* (Valley Forge, Pa.: Trinity Press International).

Clarysse, W. (1994), 'Gospel of Thomas Logion 13: "The Bubbling Well Which I Myself Dug"', in C. Laga, A. Schoors and P. van Deun (eds.), *Philohistôr: Miscellanea in honorem Caroli Laga septuagenarii* (Louvain: Peeters; Louvain: Departement Oriëntalistiek): 1–9.

Copenhaver, B. P. (1992), *Hermetica: The Greek Corpus Hermeticum and the Latin Asclepius in a New English Translation, with Notes and Introduction* (Cambridge/New York: Cambridge University Press).

Crossan, J. D. (1973), 'Seed Parables of Jesus', *JBL* 92: 244–66.

—— (1985), *Four Other Gospels: Shadows on the Contours of Canon* (Minneapolis: Winston Press).

Daumas, F. (1982), 'Le fonds égyptien de l'Hermetisme', in J. Ries, Y. Janssens and J.-M. Sevrin (eds), *Gnosticisme et monde hellenistique: Actes du colloque de Louvain-la-Neuve (11–14 mars 1980)* (Louvain-la-Neuve: Université catholique de Louvain; Louvain-la-Neuve: Institut orientaliste): 1–25.

Davies, S. L. (1983), *The Gospel of Thomas and Christian Wisdom* (New York: Seabury Press).

—— (1992), 'The Christology and Protology of the Gospel of Thomas', *JBL* 111: 663–82.

DeConick, A. D. (1996), *Seek to See Him: Ascent and Vision Mysticism in the Gospel of Thomas* (VCSup, 33; Leiden: Brill).

—— (2001), *Voices of the Mystics: Early Christian Discourse in the Gospels of John and Thomas and Other Ancient Christian Literature* (JSNTSup 157; Sheffield: Sheffield Academic Press).

—— (2002), 'The Original Gospel of Thomas', *VC* 56: 167–99.

—— (2005), *Recovering the Original Gospel of Thomas: A History of the Gospel and its Growth* (ECC 286; London/New York: T. & T. Clark).

—— (2006), *The Original Gospel of Thomas in Translation: With a Commentary and New English Translation of the Complete Gospel* (ECC 287; London/New York: T. & T. Clark).

Dehandschutter, B. (1975), 'Le lieu d'origine de l'Évangile selon Thomas', *OLP* 6: 125–31.

Donelson, L. R. (1986), *Pseudepigraphy and Ethical Argument in the Pastoral Epistles* (HUT 22; Tübingen: Mohr).

Drijvers, H. J. W. (1966), *Bardaisan of Edessa* (Assen: Van Gorcum).

—— (1970), 'Bardaisan of Edessa and the Hermetica: The Aramaic Philosopher and the Philosophy of His Time', in *Jaarbericht: Voorazaitisch-Egyptisch Genootschap Ex Oriente Lux, 21* (Leiden: Brill): 190–210.

—— (1972), *Old-Syriac (Edessean) Inscriptions* (SS 3; Leiden: Brill).

—— (1982), 'Facts and Problems in Early Syriac-Speaking Christianity', *SecCent* 2: 157–75.

—— (1984), *East of Antioch: Studies in Early Syriac Christianity* (London: Variorum Reprints).

—— (1992), 'Syrian Christianity and Judaism', in J. Lieu, J. North and T. Rajak (eds.), *The Jews among Pagans and Christians: In the Roman Empire* (London/New York: Routledge): 124–46.

Dunderberg, I. (1997), 'John and Thomas in Conflict', in J. D. Turner and A. McGuire (eds.), *The Nag Hammadi Library after Fifty Years: Proceedings of the 1995 Society of Biblical Literature Commemoration* (NHS 44; Leiden: Brill): 361–80.

—— (1998a), 'Thomas and the Beloved Disciple', in R. Uro (ed.), *Thomas at the Crossroads* (Edinburgh: T. & T. Clark): 65–88.

—— (1998b), 'Thomas' I-sayings and the Gospel of John', in R. Uro (ed.), *Thomas at the Crossroads* (Edinburgh: T. & T. Clark): 33–64.

Dunn, J. D. G. (2003), *Jesus Remembered* (Grand Rapids, Mich.: Eerdmans).

Ehlers, B. (1970), 'Kann das Thomasevangelium aus Edessa Stammen', *NovT* 12: 284–317.

Elze, M. (1960), *Tatian und seine Theologie* (Göttingen: Vandenhoeck & Ruprecht).

Evans, C. A. (2006), 'Assessing Progress in the Third Quest of the Historical Jesus', *JSHJ* 4: 35–54.

Fallon, F. T. and R. Cameron. (1989), 'The Gospel of Thomas: A Forschungsbericht and Analysis', in W. Haase and H. Temporini (eds.), *ANRW* 2.25.6 (New York: de Gruyter): 4195–251.

Fieger, M. (1991), *Das Thomasevangelium: Einleitung, Kommentar und Systematik* (NTAbh 22; Münster: Aschendorff).

Fitzmyer, J. A. (1959), 'The Oxyrhynchus Logoi of Jesus and the Coptic Gospel According to Thomas', *TS* 20: 505–60.

Fowden, G. (1985), *The Egyptian Hermes: A Historical Approach to the Late Pagan Mind* (Cambridge/New York: Cambridge University Press).

Funk, R. W. (1971), 'Beyond Criticism in Quest of Literacy: The Parable of the Leaven', *Int* 25: 149–70.

Funk, R. W. and R. W. Hoover. (1996), *The Five Gospels: The Search for the Authentic Words of Jesus: New Translation and Commentary* (New York: Scribner).

Funk, W. P. (2002), '"Einer aus Tausend, Zwei aus Zehntausend": Zitate aus dem Thomasevangelium in den koptischen Manichaica' in H.-G. Bethge et al. (eds.), *For the Children, Perfect Instruction: Studies in Honor of Hans-Martin Schenke on the Occasion of the Berliner Arbeitskreis für koptisch-gnostische Schriften's Thirtieth Year* (NHS 54; Leiden/Boston: Brill): 67–94.

Garitte, G. (1960) 'Les "Logoi" d'Oxyrhynque sont traduits du Copte', *Mus* 73: 335–49.

Gärtner, B. (1961), *The Theology of the Gospel of Thomas*, trans. E. J. Sharpe (London: Collins).

Gasparro, G. S. (1972), 'L'Ermetismo nelle testimonianze dei padri', in F. L. Cross (ed.), *Papers Presented to the Fifth International Conference on Patristic Studies Held in Oxford 1967* (StPatr 11; Berlin: Akademie-Verlag): 58–64.

—— (1985), 'Le motivazioni protologiche dell'enkrateia nel cristianemiso dei primi secoli e nello gnosticismo', U. Bianchi (ed.), *Tradizione dell'enkrateia: Motivazioni ontologiche e protologiche* (Rome: Edizione dell'Ateneo): 149–237.

Gathercole, S. J. (2006), *The Preexistent Son: Recovering the Christologies of Matthew, Mark, and Luke* (Grand Rapids: Eerdmans).

Gerhardsson, B. (1961), *Memory and Manuscript: Oral Tradition and Written Transmission in Rabbinic Judaism and Early Christianity* (Uppsala: Uppsala Universitet).

Goodacre, M. S. and N. Perrin. (2004), *Questioning Q: A Multidimensional Critique* (Downers Grove, Ill: InterVarsity Press).

Goodenough, E. R. (1968), *The Theology of Justin Martyr: An Investigation into the Conceptions of Early Christian Literature and its Hellenistic and Judaistic Influences* (Amsterdam: Philo Press).

Goulet, R. (1987), *La Philosophie de Moïse: Essai de reconstitution d'un commentaire philosophique préphilonien du Pentateuque* (HistDAC 11; Paris: Vrin).

Grant R. (1953), 'The Date of Tatian's Oration', *HTR* 46: 99–101.

Grant, R. and D. Freedman. (1960), *The Secret Sayings of Jesus* (New York: Doubleday).

Grenfell, B. P. and A. S. Hunt. (1897), *ΛΟΓΙΑ ΙΗΣΟΥ: Sayings of Our Lord* (London: Henry Frowde).

Guey, J. (1960), 'Comment le "Denier de César" de l'Évangile a-t-il pu devenir une pièce d'or', *BSFN* 15: 478–9.

Guillaumont, A. (1958), 'Sémitismes dans les logia de Jésus retrouvés à Nag-Hamâdi', *JA* 246: 113–23.

—— (1960), 'Les "Logoi" d'Oxyrhynque sonts-ils traduits du Copte', *Mus* 73: 325–33.

—— (1981), 'Les sémitismes dans l'Évangile selon Thomas: Essai de Classement', in R. van den Broeck and M. J. Vermaseren (eds.), *Studies in Gnosticism and Hellenistic Religions Presented to Gilles Quispel on the Occasion of his 65th Birthday* (EPRO 91; Leiden: Brill): 190–204.

Gundry, R. H. (1993), *Mark: A Commentary on His Apology for the Cross* (Grand Rapids, Ill.: Eerdmans).

Haenchen, E. (1961), *Die Botschaft des Thomas-Evangeliums* (Berlin: Töpelmann).

Harl, M. (1963), 'Á propos des "Logia" de Jésus: Le sens du mot Monachos', *REG* 73: 464–74.

Harnack, A. von (1958 [1897]), *Geschichte des altchristlichen Literatur bis Eusebius* (4 vols; Leipzig: Deichert).

Hartin, P. J. (1999), 'The Search for the True Self in the Gospel of Thomas: The Book of Thomas and the Hymn of the Pearl', *HvTSt* 55: 1001–21.

—— (2006), 'The Role and Significance of the Character of Thomas in the Acts of Thomas', in J. M. Asgeirsson, A. D. DeConick and R. Uro (eds.), *Thomasine Traditions in Antiquity: The Social and Cultural World of the Gospel of Thomas* (NHS 59; Leiden: Brill): 239–53.

Heim, F. (2003), 'Le dieu et sa statue: Des traces d'Hermétisme chez les apologistes latins', *RevScRel* 77: 31–42.

Heim, K. M. (2001), *Like Grapes of Gold Set in Silver: An Interpretation of Proverbial Clusters in Proverbs 10:1–22:16* (BZAW 273; Berlin/New York: de Gruyter).

Helderman, J. (1997), 'Die Herrenworte über das Brautgemach im Thomasevangelium und im Dialog des Erlösers', in W. L. Petersen, J. S. Vos and H. J. de Jonge (eds.), *Sayings of Jesus: Canonical and Non-Canonical: Essays in Honor of Tjitze Baarda* (Leiden: Brill): 69–88.

Hengel, M. (2000), *The Four Gospels and the One Gospel of Jesus Christ: An Investigation of the Collection and Origin of the Canonical Gospels* (Harrisburg, Pa: Trinity Press International).

Hilhorst, A. (2004), *The Apostolic Age in Patristic Thought* (VCSup 70; Leiden/Boston: Brill).

Howard, G. (1981), *The Teaching of Addai* (Chico, Calif.: Scholars Press).

Hunt, E. J. (2003), *Christianity in the Second Century: The Case of Tatian* (London/New York: Routledge).

Jackson, H. M. (1985), *The Lion Becomes Man: The Gnostic Leontomorphic Creator and the Platonic Tradition* (SBLDS 81; Atlanta: Scholars Press).

Johnson, S. R. (2002), 'The Hidden/revealed Saying in the Greek and Coptic Versions of Gos. Thom. 5 & 6', *NovT* 44: 176–85.

Jones, F. S. (1995), *An Ancient Jewish Christian Source on the History of Christianity: Pseudo-Clementine Recognitions 1.27–71* (Atlanta: Scholars Press).

Joynes, C. E. (1998), 'A Question of Identity: "Who do People Say that I Am?" Elijah, John the Baptist and Jesus in Mark's Gospel', in C. Rowland and C. H. T. Fletcher-Louis (eds.), *Understanding, Studying and Reading: New Testament Essays in Honour of John Ashton* (Sheffield: Sheffield Academic Press).

Kammler, H.-C. (1996), 'Jesus Christus und der Geistparaklet: Eine studie zur johanneischen Verhältnisbestimmung von Pneumatologie und Christologie', in O. Hofius and H.-C. Kammler (eds.), *Johannesstudien: Untersuchungen zur Theologie des vierten Evangeliums* (WVNT 88; Leiden: Brill): 87–190.

Kasser, R. (1961), *L'Évangile selon Thomas: Présentation et commentaire théologique* (Neuchatel: Delachaux & Niestlé).

Kelber, W. H. (1983), *The Oral and the Written Gospel: The Hermeneutics of Speaking and Writing in the Synoptic Tradition, Mark, Paul, and Q* (Philadelphia: Fortress Press).

Kerr, F. (1986), *Theology after Wittgenstein* (Oxford/New York: Blackwell).

Klijn, A. F. J. (1961), 'Das Thomasevangelium und das altsyrische Christentum', *VC* 15: 146–59.

—— (1962), 'The "Single One" in the Gospel of Thomas', *JBL* 81: 271–8.

—— (1970), 'John 14:22 and the Name Judas Thomas', in *Studies in John: Presented to Professor D. J. N. Sevenster on the Occasion of his Seventieth Birthday* (NovTSup 24; Leiden: Brill).

—— (1972), 'Christianity in Edessa and the Gospel of Thomas: On Barbara Ehlers, Kann des Thomasevangelium aus Edessa Stammen?' *NovT* 14: 70–7.

Koester, H. (1971 [1965]), 'GNOMAI DIAPHORA: The Origins and Nature of Diversification in the History of Early Christianity', in H. Koester and J. M. Robinson (eds.), *Trajectories through Early Christianity* (Philadelphia: Fortress Press): 114–57. Originally printed in *HTR* 58 (1965): 279–318.

—— (1971 [1968]), 'One Jesus and Four Primitive Gospels', in H. Koester and J. M. Robinson (eds.), *Trajectories through Early Christianity* (Philadelphia: Fortress Press): 158–204. Originally printed in *HTR* 61 (1968): 203–47.

—— (1979), 'Dialog und Spruchüberlieferung in den gnostischen Texten von Nag Hammadi', *EvTh* 34: 532–56.

—— (1980), 'Apocryphal and Canonical Gospels', *HTR* 73: 105–30.

—— (1989), 'Introduction' [to the Gospel of Thomas], in B. Layton (ed.), *Nag Hammadi Codex II,2–7 together with XII,2 Brit. Lib. Or. 4926 (1), and P. Oxy 1, 654, 655* (NHS 20; Leiden: Brill): 38–49.

—— (1990), *Ancient Christian Gospels: Their History and Development* (London: SCM Press; Philadelphia: Trinity Press International).

Layton, B. (1989), *Nag Hammadi Codex II,2–7: Together with XIII,2* Brit. Lib. Or. 4926(1), and P.Oxy 1, 654, 655: Vol. 1: Gospel According to Thomas, Gospel According to Philip, Hypostasis of the Archons and Indexes* (NHS 20; Leiden: Brill).

Leloir, L. (1962), *Le témoignage d'Éphrem sur le Diatessaron* (CSCO 227; Louvain).

Liebenberg, J. (2001), *The Language of the Kingdom and Jesus: Parable, Aphorism, and Metaphor in the Sayings Material Common to the Synoptic Tradition and the Gospel of Thomas* (BZNW 102; Berlin/New York: de Gruyter).

Lierman, J. (2004), *The New Testament Moses: Christian Perceptions of Moses and Israel in the Setting of Jewish Religion* (WUNT 2.173; Tübingen: Mohr [Siebeck]).

Löw, A. (2002), *Hermes Trismegistos als Zeuge der Wahrheit: Die christliche Hermetikrezeption von Athenagoras bis Laktanz* (Theoph 36; Vienna: Philo).

Luck, G. (1985), 'The Doctrine of Salvation in the Hermetic Writings', *Society of Biblical Literature 1985 Seminar Papers* (SBLSP, 24; Atlanta: Scholars Press): 315–20.

Luomanen, P. (2006), '"Let Him Who Seeks, Continue Seeking": The Relationship between the Jewish-Christian Gospels and the Gospel of Thomas', in J. M. Asgeirsson, A. D. DeConick and R. Uro (eds.), *Thomasine Traditions in Antiquity: The Social and Cultural World of the Gospel of Thomas* (NHS 59; Leiden: Brill): 119–53.

Luttikhuizen, G. P. (2004), 'Witnesses and Mediators of Christ's Gnostic Teachings', in A. Hilhorst (ed.), *Apostolic Age in Patristic Thought* (VCSup 70; Leiden/Boston: Brill): 104–14.

Mack, B. L. (1988), *A Myth of Innocence: Mark and Christian Origins* (Philadelphia: Fortress Press).

—— (1985), 'Moses on the Mountaintop: A Philonic View', in J. P. Kenney (ed.), *The School of Moses: Studies in Philo and Hellenistic Religion: In*

Memory of Horst R. Moehring (BJS 304; Atlanta, Ga.: Scholars Press): 16–28.

Mahé, J.-P. (1976), 'Les Définitions d'Hermès Trismégiste à Asclépius (Trad de l'Arménien et Commentaire)', *RevScRel* 50: 193–214.

—— (1978), *Hermès en Haute-Egypte: Les textes hermétiques de Nag Hammadi et leurs parallèles grecs et latins* (BCNH 3; Quebec: Presses de l'Université Laval).

—— (1984), 'Fragments hermétiques dans les Papyri Vindobonenses Graecae 29456 ruo et 29828 ruo', in A. J. Festugière, E. Lucchesi and H. D. Saffrey (eds.), *Mémorial André-Jean Festugière: Antiquité païenne et chrétienne, vingt-cinq études* (Geneva: Cramer): 51–64.

—— (1991), 'La voie d'immortalité á la lumière des Hermetica de Nag Hammadi et de découvertes plus récentes', *VC* 45: 347–75.

Marjanen, A. (1998a), 'Is Thomas a Gnostic Gospel?', in R. Uro (ed.), *Thomas at the Crossroads: Essays on the Gospel of Thomas* (Edinburgh: T. & T. Clark): 107–39.

—— (1998b), 'Thomas and Jewish Religious Practices', in R. Uro (ed.), *Thomas at the Crossroads: Essays on the Gospel of Thomas* (Edinburgh: T. & T. Clark): 163–82.

—— (1998c), 'Women Disciples in the Gospel of Thomas', in R. Uro (ed.), *Thomas at the Crossroads: Essays on the Gospel of Thomas* (Edinburgh: T. & T. Clark): 89–106.

—— (2006), 'The Portrait of Jesus in the Gospel of Thomas', in J. M. Asgeirsson, A. D. DeConick and R. Uro (eds.), *Thomasine Traditions in Antiquity: The Social and Cultural World of the Gospel of Thomas* (NHS 59; Leiden: Brill): 209–19.

Martens, J. W. (2003), *One God, One Law: Philo of Alexandria on the Mosaic and Greco-Roman Law* (StudPhil 2; Leiden/Boston: Brill).

Martín, J. P. (1987), 'Taicano de Siria y el origen de la oposicion de materia y espiritu', *Str* 43:71–107.

—— (1988), 'Filon y las ideas cristianas del siglo II: Estado de la cuestion', *RevistB* 50: 263–94.

McArthur, H. K. (1959–60), 'Dependence of the Gospel of Thomas on the Synoptics', *ExpTim* 71: 286–7.

McKane, W. (1977), *Proverbs: A New Approach* (Philadelphia: Westminster Press).

—— (1986), *A Critical and Exegetical Commentary on Jeremiah* (ICC; Edinburgh: T. & T. Clark).

Ménard, J.-E. (1968), 'Le milieu syriaque de l'Évangile selon Thomas et de l'Évangile selon Philippe', *RevScRel* 42: 261–6.

—— (1975a), *L'Évangile selon Thomas* (NHS 5; Leiden: Brill).

—— (1975b), 'Der syrische Synkretismus und das Thomasevangelium', in A. Dietrich (ed.), *Synkretismus im syrisch-persischen Kulturgebiet: Bericht über ein Symposion in Reinhausen bei Göttingen in der Zeit vom 4. bis 8. Oktober 1971* (AAWG 96; Göttingen: Vandenhoeck & Ruprecht): 65–79.

—— (1976), 'Les problèmes de l'Évangile selon Thomas', in E. A. Livingstone (ed.), *Papers Presented to the Sixth International Conference on Patristic Studies, Held in Oxford, 1971* (StPatr 14; Berlin: Akademie): 209–28.

—— (1980), 'Beziehungen des Philippus- und des Thomas-Evangeliums zur syrischen Welt', in K. Tröger (ed.), *Altes Testament, Frühjudentum, Gnosis* (Gütersloh: Mohr [Siebeck]): 317–26.

Meyer, M. W. (2002), 'Gospel of Thomas Logion 114 Revisited', in H.-G. Bethge et al. (eds.), *For the Children, Perfect Instruction: Studies in Honor of Hans-Martin Schenke on the Occasion of the Berliner Arbeitskreis für koptisch-gnostische Schriften's Thirtieth Year* (NHS 54; Leiden/Boston: Brill): 101–11.

—— (2003 [1990]), 'The Beginning of the Gospel of Thomas', in *Secret Gospels: Essays on Thomas and the Secret Gospel of Mark* (Harrisburg, Pa.: Trinity Press International): 39–53. Originally printed in *Semeia* 52 (1990): 161–73.

—— (2006), '"Be Passersby": Gospel of Thomas 42, Jesus Traditions, and Islamic Traditions', in J. M. Asgeirsson, A. D. DeConick and R. Uro (eds.), *Thomasine Traditions in Antiquity: The Social and Cultural World of the Gospel of Thomas* (NHS 59; Leiden: Brill): 255–71.

Millar, F. (1971), 'Paul of Samosata, Zenobia and Aurelian: The Church, Local Culture and Political Allegiance in Third-Century Syria', *JRS* 61: 1–17.

Mirecki, P. A. (1991), 'Coptic Manichaean Psalm 278 and the Gospel of Thomas 37', in J. Ries, A. van Tongerloo and S. Giversen (eds.), *Manichaica Selecta: Studies Presented to Professor Julien Ries on the Occasion of His Seventieth Birthday* (MS 1; Louvain: International Association of Manichaean Studies): 243–62.

Moehring, H. R. and J. P. Kenney. (1995), *The School of Moses: Studies in Philo and Hellenistic Religion: In Memory of Horst R. Moehring* (BJS 304; Atlanta: Scholars Press).

Morard, F. (1980), 'Encore quelques réflexions sur *monachos*', *VC* 34: 395–401.

Moravcsik, G. (1964), 'Hund in der Krippe: Zur Geschichte eines griechischen Sprichwortes', *AcA* 12: 77–86.

Moreland, M. (2006), 'The Twenty-Four Prophets of Israel are Dead: Gospel of Thomas 52 as a Critique of Early Christian Hermeneutics', in J. M. Asgeirsson, A. D. DeConick and R. Uro (eds.), *Thomasine Traditions in Antiquity: The Social and Cultural World of the Gospel of Thomas* (NHS 59; Leiden: Brill): 75–91.

Munck, J. (1960), 'Bemerkungen zum koptischen Thomasevangelium', *ST* 14: 130–47.

Murray, R. (1975), *Symbols of Church and Kingdom: A Study in Early Syriac Tradition* (London/New York: Cambridge University Press).

Mussies, G. (1982), 'The Interpretatio Judaica of Thot-Hermes', in V. H. van Heerman, D. J. Hoens and G. Mussies (eds.), *Studies in Egyptian Religion: Dedicated to Professor Jan Zandee* (SHR 43; Leiden: Brill): 89–120.

Nagel, P. (1966), *Die Motivierung der Askese in der alten Kirche und der Ursprung des Mönchtums* (Berlin: Akademie-Verlag).

—— (1969), 'Erwägung zum Thomas-Evangelium', in F. Altheim and R. Stiehl (eds.), *Der Araber in der alten Welt* (Berlin: de Gruyter): 368–92.

Najman, H. (2003), *Seconding Sinai: The Development of Mosaic Discourse in Second Temple Judaism* (JSJSup 77; Leiden/Boston: Brill).

Neller, K. V. (1989), 'Diversity in the Gospel of Thomas: Clues for a New Direction' *SecCent* 7: 1–18.

Neusner, J. (1987), *Oral Tradition in Judaism: The Case of the Mishnah* (New York: Garland).

Nock, A. C. (1962), 'The Exegesis of Timaeus 28C', *VC* 16: 79–86.

Nordsieck, R. (2004), *Das Thomas-Evangelium* (Neukirchen-Vluyn: Neukirchener).

Onuki, T. (1991), 'Traditionsgeschichte von Thomas 17 und ihre christologische Relevanz', in C. Breytenbach and H. Paulsen (eds.), *Anfänge der Christologie: FS für Ferdinand Hahn zum 65. Geburtstag* (Göttingen: Vandenhoeck & Ruprecht): 399–415.

Pagels, E. (1999 [2000]), 'Exegesis of Genesis 1 in the Gospels of Thomas and John', *JBL* 118: 477–96. Reprinted in R. Argall, B. A. Bow and R. A. Werline (eds.), *For a Later Generation: The Transformation of Tradition in Israel, Early Judaism and Early Christianity* (Harrisburg, Pa.: Trinity Press International, 2000): 196–215.

—— (2003), *Beyond Belief: The Secret Gospel of Thomas* (New York: Random House).

Patterson, S. J. (1993), *The Gospel of Thomas and Jesus* (FF; Sonoma: Polebridge Press).

—— (1995a), 'The Gospel of Thomas and Jesus', *Dialogue* 28: 111–19.

—— (1995b), 'The End of Apocalypse', *ThTo* 52: 29–58.

—— (1998), *The God of Jesus: The Historical Jesus and the Search for Meaning* (Harrisburg, Pa.: Trinity Press International).

—— (2004), *Beyond the Passion: Rethinking the Death and Life of Jesus* (Minneapolis: Fortress Press).

Patterson, S. J., J. M. Robinson and H-.G. Bethge. (1998), *The Fifth Gospel: The Gospel of Thomas Comes of Age* (Harrisburg, Pa.: Trinity Press International).

Perrin, N. (2002), *Thomas and Tatian: The Relationship between the Gospel of Thomas and the Diatessaron* (AcBib 5; Atlanta: Society of Biblical Literature; Leiden: Brill).

—— (2004), 'NHC II,2 and the Oxyrhynchus Fragments (P.Oxy 1, 654, 655): Overlooked Evidence for a Syriac Gospel of Thomas', *VC* 58: 138–51.

—— (2006), 'Thomas: The Fifth Gospel?' *JETS* 49: 67–80.

—— (2007), 'Recent Trends in *Gospel of Thomas* Research (1991–2006): Part 1, The Historical Jesus and the Synoptic Gospels', *CurBS* 5: 186–212.

Petersen, S. (1999), 'Adolf Jülicher und die Parabeln des Thomasevangeliums', in *Gleichnisreden Jesu 1899–1999* (Berlin: de Gruyter): 179–207.

Petersen, W. L. (1994), *Tatian's Diatessaron: Its Creation, Dissemination, Significance, and History in Scholarship* (VCSup 25; Leiden/New York: Brill).

—— (2005), 'Tatian the Assyrian', in A. Marjanen and P. Luomanen (eds.), *A Companion to Second-Century Christian 'Heretics'* (VCSup 76; Leiden: Brill): 125–58.

Plooij, D. (1929), *The Liège Diatessaron* (Verhandelingen der Koninklijke Akademie van Wetenschappen te Amsterdam, Afdeeling Letterkunde 31–38; Amsterdam).

Poirier, P. H. (1997), 'The Writings Ascribed to Thomas and the Thomas Tradition', in J. D. Turner and A. McGuire (eds.), *The Nag Hammadi Library after Fifty Years: Proceedings of the 1995 Society of Biblical Literature Commemoration* (NHS 44; Leiden: Brill): 295–307.

Priest, J. F. (1985), 'The Dog in the Manger: In Quest of a Fable', *CJ* 81: 49–58.

Puech, H.-C. (1978 [1957]), 'Une collection de paroles de Jesús récemment retrouveé: L'Évangile selon Thomas', in *En quête de la gnose* (Paris: Gallimard): 28–48. Originally published in *Comptes rendus de l'académie des inscriptions et belles-lettres* (Paris: Institute de France, 1957).

Quecke, H. (1963), ' "Sein Haus seines Königreiches": Zum Thomasevangelium 85,9f.', *Mus* 76: 51–3.

Quispel, G. (1959), 'L'Évangile selon Thomas et le Diatessaron', *VC* 13: 87–117.

—— (1975), *Tatian and the Gospel of Thomas: Studies in the History of the Western Diatessaron* (Leiden: Brill).

—— (1981), 'The Gospel of Thomas Revisited' in B. Barc (ed.), *Colloque international sur les textes de Nag Hammadi (Québec, 22–25 août 1978)* (BCNH 1; Quebec: Presses de l'Université Laval): 218–66.

—— (1985), 'The Study of Encratism: A Historical Survey', in U. Bianchi (ed.), *Tradizione dell'enkrateia: Motivazioni ontologiche e protologiche* (Rome: Edizioni dell'Ateneo): 35–82.

Riley, G. J. (1995), *Resurrection Reconsidered: Thomas and John in Controversy* (Minneapolis: Fortress Press).

Rist, M. (1972), 'Pseudepigraphy and the Early Christians', in A. P. Wikgren and D. E. Aune (eds.), *Studies in New Testament and early Christian Literature: Essays in Honor of Allen P. Wikgren* (NovTSup 33; Leiden: Brill): 75–91.

Roberts, C. H. (1979), *Manuscript, Society, and Belief in Early Christian Egypt* (London/New York: Oxford University Press).

Robinson, J. A. T. (1958), 'Elijah, John and Jesus: An Essay in Detection', *NTS* 4: 263–81.

Robinson, J. M. (1971 [1964]), 'LOGOI SOPHON: On the Gattung of Q', in J. M. Robinson and H. Koester (eds.), *Trajectories through Early Christianity* (Philadelphia: Fortress Press): 71–113. Originally printed in German in 'LOGOI SOPHON: Zur Gattung der Spruchquelle', in E. Dinkler (ed.), *Zeit und Geschichte: Dankesgabe an Rudolf Bultmann* (Tubingen: Mohr [Siebeck], 1964).

Robinson, J. M. and H. Koester. (1971), *Trajectories through Early Christianity* (Philadelphia: Fortress Press).

Rudolph, K. (1969), 'Gnosis und Gnosizismus: Ein Forschungsbericht', *TRu* 34: 21–75, 181–231, 359–61.

Runia, D. T. (1993), *Philo in Early Christian Literature: A Survey* (JTECL 3; Assen: Van Gorcum; Minneapolis: Fortress Press).

—— (1995), *Philo and the Church Fathers: A Collection of Papers* (VCSup 32; Leiden/New York: Brill).

Schenke, H.-M. (1994), 'On the Compositional History of the Gospel of Thomas', *FFF* 10: 9–30.

Schippers, R. (1960), *Het Evangelie van Thomas: Apocriefe woorden van Jezus* (Kampen: Kok).

Schmitt, R. (1980), 'Die Ostgrenze von Armenien über Mesopotamien: Syrien bis Arabien', in G. Neumann and J. Untermann (eds.), *Die Sprachen im romischen Reich der Kaiserzeit: Kolloquium vom 8.–10. April 1974* (BBJ 40; Cologne: Rheinland-Verlag; Bonn: Habelt): 187–214.

Schnackenburg. R. (1982), *The Gospel According to St John* (3 vols; New York: Crossroad).

Schrage, W. (1964), *Das Verhältnis des Thomas-Evangeliums zur synoptischen Tradition und zu den koptischen Evangelien-Übersetzungen* (BZNW 29; Berlin: Töpelmann).

Schröter, J. (1997), *Erinnerung an Jesu Worte: Studien zur Rezeption der Logienüberlieferung in Markus, Q und Thomas* (WMANT 76; Neukirchen-Vluyn: Neukirchener Verlag).

Schweitzer, A. (1968 [1930]), *The Mysticism of Paul the Apostle* (London: A. & C. Black; New York: Seabury Press).

Segal, J. B. (1970), *Edessa: 'The Blessed City'* (Oxford: Clarendon Press).

Sellew, P. H. (1997a), 'The Gospel of Thomas: Prospects for Future Research', in J. D. Turner and A. McGuire (eds.), *The Nag Hammadi Library after Fifty Years: Proceedings of the 1995 Society of Biblical Literature Commemoration* (NHS 44; Leiden: Brill): 327–46.

—— (1997b), 'Death, the Body, and the World in the Gospel of Thomas', in E. A. Livingstone (ed.), *Proceedings of the XII International Patristics Conference, Oxford, 1995* (StPatr 31; Louvain: Peeters): 530–4.

—— (2001), 'Thomas Christianity: Scholars in Quest of a Community,' in J. N. Bremmer (ed.), *The Apocryphal Acts of Thomas* (SECA; Louvain: Peeters): 11–35.

—— (2006), 'Jesus and the Voice from Beyond the Grave: Gospel of Thomas 42 in the Context of Funerary Epigraphy', in J. M. Asgeirsson, A. D. DeConick and R. Uro (eds.), *Thomasine Traditions in Antiquity: The Social and Cultural World of the Gospel of Thomas* (NHS 59; Leiden: Brill): 39–73.

Sevrin, J.-M. (1992), 'La rédaction des paraboles dans l'Évangile de Thomas', in *Actes du IVe Congrès Copte, Louvain-la-Neuve, 5–10 septembre 1988: Vol 2, De la linguistique au Gnosticisme* (Louvain-la-Neuve: Institut Orientaliste de l'Université Catholique de Louvain; Louvain: Peeters): 343–54.

—— (1995), 'Remarques sur le genre littéraire de l'Évangile selon Thomas', in L. Painchaud and A. Pasquier (eds.), *Les textes de Nag Hammadi et le problème de leur classification: Actes du Colloque tenu à Québec du 15 au 19 septembre 1993* (BCNH 3; Louvain: Peeters): 263–78.

—— (1997), 'L'interprétation de l'Évangile selon Thomas, entre tradition et rédaction', in J. D. Turner and A. McGuire (eds.), *The Nag Hammadi*

Library after Fifty Years: Proceedings of the 1995 Society of Biblical Literature Commemoration (NHS 44; Leiden: Brill): 347–60.

—— (1999), ' "Ce que l'œil n'a pas vu . . .": 1 Co 2,9 comme parole de Jésus', in J.-M. Auwers and A. Wenin (eds.), *Lectures et relectures de la Bible: FS P.-M. Boguert* (BETL 144; Louvain: Louvain University Press; Louvain: Peeters): 307–24.

Siegert, F. (1988), *Philon von Alexandrien: über die Gottesbezeichnung 'wohltätig verzehrendes Feuer' (De Deo): Rückübersetzung des Fragments aus dem armenischen, deutsche Übersetzung und Kommentar* (Tübingen: Mohr [Paul Siebeck]).

Sivertsev, A. (2000), 'The Gospel of Thomas and Early Stages in the Development of the Christian Wisdom Literature', *JECS* 8: 319–40.

Snell, D. C. (1993), *Twice-Told Proverbs and the Composition of the Book of Proverbs* (Winona Lake, Ind.: Eisenbrauns).

Speyer, W. (1971), *Die literarische Fälschung im heidnischen und christlichen Altertum: Ein Versuch ihrer Deutung* (Munich: Beck).

Stanton, G. N. (2003), 'Jesus Traditions and Gospels in Justin Martyr and Irenaeus', in J.-M. Auwers and H. J. de Jonge (eds.), *The Biblical Canons* (BETL 163; Louvain: Peeters): 353–70.

Stendahl, K. (1968), *The School of St. Matthew, and its Use of the Old Testament* (Philadelphia: Fortress Press).

Strobel, A. (1963), 'Textgeschichtles zum Thomas–Logion 86 (Mt 8,20/Luk 9,58)', *VC* 17: 211–24.

Taylor, V. (1949), *The Formation of the Gospel Tradition: Eight Lectures* (2nd edition; New York: Macmillan; London: St. Martin's Press).

Theissen, G. (1977 [1978]), *Soziologie der Jesus Bewegung* (Munich: Chr. Kaiser Verlag). ET: *The Sociology of Early Palestinian Christianity*, trans. J. Bowen (Philadelphia: Fortress Press).

—— (1987), *The Shadow of the Galilean: The Quest of the Historical Jesus in Narrative Form* (Philadelphia: Fortress Press).

Trakatellis, D. (1976), *The Pre-Existence of Christ in the Writings of Justin Martyr* (HDR, 6; Missoula, Mont.: Scholars Press).

Trevijano Etcheverría, R. M. (1992), 'Santiago el Justo y Tomás el Mellizo (Evangelio de Tomás, Log 12 y 13)', *Salm* 39: 97–119.

—— (1993a), 'La Reconversión de la escatología en protología (EvTom Log 18, 19, 24, 49 y 50)', *Salm* 40: 133–63.

—— (1993b), 'La valoración de los dichos no canónicos: El caso de 1 Cor 2.9 y Ev Tom Log 17', in E. A. Livingstone (ed.), *Papers Presented at the Eleventh International Conference on Patristic Studies held in Oxford, 1991* (StPatr 24; Louvain: Peeters): 406–14.

Tuckett, C. M. (1991), 'Q and Thomas: Evidence of a Primitive "Wisdom Gospel"? A Response to H. Koester', *EThL* 67: 346–60.

Turner, J. D. (1975), *The Book of Thomas the Contender from Codex II of the Cairo Gnostic Library from Nag Hammadi* (CGII, 7) (SBLDS 23; Missoula, Mont.: Scholars Press).

Turner, J. D. and A. McGuire (1997), *The Nag Hammadi Library after Fifty Years: Proceedings of the 1995 Society of Biblical Literature Commemoration* (NHS 44; Leiden: Brill).

Uro, R. (1997), 'Asceticism and Anti-familial Language in the Gospel of Thomas', in H. Moxnes (ed.), *Constructing Early Christian Families: Family as Social Reality and Metaphor* (London: Routledge): 216–34.

—— (1998a), *Thomas at the Crossroads: Essays on the Gospel of Thomas* (Edinburgh: T. & T. Clark).

—— (1998b), 'Is Thomas an Encratite Gospel?, in R. Uro (ed.), *Thomas at the Crossroads: Essays on the Gospel of Thomas* (Edinburgh: T. & T. Clark): 140–62.

—— (1998c), 'Thomas and Oral Tradition', in R. Uro (ed.), *Thomas at the Crossroads: Essays on the Gospel of Thomas* (Edinburgh: T. & T. Clark): 8–32.

—— (2002), '"Who Will Be Our Leader?": Authority and Autonomy in the Gospel of Thomas', in I. Dunderberg, K. Syreeni and C. Tuckett (eds.), *Fair Play: Diversity and Conflicts in Early Christianity: Essays in Honour of Heikki Räisänen* (NovTSup 103; Leiden: Brill): 457–85.

—— (2003), *Thomas: Seeking the Historical Context of the Gospel of Thomas* (London: T. & T. Clark).

Vööbus, A. (1958), *History of Asceticism in the Syrian Orient: A Contribution to the History of Culture in the Near East* (3 vols; CSCO 184, 197, 500: Louvain: Secrétariat deu CorpusSCO/Peeters).

Walls, A. F. (1960–1), 'The References to Apostles in the Gospel of Thomas', in *NTS* 7: 266–70.

Watson, F. (1997), *Text and Truth: Redefining Biblical Theology* (Edinburgh: T. & T. Clark).

Wayment, T. A. (2004), 'Christian Teachers in Matthew and Thomas: The Possibility of Becoming a "Master"', *JECS* 12: 289–311.

Weeks, S. (1994), *Early Israelite Wisdom* (OTM; Oxford: Clarendon Press; New York: Oxford University Press).

Williams, M. A. (1996), *Rethinking "Gnosticism": An Argument for Dismantling a Dubious Category* (Princeton, N.J.: Princeton University Press).

Wilson, R. M. (1960), *Studies in the Gospel of Thomas* (London: Mowbray).

Witherington, B. (1995), *The Jesus Quest: The Third Search for the Jew of Nazareth* (Downers Grove, Ill.: InterVarsity Press).

Wrede, W. (1971 [1901]), *The Messianic Secret* (London and Cambridge: James Clarke; Greenwood, S.C.: Attic).

Wright, N. T. (1996), *Christian Origins and the Question of God: Vol. 2. Jesus and the Victory of God* (Minneapolis: Fortress Press; London: SPCK).

—— (2003), *Christian Origins and the Question of God: Vol. 3. The Resurrection of the Son of God* (Minneapolis: Fortress Press; London: SPCK).

Zahn, T. (1881) *Tatian's Diatessaron* (FGNK 1; Erlangen).

Zöckler, T. (1999), *Jesu Lehren im Thomasevangelium* (NHS 47; Leiden: Brill).

Index of ancient and biblical sources

Index of subjects and modern authors